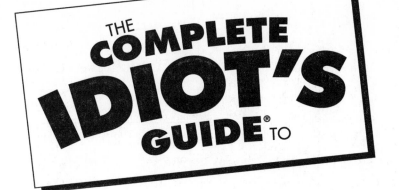

THE COMPLETE IDIOT'S GUIDE® TO

Selling Your Own Home

by Jeff Wuorio, Marcia Layton Turner, with
ForSalebyOwner.com

ALPHA

A member of Penguin Group (USA) Inc.

ALPHA BOOKS

Published by the Penguin Group

Penguin Group (USA) Inc., 375 Hudson Street, New York, New York 10014, U.S.A.

Penguin Group (Canada), 10 Alcorn Avenue, Toronto, Ontario, Canada M4V 3B2 (a division of Pearson Penguin Canada Inc.)

Penguin Books Ltd., 80 Strand, London WC2R 0RL, England

Penguin Ireland, 25 St Stephen's Green, Dublin 2, Ireland (a division of Penguin Books Ltd.)

Penguin Group (Australia), 250 Camberwell Road, Camberwell, Victoria 3124, Australia (a division of Pearson Australia Group Pty Ltd.)

Penguin Books India Pvt Ltd., 11 Community Centre, Panchsheel Park, New Delhi—110 017, India

Penguin Group (NZ), cnr Airborne and Rosedale Roads, Albany, Auckland 1310, New Zealand (a division of Pearson New Zealand Ltd.)

Penguin Books (South Africa) (Pty) Ltd., 24 Sturdee Avenue, Rosebank, Johannesburg 2196, South Africa

Penguin Books Ltd., Registered Offices: 80 Strand, London WC2R 0RL, England

International Standard Book Number: 1-59257-440-8
Library of Congress Catalog Card Number: 2005930988

08   07   06   05   8   7   6   5   4   3   2   1

Interpretation of the printing code: The rightmost number of the first series of numbers is the year of the book's printing; the rightmost number of the second series of numbers is the number of the book's printing. For example, a printing code of 05-1 shows that the first printing occurred in 2005.

Printed in the United States of America

Note: This publication contains the opinions and ideas of its authors. It is intended to provide helpful and informative material on the subject matter covered. It is sold with the understanding that the authors and publisher are not engaged in rendering professional services in the book. If the reader requires personal assistance or advice, a competent professional should be consulted.

The authors and publisher specifically disclaim any responsibility for any liability, loss, or risk, personal or otherwise, which is incurred as a consequence, directly or indirectly, of the use and application of any of the contents of this book.

Most Alpha books are available at special quantity discounts for bulk purchases for sales promotions, premiums, fundraising, or educational use. Special books, or book excerpts, can also be created to fit specific needs.

For details, write: Special Markets, Alpha Books, 375 Hudson Street, New York, NY 10014.

Publisher: *Marie Butler-Knight*	**Copy Editor:** *Sarah Cisco*
Editorial Director: *Mike Sanders*	**Cartoonist:** *Shannon Wheeler*
Senior Managing Editor: *Jennifer Bowles*	**Cover/Book Designer:** *Trina Wurst*
Acquisitions Editor: *Michele Wells*	**Indexer:** *Tonya Heard*
Development Editor: *Nancy D. Lewis*	**Layout:** *Becky Harmon*
Senior Production Editor: *Billy Fields*	**Proofreading:** *Mary Hunt*

Contents at a Glance

Contents

Foreword

As founder and president of ForSaleByOwner.com, the world's leading for sale by owner website and one of the largest real estate sites in the country, I jumped at the chance to assist in the creation of this extremely helpful book.

When it came to business, I had two passions in life, real estate and the Internet. As a serial entrepreneur, I have founded several Internet companies and managed my own portfolio of residential real estate. I must say I did get an early start. I was only 17 years old when I made my first real estate purchase. It definitely took some fancy negotiating and a small loan from my mother. So I thank God my mother and father believed in me because everyone else thought I was crazy to be making this kind of investment and commitment at such a young age.

Well, that first investment turned out great and that's what led me to my passion for real estate. During the next few years, I bought and sold real estate and realized that by selling my properties without the use of a real estate agent, I would greatly increase my profits by pocketing the 6% commission I would have normally given to an agent. This was my early experience with the For Sale By Owner method and I was intrigued and excited with the whole concept. I always thought, "Why would anyone do anything different when it really wasn't very difficult at all?"

Then came my second passion, my fascination with the Internet and its never ending possibilities. I could see the writing on the wall and predicted the Internet would change the way millions of people did so many things, from finding a date and booking travel to buying stocks and researching homework assignments. It was an endless stream of possibilities and my mind would run wild and I just loved it.

That's when it hit me. What if I combined my two passions into one concept? What if I utilized the Internet to create a For Sale By Owner marketplace utilizing my knowledge and experience buying and selling real estate By Owner? It was the single best idea I have ever had. I could help hundreds of thousands of people sell their own home and save them hundreds of millions of dollars. So I did just that with the creation of ForSaleByOwner.com and to date ForSaleByOwner.com has helped consumers save over a billion dollars in would be commissions.

This is why I jumped at the chance to play a role in the creation of *The Complete Idiot's Guide to Selling Your Own Home* because I knew that I'd be part of another outlet that would help so many people successfully sell their own home and save thousands of dollars that they can now use for so many other great things.

This book is not only a guide but it's also an education in the For Sale By Owner real estate marketplace. This *Complete Idiot's Guide* will not only teach you everything you need to know about selling your own home, it will give you the tools and resources needed to help make the process simple and effective.

I truly believe that if you educate yourself by reading this guide and implement the strategies and services outlined, your rate of success will greatly improve and you, too, will be one of the many people who have saved thousands in would-be commissions.

Damon Giglio, Founder & President
ForSaleByOwner.com. No Commission, Lots of Help.

Introduction

If you're thinking of selling your home without a real estate agent, there's a good chance you're getting a lot of feedback—much of it questioning your good sense. To wit …

◆ You can't sell your home without an agent (it's illegal or something like that).

◆ You'll never get any buyers (the agents have them all hidden away, as everyone knows).

◆ You'll never get through all that paperwork (it's all written in some dead language, like Sanskrit).

And so on.

If it sounds like some people are a bit misinformed, you could not be more on the mark. The fact is, the number of people selling their home without a real estate agent is growing all the time. And armed with the material we've provided in this book, you're poised to join them.

We've crafted this book to offer a systematic, step-by-step approach to walk you through every issue and element attached to selling your home without an agent. From powerful sales strategies to every last scrap of paperwork you'll need, we've got you covered. In fact, we've gone well beyond that. For one thing, we conclude each chapter with several Internet sites that address some of the topics we discuss. They're designed to augment the material and provide you with additional resources—whether it's information, interactive search engines, calculators, or other useful tools.

One of the nice things about writing a book such as this one is that we're able look back a bit and examine the successes and frustrations of those who've gone before us. In so doing, we see what's worked and what has not. While we pay exhaustive attention to those tips and strategies that others who have taken the FSBO route have put to good use, we also focus on those common mistakes that can trip up any sale. Just as important, we go in-depth to show you ways to avoid those problems.

Although, naturally, you're free to read as you wish, we urge you to try to make your way through most, if not all, of this book before getting started with the sale of your home. While we've generally arranged things in chronological order, examining the topic as a whole puts all the individual parts into perspective and balance. And that can help you map out your thinking and planning in the most organized and thoughtful way possible—from the first moment you consider selling your home without an agent to the instant the last dab of ink has dried on the final sales documents.

How This Book Is Organized

This book is presented in five sections:

In **Part 1, "The Nuts and Bolts,"** you get your first glimpse into the world of selling your home without a real estate agent. We help you decide whether a FSBO is right for you. If it's a match, we move on to other basics, including getting your home in shape, others you'll work with in selling your home, and the importance of setting the right price.

Part 2, "Let The Selling Begin!," moves us into the actual mechanics of the sales process. Starting with advertising strategies—including how to write the best newspaper ad ever—we discuss open houses, tips, and techniques when buyers come calling, and what to do if you want to move your sales effort onto the Internet.

Part 3, "Setting Up the Deal," does just that. Here, you'll be getting a handle on the nuts and bolts of the sale itself. You learn about the do's and don'ts of fielding offers, negotiation strategies, the basics of home loans and mortgages, and alternatives you can consider to sweeten the financial terms of your sale.

Part 4, "That Sweet, Sweet Closing and What Comes After," leads you through the closing stages to the closing itself. First, we discuss the mechanics of the home inspection and various other tests that may take place. That can lead to some problems and misunderstandings, so we address those next. But, after those are ironed out, we enjoy the details of the closing itself (accompanied by the not-so-palatable tax discussion that follows).

Not every home is perfect. **Part 5, "The Problem House: The Less Than Perfect Buyer and Other Final Details,"** hits on some issues you may encounter in your sale and strategies to work them out. Ranging from the home that just won't sell to the buyer from, shall we say, the fiery regions below, you'll be well-prepared to meet most any challenge.

Bonus FSBO Features

Not surprisingly, certain parts of our discussion warrant additional attention. To make sure nothing gets lost in the shuffle, we've included four special boxes throughout the text highlighting key points, terms, and other details.

Selling Smarts

Certain sales ideas and strategies are particularly effective. Here's where you'll find them.

Tools of the Trade

These point out and explain important real estate and home sales terms you'll want to know.

Sales Snafu

Here, we highlight potential problems and pitfalls that many home sellers encounter and, of course, ways to head them off.

FSBO Facts

Not every part of selling your home on your own is as obvious as it might first appear. Here, we point them out and show how you can put them to your advantage.

Special Thanks to the Technical Reviewer

The Complete Idiot's Guide to Selling Your Own Home was reviewed by an expert, who double-checked the accuracy of what you learn here, to help ensure this book gives you everything you need to know about selling your home yourself. Special thanks are extended to Doug Jones.

Doug Jones has been a residential and commercial developer and broker in Indiana for 12 years. Doug specializes in urban "in-fill" projects that require a bit of imagination, diplomatic skills, and stick-to-it-iveness to get the projects done. You can see examples of his work at urbanforward.com. Doug is a 1990 graduate of Indiana University and got his "MBA of Sorts" while serving as a Peace Corps volunteer in West Africa.

Trademarks

All terms mentioned in this book that are known to be or are suspected of being trademarks or service marks have been appropriately capitalized. Alpha Books and Penguin Group (USA) Inc. cannot attest to the accuracy of this information. Use of a term in this book should not be regarded as affecting the validity of any trademark or service mark.

Part 1

The Nuts and Bolts

This part begins by addressing what's likely to be the most central question in many minds … what are the pluses and minuses of trying to sell your home yourself as opposed to using a real estate agent? Equally important, we'll also lead you through some issues and questions to help you determine if you're a good match for the task ahead. From there, you need to get your house in shape and find others with whom you can partner. We close with a chapter on strategies that can help you set the right price for your home, a critical decision as you move into the actual selling phase.

Chapter 1

Why Bother?

In This Chapter

- The choice to go For Sale By Owner (FSBO)
- Getting to know you
- Getting the timing right
- It's not for everyone (and that's okay)

No matter how you do it, selling a home; and doing it to your satisfaction; raises a number of questions and involves making some decisions. What price should you ask? How quickly should you sell the house? What sort of marketing and advertising do you need? And the list goes on.

So why bother going to all the trouble of selling your home yourself? That's the question we address in this chapter. We hit on the advantages and drawbacks of using an agent to sell your home and then discuss a few of the more appealing advantages that come from selling your home yourself.

We also spend considerable time helping you answer this central question; is selling your home the right decision for you? Strategies and skills can always be learned, but knowing whether or not you're the kind of person who can put those skills into effective practice is every bit as critical.

You or an Agent? (That Is the Question)

Choosing to sell your home on your own involves weighing a variety of issues, but none is more central than weighing the advantages and disadvantages of going on your own—that is, not having the help of a real estate agent to sell your house and manage the entire transaction. In effect, it's a choice between going with an agent or choosing a *FSBO*.

Tools of the Trade

The term **FSBO** (pronounced *Fizz-bo*) is an acronym for For Sale By Owner. We use it throughout the book.

We get into the meat of the FSBO versus agent discussion in the section "Why Use an Agent," later this chapter. But, first, let's look at a couple of the central issues pertaining to both options.

Show Me the Money!

By selling your home on your own, you bypass commissions paid to real estate agents. Most FSBOs cite this as the number one reason for taking on the job themselves. Rates vary, but you can expect to pay about 6 percent of the selling price of your home in real estate commissions. That's money that comes directly from whatever proceeds you get from the sale.

Six percent may not seem like much on the surface, but it adds up, particularly if you're selling an expensive home. Check out the following chart for a breakdown of various commissions:

Sales Price	Commission at 6%
$100,000	$6,000
$175,000	$10,500
$250,000	$15,000
$350,000	$21,000
$450,000	$27,000

Some additional good news and bad news. First, the good—the higher the purchase price of a home, the more open many agents may be to trimming their commission somewhat. That, in the end, may trim your out of pocket expenses.

Still, any significant commission can prove a discouraging factor for any homeowner. Say an owner bought a home for $210,000, then sunk some $10,000 into improvements. While that boosted the home's value to $220,000 in the marketplace, the $15,000 she'll have to pay on commission cancels out the investment in improvements.

It doesn't take long for a 6 percent commission to add up to a significant chunk of change, does it? It can get even costlier. More expensive homes with higher selling prices result in very handsome commissions for the agent, but mean less left over for the owner at the end of the sale.

As the Internet has grown and matured, so have the websites available that offer information, calculators, and other valuable tools for homesellers. See the figure that follows.

For Sale By Owner websites, such as this one in Bellingham, Washington, have handy calculators you can use to quickly add up your savings.

FSBO Facts

Why do real estate agents usually charge a 6 percent commission? Simple—it's always been done that way. Agents benefit because it's an automatic means of making the most of rising real estate prices. As opposed to a flat fee, a percentage naturally translates into a higher commission for the agent as home prices increase. However, it also means less commission when the real estate market isn't doing well, and the more work an agent must put into selling your house, the less his or her hourly wage works out to be.

The potential problem of real estate commissions becomes even more acute if you only have a modest amount of equity in your home.

The term equity refers to the difference between the market value of your home and the claims that exist against it, such as the outstanding amount of a mortgage, a home equity loan or line of credit, and other charges. To illustrate: a homeowner with a $200,000 home and a $150,000 mortgage is said to have $50,000 worth of equity.

See how the issue of equity becomes so important? The less equity you have in your home, the smaller the profit margin, and the greater the impact of a sales commission. In fact, the prevalence of low interest rates has, in many cases, worked to reduce many homeowners' equity. Because refinancing is easy and cheap, many homeowners roll high credit card debt and even the expense of refinancing into the new loan. Taking advantage of lower interest rates may lower their monthly mortgage payments and personal debt, but it also trims the amount of equity they have in their home.

You're the One at the Controls

Another plus to selling your home by yourself is that you're in complete charge of everything. That means every last decision comes down to you. You decide when to sell your home, when to take it off the market if you so choose, where to set the price, and every other element attached to the sale. A lot of people enjoy that sense of command and autonomy.

Sales Snafu

Other aspects of a sense of control can come into play depending on whether or not you're using an agent. For instance, many real estate agents prefer that you not be home when they're showing your house to a potential buyer. For some, that's OK, but there are others who are less than comfortable with the idea of strangers traipsing about their home without them there. With a FSBO, of course, you're always going to be there when a buyer comes calling.

It's a Great Education

Although saving money and having control over every part of the process are important, don't overlook the sorts of skills you stand to gain by learning how to handle a FSBO. Not only are you likely to sharpen your math skills—no fuzzy math here!— you also stand to learn negotiation techniques, as well as sales and marketing strategies, not to mention a good dose of dealing effectively with people on top of it all. Those are attributes you can use to your advantage, not merely in any future home sales in which you may become involved, but in any number of professional and personal situations as well. Not a bad deal.

Why Use an Agent?

Onward we go into our examination of the various ways you can sell your home. Here, we touch on a couple of the advantages of using the traditional real estate agent system to list, market, and, ultimately, sell your home.

The Price Is Right

Research shows that one of the biggest problems encountered by FSBOs was setting the correct selling price for their home. Fans of the agent system contend that a good agent takes that worry out of the mix by staying on top of fluctuating market conditions, factoring in other comparable homes also up for sale, and taking into account other elements that impact exactly what goes into determining the right price. A good agent can prove to be an effective sounding board, helping the homeowner keep his or her goals and objectives aggressive yet reasonable.

FSBO Facts

A 2004 survey by the National Association of Realtors found that the median selling price of a FSBO home was 15.4 percent less than homes sold when an agent was involved. However, the same survey found that one-half of all recent FSBOs were comfortable in selling another home in the future without the assistance of a real estate agent.

You're Paying for Experience

Knowing what price makes for a good sale is another often-cited advantage to working with an agent—they are experienced with the process. Although quality naturally differs from one agent to the next, commission expenses should at least buy you a sales representative who's not only trained in all elements of the home selling process, but one who has picked up experience and savvy along the way. That, say fans of agents, more than justifies commission costs.

Tools of the Trade

An important part of our discussion is recognizing that a real estate agent and a Realtor are not one and the same. Although both are trained and have to be licensed, a Realtor has taken certain training courses and shown expertise in a particular area of real estate. All Realtors are members of the National Association of Realtors and subscribe to that group's code of ethics. Among other issues, the code pledges loyalty to clients, fiduciary honesty, and cooperation with competitors.

Obtaining all this experience and know-how doesn't always have to mandate the going commission rate of 6 percent. Depending on the circumstances, there may be some room to negotiate a lower commission. Some agents are willing to do this. A recent report by the National Association of Realtors found the negotiated commission rate had dropped to an average of 5.1 percent—nearly a full percentage point below the usual going rate—and sometimes more.

That's something, but it's not exactly a windfall. Using the commission chart that we saw earlier in this chapter, a $250,000 home sold at a 5.1 percent fee takes $12,750 in commission. That's $2250 less than you'd pay under the usual 6 percent cut. In fact, the dynamics of commission runs against you here—the less your home costs, the less you stand to save with a discounted commission. Only with exceedingly expensive homes do the savings become genuinely substantial. Using the $450,000 home sale example, the owner would save approximately $4000 by opting for the 5.1 discount ($22,950) versus the conventional 6 percent commission ($27,000).

There are real estate agents out there who charge considerably less than conventional agents—either a flat fee or significantly less than the going 6 percent. The trouble is, you pay less but get a great deal less in service. Advertising and marketing efforts may be haphazard or downright nonexistent, not to mention cutbacks in other programs or services that a full-service agent always provides.

So, it's clear that FSBOs and the traditional real estate agent system have their various advantages and drawbacks. But there are other issues that factor into the equation—considerations that can greatly boost the case for opting for a FSBO.

Speed and Sales Savvy

Money saved or money paid in commissions, of course, are not the only considerations in selling your home on your own and doing so successfully. The speed with which all this happens is often of great importance as well. A well-planned and executed FSBO can take advantage of speed in any number of ways.

Selling your home yourself can be the perfect answer to a home that needs to be sold as soon as possible. Look at it one way, you're the primary person involved in getting the home on the market and attracting a suitable buyer. You don't have to conform to a real estate agent's calendar or work schedule. You don't have to wait on someone else to draw up an ad or find the time to arrange an open house or a showing. It's up to you, including the speed with which you want those various things to occur.

> **Sales Snafu**
>
> When tackling the issue of the speed with which you can expect to sell your home, it's essential to bear in mind that speed is, in this case, a very relative term. The average American home takes about four months to sell. Keep that realistic benchmark in mind when considering just how quickly you can expect things to progress.

Other elements play into a home that needs to be sold ASAP. Let's say you've already found a new home that you want to close on as quickly as possible. Because the pressure is now on to find a buyer for your existing home, selling it on your own provides you complete leeway in setting the price you think will attract a buyer quickly. You may even go so far as to set the price below the reasonable market value you could expect to get if you want to move things along. A low price can attract a lot of buyers who recognize they're getting a value. You, on the other hand, benefit by turning things over fast (and, by the way, still pocketing a reasonable profit since you're saving a 6 percent sales commission.)

This table illustrates how a lower price moved a home faster but, in the end, provided a FSBO with a greater profit due to the absence of a commission.

Sale Price	Less Commission	Net to Seller	Time on Market
$250,000	$15,000	$235,000	45 days
$240,000	0	$240,000	30 days

The other end of the speed spectrum also fits nicely with the workings of selling your home yourself. Although many owners want to turn around their sale as reasonably fast as they can, others want to take their time. For instance, some homeowners aren't certain what they want to do after selling their home. Other homeowners are interested in dipping their big toe in the home sales market to see just how much they might be able to get.

If you're not in a breakneck hurry to get the deal done, selling your home on your own can make a world of sense. Like other elements of the process, you're the one who decides what and when. You may want to take your time in drawing up a marketing and advertising plan. You can be as picky as you wish about potential buyers and what they bring to the sale. It's entirely up to you.

Remember, freedom is a wonderful thing, but you're as bound as anyone to adhere to the law. That means following anti-discrimination guidelines in selecting buyers with whom you deal. If you have any concerns, check with an attorney.

Sales Snafu

Here, even the most ardent FSBO fan would have to sympathize with a real estate agent. After all, they're in it to make a living, and nothing can prove more maddening than a seller who wants to take his own sweet time about getting the sale completed. It's not hard to understand that agents would prefer devoting their time and energies to homes whose owner are a good deal more eager to get the sale done ASAP.

Who Better Than You?

Another important issue to bear in mind is that you're likely your home's best salesperson. Who could possibly know more about it than you—its charming little nuances and features, advantages, and joys that may not be readily apparent on the surface?

That, in turn, puts you in the best possible position to know exactly what sort of sales and marketing strategy will ultimately put your home in the best light. Granted, a skilled real estate agent can learn some, if not all, of those advantages. But as the homeowner, you know them through the power of your own experience. And that adds up to another advantage to FSBOs: at the end of the day, you know more about your own home than anyone else possibly could.

We'll look at this in greater detail later in this chapter, but knowing everything there is to know about your home shouldn't come at the expense of objectivity. In-depth knowledge can be undercut by an inability to acknowledge problems or becoming too emotional about the process—in other words, not being able to detach from your home. It's essential to approach the sale of your home as a *house*—a commodity than you know very well, but a commodity nonetheless.

Is It Right for You?

By now, you're hopefully sold on some of the advantages of selling your home on your own. But, truth be told, not everyone is cut out to sell their own home. This can be due to any number of reasons. Perhaps you just don't have the patience or the attitude necessary to steer a home sale from beginning to end. Many would-be FSBOs were nothing but enthusiastic at the outset of the project, only to abandon their efforts in failure and frustration. So it's essential to do a bit of soul searching to see if you're the kind of person who can make the most of the FSBO experience.

First, Know Thyself

That ancient bit of wisdom applies to various aspects of our lives, and it's very much the case in determining whether or not you're the sort of person who can sell their own home successfully. Even the best intentioned homeowners can have a tough time preparing, marketing, and, ultimately, selling their homes if their personal attributes aren't compatible with the responsibilities they'll be taking on.

The key to evaluating yourself and your potential to be a winning FSBO is complete honesty. Don't sugar coat or rationalize your thoughts! Take the process outside yourself—ask friends and loved ones to point out those things about you that may be positive or negative.

It's All in Your Mind

There's an old saying: attitude is everything. It's true—no matter how many outside obstacles you confront, how you process those problems can make all the difference between coming out on top or letting elements beyond your control get the best of you.

That's absolutely central to how you approach selling your own home. One of the most common attributes among successful FSBOs is a positive, solve-the-problem-don't-just-complain attitude. Think about that for a moment. If you're selling your home through a real estate agent and a problem crops up, it's often up to the agent to devise a solution. In a very real sense, when you hire an agent, you're allocating the problem solving responsibility to someone else.

Not so with a FSBO. For the most part, if you encounter a problem—say, your home just doesn't seem to be attracting enough attention or a potential buyer's being a pain in the you-know-what—it comes down to you to deal with it. And how you deal with it boils down to attitude. If you approach problems constructively and with confidence that you will find a solution, you're on your way to selling your home. But, if problems frustrate you and the particular whims of the home buying public drive you up a wall, that's not an attitude that encourages a successful sale.

Sales Snafu

Know that keeping a positive attitude is particularly important when dealing with potential buyers. Although it's changing, many home shoppers prefer to work through a real estate agent rather than with a seller directly. So, your attitude can make a big difference in winning over an otherwise wary buyer. That means it's particularly important to be as patient and professional as possible to convince any prospective buyer that you do, in fact, know what you're doing.

So, examine your attitude as a whole on top of individual advantages and drawbacks. How you approach the process likely will influence every single element—and, the likelihood of a "sold" sticker eventually crowning your signage.

Remember: It's a House

Needless to say, every homeowner trying to sell his or her house wants the process to be a rousing success. Many sellers make every effort toward that goal—an immaculate house to show, killer marketing and advertising, and top-notch open houses.

However, one overriding problem derails all that terrific effort—being too emotionally attached to the process. As we discussed earlier, some sellers are not just selling a *house*—they're selling their *home*.

The problem with this is one of objectivity. Because what they're trying to sell is very much theirs—perhaps something in which they have a substantial financial and emotional investment—they forget that what they're trying to sell is a commodity, pure and simple.

This can cause real problems. Perhaps an owner rejects a fairly reasonable offer because the money, somehow or other, isn't sufficient for his "baby." Maybe an owner takes offense when an otherwise interested buyer remarks that she doesn't care for the paint scheme. The seller may even go so far that he rejects a buyer simply because he doesn't care for the way the buyer looks. He can't leave his precious home in the hands of someone like that! (Not only illogical, but potentially illegal as well.)

The ability to approach the process as objectively as possible is an essential skill for being a successful FSBO. This is not arranging your child's marriage. You're trying to sell a home that, no matter how much it might mean to you, is nothing more than a collection of wood, cement, and brick.

Let's Check You Out!

Our discussion in this chapter boils down to a simple truth. Like everything else in life, not every homeowner is in the right position to sell his or her home. So to wrap up, here's a checklist of 20 questions that hit on many of the essential issues that are important to a successful FSBO. Some we've already raised; others are new. Regardless of whether you're familiar with a few of these questions, approach each one as thoughtfully and honestly as you possibly can.

The FSBO 20

❏ Do you consider yourself an independent person?

❏ Do you enjoy working with numbers?

❏ Would you say you're detail oriented?

❏ Would you say you have any sales ability?

❏ Do you enjoy in-depth, detailed research?

❏ Do you have a sense of humor (seriously, this is an important one!)?

❏ Are you good at dealing with difficult people?

❏ Do you generally have a positive attitude about things?

❏ Do you prefer acting on your own rather than waiting for others to act on your behalf?

❏ Would you say you're a practical person?

❏ Do you enjoy handling a number of details at once?

❏ Do you consider yourself a patient person?

❏ Does your life offer adequate time to take on an involved project?

❏ If need be, are you flexible if it helps solve a problem?

❏ Are you comfortable asking someone for help if you need it?

❏ Do you take critical feedback well?

❑ Do you recover from setbacks and disappointment easily?

❑ Are you handy with home repairs and fix-ups?

❑ If you're not, are you willing to spend some money in hopes of recouping it later?

❑ Would you say you're a good negotiator?

Add up your yes and no answers. If you're more on the yes side, chances are excellent that you're the right kind of person to sell your home on your own. If, on the other hand, there are more no's, think carefully about whether you wish to proceed on your own or pursue other options.

Is the Time Right?

One final issue winds up our discussion of FSBO—time. In fact, that's actually more than one single issue. As we've seen, time is an important part of the FSBO process—for instance, how quickly or deliberately a homeowner wants to sell his or her home.

But time plays other roles as well. The first issue is the time of year you put your house on the market because this can impact your efforts in several ways. Keep in mind that certain times of year are better than others for selling a home. While that depends in part on where you live and other factors, spring is generally considered optimal. By this point, winter is finally over, and buyers are looking to make a fresh start in a new home.

Selling Smarts

Local market conditions also can effect when conditions are optimal to sell a home. If, for instance, you live in a warm climate, a backyard pool is going to look awfully enticing to buyers cutting through the heat of the summer. The same can hold true for homes that accent the changing of the leaves in the fall.

Not only does the time of year influence your chances for success, it also effects your preparation time. If spring is around the corner and you're looking to sell, will you have enough time to get ready? If you're approaching a slower time of year, are you in a position to wait for a more favorable selling period?

The time of year isn't the only issue. The time involved in the process is just as important—not to mention your commitment to meeting those time demands. A FSBO can be a time-intensive task. As we'll see in subsequent chapters, there are many steps involved—many of which mandate significant time and effort—and each unto itself can be demanding in any number of ways.

So think about your commitment to that time-consuming process, not to mention your own circumstances. Will your home and professional life afford you enough time to do the job correctly? Will you have to travel any significant amount of time, either for business or pleasure? We'll offer some tips and powerful strategies to help meet the time demands of a FSBO, but it's important to acknowledge that you'll need adequate time to see the process through to the best conclusion possible.

But know that, no matter how time-consuming, the investment is usually worth the end result—not only in money in your pocket, but in the satisfaction and personal reward that a successful FSBO can offer. Now that you know some of the ways a FSBO can pay off in a big way—not to mention whether you're suitable for the challenges ahead—we can move on to the first practical steps in preparing your home for a successful, and hopefully brief, stint on the market.

Online Resources for the Basics

Here are a few websites that can introduce you to FSBOs and further your understanding of the differences between selling your home yourself and using a real estate agent:

- ForSalebyOwner.com (www.forsalebyowner.com)—A terrific resource for learning about the FSBO process. Free FSBO manual available for download. Also a powerful vehicle for listing and selling your FSBO.

- Realtor.com (www.realtor.com)—The online home of the National Association of Realtors. Lots of information on using a realtor to sell your home.

- SellYourHomeYourself.com (www.sellyourhomeyourself.com)—Another substantial guide for using the FSBO process to best advantage. Home seller's manual for sale.

- U.S. Department of Housing and Urban Development (www.hud.gov/selling/index.cfm)—A terrific overview of the various steps involved in selling your home. Also refers to a variety of additional resources.

- OurBroker.com (www.ourbroker.com)—Offered by real estate author Peter Miller, this site provides a wealth of information on the entire home selling process, including FSBOs. Also includes on-site calculators and links to valuable resources.

The Least You Need to Know

- ◆ Saving money by not paying a commission isn't the only advantage to selling your home yourself. You control the entire process and can dictate what you want to happen and when.

- ◆ It's important to know whether you're the right kind of person to oversee a FSBO. Successful sellers are detail-minded, patient, and comfortable with overcoming problems and obstacles.

- ◆ Don't underestimate the time commitment involved in a FSBO. There are many steps, many of them exceedingly time-consuming, so enter the FSBO process with an understanding that the road ahead, however rewarding, may prove long.

Chapter **2**

Start Shaping Up!

In This Chapter

- ◆ Sprucing up your space
- ◆ Improvements that boost your home's value
- ◆ Staging a sale
- ◆ Home guarantee pros and cons

The old adage, "You never get a second chance to make a first impression" is never more applicable than with home sales. Home buyers want to be "wowed" at first sight by your place—anything less is likely to turn them off.

Fortunately, there is a lot you can do yourself to impress potential buyers. Some improvements, like repairing serious plumbing leaks or updating electrical work, may require professional help. But most projects, like getting rid of clutter and cleaning, you'll be able to tackle yourself.

Investing muscle, and a little money, will pay big dividends when it comes time to put your place on the market. An attractive home yields more interested buyers and increases the likelihood you'll get offers close to— or above—your asking price.

To Improve or Not?

Homebuyers are attracted to homes that are bright, spacious, and clean. Though you can't change your home's layout to make it bigger, you can easily make it sparkle.

Unless you're content to accept less than the market value for your home, get ready to invest some time and energy readying your home for sale.

Why Appearance Can Kill a Sale

Think a little clean up doesn't matter? Think again. Although you may be totally comfortable living with dirty dishes piled high in the sink and kids' toys strewn about the house, a disheveled house suggests to buyers that you haven't been taking care of the place. No one wants to move into a home that has not been maintained properly or regularly. And even if they can see past the dirt and items needing repair, they're going to offer you far less to take on those projects themselves.

> **FSBO Facts**
>
> The typical buyer takes an average of three minutes to see a home the first time, according to Julie Dana of TheHomeStylist.com.

> **FSBO Facts**
>
> Preparing and fixing up a home for sale is the second most difficult task for FSBO sellers, reports a 2003 National Association of Realtors "Profile of Homebuyers and Sellers." The first is understanding the paperwork.

Your challenge is to look at your property with the eye of a buyer. Try and take a step back, or ask a friend or neighbor to help you, and tour your home as buyers will. What stands out? What are any negatives they may spot? Where does your eye go as you enter each room? What do you smell as you first enter the home? Be ruthless.

Your goal is not to show your house as you've lived in it, but to show your house in the best possible light—so it will sell. There's a difference. And when selling your home, the littlest things can matter most.

To ensure you're covering all your bases, or uncovering all your eyesores, use this handy checklist as you tour your home:

Improvements Checklist

❏ Curbside view   ❏ Front walkway

❏ Family room   ❏ Living room

- ❏ Front door and entryway
- ❏ Kitchen
- ❏ Front landscaping
- ❏ Mudroom/pantry
- ❏ Roofline
- ❏ Garage door and front
- ❏ Sides of property
- ❏ Garage interior
- ❏ Standalone mailbox
- ❏ Powder room
- ❏ Back deck/patio

- ❏ Master bedroom
- ❏ Back yard
- ❏ Additional bedrooms
- ❏ Front foyer
- ❏ Bathrooms
- ❏ Dining room
- ❏ Laundry area
- ❏ Hallways
- ❏ Attic
- ❏ Closets
- ❏ Basement

As you enter each room, what is your first impression? What could you do to improve the room's appearance? And what would make the space seem bigger or brighter?

You've just drafted your basic to-do list.

> **FSBO Facts**
>
> Buyers make up their minds in the first 15 seconds. The rest of the time is spent justifying their initial decision, says Julie Dana of TheHomeStylist.com.

Research, Research, Research

"People who are buying a home are comparing available homes on the market. Sellers should, too," says James Thomas Webb, CEO of CitiRise Redevelopment Corp. in Weston, Florida. Webb, who has decades of experience buying and refurbishing homes for investment purposes, strongly recommends that sellers look at comparable homes on the market to see what kinds of improvements will yield the best return. Before you go replacing perfectly good plumbing fixtures or installing a new high-end sink, find out what the standards are for your neighborhood.

For example, look for information about the type of flooring in area homes—is it hardwood, linoleum, tile, or carpeting? Do the homes have central air? What kinds of kitchen appliances are frequently mentioned? Are they Kenmore, GE, or Viking? And what kind of countertop is common? Do most homes have laminate, Corian, or granite? Make sure you're comparing apples-to-apples in terms of home features so you can spot the strengths and weaknesses of your home. One tool for finding like homes in your area is www.forsalebyowner.com.

To learn what features homes in your area have, turn to your local Multiple Listing Services (MLS) website. For instance, in Rochester, New York, www.homesteadnet.com lists all homes in the area for sale with complete descriptions and photos (see the figure that follows). If you can't find an online source with local real estate listings, you can purchase a list of comparable properties at www.forsalebyowner.com/appraisals for between $5 and $30. This information also will help you determine an appropriate price for your home.

MLS websites like this one in Rochester, New York, are an excellent resource for researching properties like yours.

Researching what most homes feature will help you assess where your home may fall short in a buyer's eyes. And that's where you should start your improvement efforts in order to get the biggest bang for your buck.

On the Outside—Improve Curb Appeal

The initial decision to look at your home is frequently made based on its outward appearance. Some buyers will do a "drive-by" to scope out the exterior of your home. And based on its curb appeal—what they see from the street—they'll decide whether or not to go inside.

Assuming your home is already in decent structural shape, there are many things you can do to spiff up its appearance.

The Exterior

Improving your home's exterior appearance may take a little effort, but if you've been keeping up with needed repairs, it shouldn't be very involved.

A fresh coat of paint is always a good idea, especially if the home's wood siding is chipped or peeling. If you have aluminum siding, soapy water or a professional pressure wash will help get rid of built-up dirt and dust.

A doorway that stands out is also a plus, so consider giving it a fresh coat of paint, or wash, too. Torn window or door screens should be replaced, which isn't hard to do, and windows should be cleaned.

If you have a front porch or landing, clean it off and make it more inviting, such as with a small chair or table with flowers. Or if you've been using it as a storage area, clear it out.

Flowers and plants add charm and life to a front stoop or door, but don't go overboard. Too much of anything is distracting and causes a cluttered appearance.

Seasonal decorations, such as holiday lights strung across the roofline or fabric ghosts hanging from nearby trees, should be taken down. Again, it's just too distracting.

Selling Smarts

Unless it's winter and your walkway is covered with snow, spend a little money on colorful perennials and plant them. You'll draw attention to your home and suggest to potential buyers that you're meticulous, which boosts the value of your home.

The Yard

Spending a little time to make your yard neat and clean is also worth it. Some buyers have told us they have refused to even enter homes with overgrown or unkempt yards. The house may have been neat-as-a-pin inside, but the yard full of tall grass and weeds was a major turnoff.

Here are some of the simplest things to do to get your yard ship-shape:

♦ Mow the lawn, especially right before a showing or open house.

Sales Snafu

A big mistake some homeowners make is tackling too much all at once. Instead, start small or stagger your efforts. For instance, mulch your flower beds one weekend, install flowers the next, and trim all the bushes the following weekend, rather than planning to do it all at once.

- Pick up any dog droppings—preferably before you get the lawn mower out.

- During the winter, make sure all the snow is neatly shoveled from walkways.

- Cut back any trees or shrubs blocking front windows.

- Trim overgrown trees or bushes.

- Pull weeds from the flower beds and loosen the soil with a hoe or spade.

- Replace any burned out light bulbs in front lights or lanterns.

- Consider installing low voltage lighting to edge a walkway or as an uplight beneath a tree to show off its height.

- Edge the lawn, trimming any grass hanging over on the driveway or sidewalk.

- Sweep the front sidewalk and driveway.

- Store kids toys, sports equipment, and other outdoor accessories that may be laying around.

Your lawn may not make or break a sale, but a clean, neat one will add to the overall positive image of your home.

More Than a Pretty Face

Although home improvements generally increase the overall value of your home, some improvements are better than others. The average amount recouped from home improvement projects in 2004 was 80.3 percent, according to *Remodeling* magazine's "Cost vs. Value Report," which is down slightly from the 2003 average of 86.4 percent. That means for every $1,000 invested in improvements, homeowners earned back an average of $803.

Selling Smarts _____

The appearance of some home finishes are more important than the brand name, says James Thomas Webb, CEO of CitiRise Redevelopment Corp., which specializes in renovating homes. For instance, you don't need to invest in a $2,000 high-end kitchen faucet if you can find a similar looking one for $200 at Home Depot. Nor do you need to overpay for a new fancy showerhead or dovetailed kitchen cabinet drawers. Instead, come close to the look of the upscale features by buying their lower-priced cousins.

Remodeling magazine reports the following national averages for the top 15 home improvements in 2004:

Project	Typical Cost	% Recouped
Minor kitchen remodel	$15,273	92.9%
Siding replacement	$6,946	92.8%
Bathroom remodel	$9,861	90.1%
Deck addition	$6,917	86.7%
Bathroom addition	$21,087	86.4%
Bathroom remodel, upscale	$25,273	85.6%
Window replacement	$9,273	84.5%
Window replacement, upscale	$15,383	83.7%
Attic bedroom	$35,960	82.7%
Roofing replacement	$11,376	80.8%
Family room	$52,562	80.6%
Master suite	$70,245	80.1%
Major kitchen remodel	$42,660	79.4%
Basement remodel	$47,888	76.1%
Sunroom addition	$31,063	70.8%

If you're not up for one of these major renovations, take heart. You can significantly improve the appeal of your home without adding another bathroom or increasing the square footage of the home.

Basic Interior Improvements Worth Your Time

Beyond making repairs, it often pays to update home fixtures. Even if older features still work well, buyers are more likely to appreciate new home trimmings than old. For example, a new, white elongated toilet base and seat is worth much more than the $160 it costs to buy and install, when compared with the existing 1960s-era peach-colored unit with ratty seat.

Kitchens and baths matter most to buyers, say the pros, so any investment in new or upgraded features can boost the appeal of your home right off the bat. Webb of CitiRise advises evaluating your existing:

◆ Kitchen cabinets

◆ Countertop

◆ Faucet

◆ Appliances

◆ Toilet

◆ Bathroom sink faucet

◆ Showerhead/bath faucet

If you find from your research that other area homes have one or more features that your home is lacking, focus on finding upgrades that look like, but don't cost like, more expensive accessories. For example, swapping out an older lime green laminate refrigerator with a new stainless steel replacement, but not necessarily a top-of-the-line SubZero model. Or exchanging a very traditional kitchen faucet with a modern, more contemporary one; buying a high-end-looking faucet instead of a $600+ authentic, imported European one.

Although market conditions and housing prices vary widely, Webb has found that, on average, he can perform the most important upgrades on a 2,000 sq. ft. home for under $5,500. That includes $2,000 for new carpeting, $1,800 for kitchen and bath upgrades, and $1,200 to have a pro repaint the home, with a $400 budget for paint.

Staging Secrets the Pros Use

Buyers ask themselves three major questions when they tour a home, explains Julie Dana of TheHomeStylist.com. They want to know:

1. Can I imagine myself, or my family, living here?

2. Is this an easy, carefree home to live in?

3. Is this a good value for my money?

To help buyers answer these questions affirmatively, your home needs to be decorated and arranged in a particular way. This process is called *staging* or home or property enhancement.

Dana offers the following staging tips to make the best impression on buyers:

Tools of the Trade

Staging, which is a registered trademark of StagedHomes.com, describes the process of preparing a home for sale, making it as appealing as possible by cleaning, rearranging, and decorating it for maximum impact.

♦ Remove. You'll want to take out anything personal, so buyers can imagine themselves in your space. This includes family photographs, toiletries, mail, and special collectibles (see the figures that follow).

Before: Remove personal items.

(Photo by Julie Dana of The Home Stylist)

After: A cleaner look.

(Photo by Julie Dana of The Home Stylist)

◆ Declutter. Clear all papers, knick-knacks, and junk from countertops, tables, and corners. Either throw it out, if you know you don't need it anymore, or box it all up and store it out of sight (see the figures that follow).

Before: Declutter the living areas.

(Photo by Julie Dana of The Home Stylist)

After: A cleaner look.

(Photo by Julie Dana of The Home Stylist)

◆ Clean. "The house needs to be absolutely sparkling clean," says Dana, who advises washing windows inside and out, shining the kitchen sink, dusting baseboards, bleaching grout around tiles, in addition to a basic scrub-down. Wipe down the walls, use glass cleaner on mirrors, hanging artwork, and the fronts of kitchen appliances. Clean the carpets, mop the floors, wash the rugs.

◆ Repair. Take care of any minor patching needed on walls, regrout or retile worn areas in your bathroom or kitchen, replace broken windows, and finish any unfinished projects you've been meaning to get to.

◆ Freshen. If it's been a while since you've painted, put a new coat of paint on your walls. Neutral colors, like white, beige, and tan, are the safest choice. Removing wallpaper is also smart, replacing it with neutral paint.

◆ Air out. Buyers should not be able to smell any odors in your home, which means airing out cooking odors, emptying garbage pails, and cleaning out the litter box long before buyers stop by. Cookies baking in the oven or potpourri on the stove are two ways to mask any odors while buyers are there.

◆ Hide. "Do not have daily housekeeping supplies visible to potential buyers," says Dana. "This includes laundry baskets and dish drainers—nothing to remind people that there will be work to do in this house." Buyers want to live in an easy-to-care for home; removing signs of work helps meet that need (see the figures that follow).

Before: Hide household supplies.

(Photo by Julie Dana of The Home Stylist)

After: A cleaner look.

(Photo by Julie Dana of The Home Stylist)

♦ Reduce. Although this step is frequently overlooked by sellers, says Dana, it's one of the most important. To make your home appear spacious, with plenty of room to grow, you should take out about half of your possessions. That means taking out extra furniture as well as clearing out items in your closets. All of your closets should be no more than half full, suggesting that there is more than enough space to live in, and meeting a buyer's need to find a good value for the money (see the figures that follow).

And don't just relocate everything to somewhere else in the house—you need to get it off-site, or at least out of site. Depending on how much stuff you have, a local self-storage facility is a good option. If that doesn't work for you, try and contain everything in one area, either in the basement, attic, or garage. If you determine that you don't want to move a lot of it, hold a garage sale or donate it to a nonprofit (ask them to pick it up).

Before: Reduce visible items.

(Photo by Julie Dana of The Home Stylist)

After: A cleaner look.

(Photo by Julie Dana of The Home Stylist)

For many homes, these basic clean-up steps may be enough. The key is to clear out anything that interferes with a buyer's ability to picture themselves living there.

Hiring a pro to stage your home can cost anywhere from a few hundred dollars to a couple thousand dollars, with the return on that investment estimated to be two to three times the cost, says Neal Hribar, a California-based property enhancement professional. But by following these recommendations, you should be able to tackle many of the enhancements yourself.

Good to Guarantee?

Buyers have fears about buying a home. Is it the right one? Is it big enough? Are we paying too much? Will we like it? Will something major go wrong with it right after we buy it? You can't alleviate many of these concerns, but you can remove the risk of major repairs by purchasing a *home warranty*. At a cost of around $400, you can make your home more attractive to buyers. According to a Gallop Poll, eight out of 10 buyers would prefer to buy a warranted home over an unwarranted one.

Home warranties are attractive for several reasons, besides attracting more buyers:

Tools of the Trade

A **home warranty** is a service contract purchased to protect the seller from a major household expense while the home is listed for sale and up to a year after closing. Generally, major systems like heating and air conditioning units, plumbing, and electrical, as well as appliances, are covered against breakdown.

FSBO Facts

Homes with home warranties sell for up to 3 percent more, on average, than those without, according to a *BusinessWeek* magazine article cited on a Prudential Realtors website.

♦ You're protected against costly repairs while you're gearing up to move to a new home. A small deductible may be required for each repair call, however. The Home Warranty Association of California reports an average of 1.7 to 2 claims per contract per year occur.

♦ Homes with warranties sell faster than unwarranted ones, according to the National Home Warranty Association.

♦ You reduce the chance of a dispute over a defective appliance or mechanical system, which can delay a closing. Just call your warrantor and get it taken care of.

♦ You also reduce the odds of the buyer asking you to cover the cost of something that broke down after closing. The warranty would cover it.

Many real estate agents are now including home warranties as part of the package they offer sellers. Nearly nine out of every 10 existing home sales on the West Coast includes a home warranty, reports the Warranty Association of California, which suggests you may be at a disadvantage without one.

The Ugly Duckling—Making the Most of an Unattractive Home

So what do you do when you fear your home's appearance may scare away buyers? Follow the advice of fashionistas everywhere: downplay the negatives and highlight the positives.

Every home has its pros and cons—some are just more obvious from the road. If that's the case with your place, you'll want to do everything you can to improve your home's worst feature. And there is always something you can do.

If your home's worst side is visible from the street, you can either try and cover it up, or draw buyers' attention away from it. For example, if your home is a 12th floor condo with windows all facing the backside of a rundown industrial plant, you'll want to keep everyone's attention on the interior. Use beautiful window treatments with sheer curtains to cover up the view without blocking the light. On the other hand, if you live in a house with a bleak, unattractive front yard, you have a little more control over the environment. You may choose to punch up the color on the house or the trim, as well as add a few bushes or trees to liven the space. If the architecture is hideous, there is little you can do to fix it. However, you can cover it, by installing window awnings, for instance, or adding some tall bushes and vines.

Look for ways to play up your home's best aspects, too, whether it's the size of the yard, the ample sunlight that flows through the house, the newly renovated kitchen, or cozy fireplace. Draw attention to whatever you believe is the home's biggest selling point; that may be as obvious as hardwood floors throughout, or as intangible as being in the best school district around.

If you have no trouble drawing buyers in, but they're turned off by an aspect of the home's interior, our advice is the same—play up the positives, cover the negatives. For example, if the home seems dark, stock up on white paint and give all the rooms a facelift. Or install additional lighting wherever you can. If your home is energy efficient, or is part of a municipal utility, and has below average utility costs, set your monthly utility statements on the kitchen counter to catch the eye of fiscally responsible buyers coming through. If it seems small for the square footage quoted, take out more furniture, remove wall hangings and artwork—don't worry about it looking bare. Err on the side of empty.

Remember, all you need is one buyer, one person or family, who falls in love with your place.

Online Resources to Help Shape Up

For more information about topics covered in this chapter, check out the following websites:

◆ www.electronicappraiser.com. For a report containing comparable home information, as well as an appraisal of your home's value, check out this website. Prices start as low as $3.95, with a complete report costing $29.95.

◆ www.foresalebyowner.com. Download our e-book, *The Complete Guide to Buying and Selling Your Own Home*, for tips on readying your place for sale.

◆ www.hgtv.com. See HGTV for tutorials on home improvements and decorating, compliments of shows like *Designed to Sell* and *Curb Appeal*.

◆ www.hmsnet.com. Visit this website to learn more about home warranties, how they work, and what is covered by HMS National Home Warranty.

◆ www.homewarranty.com. For information about home warranties and to apply for one online, visit Fidelity National Home Warranty.

◆ www.lowes.com. Check out the Home Solutions section of the site for online instruction on everything from installing appliances to replacing broken tile to doing a quality paint job.

◆ www.stagedhomes.com. Visit this site to search the directory of certified staging professionals nationwide. Find someone locally who can help you put your home's best foot forward.

The Least You Need to Know

◆ The best thing you can do to improve the appearance of your home is to clear it out—your furniture and knick-knacks—and clean it up—everything from putting a fresh coat of paint on the walls to steam-cleaning the carpets, decluttering all the surfaces, and airing out the rooms.

◆ Appeal to your buyers' psychological needs for a spacious, clean, easy-to-live-in home by removing all traces of cleaning products and implements, as well as personal keepsakes and toiletries.

◆ Research what other homes in your area have feature-wise and invest in little upgrades to match those. Appearance is more important than brand name, so don't buy the top-of-the-line.

◆ Consider investing in a home warranty to eliminate any fears buyers may have about buying your home, especially if it happens to be older. Studies indicate homes with warranties sell faster and for more money.

Chapter 3

Team Up!

In This Chapter

- ◆ You're not completely alone
- ◆ How a lender can help
- ◆ The importance of an attorney
- ◆ What the heck is a title company?
- ◆ Put a home inspector on your team

Selling your home on your own is something of a misleading statement. Granted, you're overseeing the entire process yourself. But that doesn't mean you're out there completely on your own, coping with every single trial and challenge of the real estate market without a single helping hand.

Far from it. In this chapter, we introduce you to various people who will ultimately make up your overall FSBO team. Although a FSBO puts control of the sale of your home directly in your lap, there are certain services and skills that are best deferred to others whose expertise lies in that specialty. Here's who they are, where you can find them, and what to look for.

Ready to Lend—Partnering with a Lender

This may seem something of a surprise to many new to the FSBO process. If you're the one selling the home rather than buying it, why should you concern yourself with finding an appropriate *mortgage lender*? Well, there are several good reasons, all of which can impact the entire selling process from beginning to end.

Tools of the Trade

It's important to know the difference between a mortgage banker and a mortgage lender. A mortgage banker lends its own money, although it can also sell the loan later. A **mortgage lender** is a go-between. He or she shops for loan providers and partners them with the buyer. While mortgage bankers may have fewer loan programs, they are often less expensive than a broker who charges for his services. **Prequalifying** a buyer involves various financial calculations to determine whether a particular buyer is in a financial position to afford a home. As the term suggests, prequalifying happens relatively early in the sales process. Be aware this doesn't guarantee a loan—other factors such as employment and credit history figure into whether a lender will actually approve a loan.

Prequalify Potential Buyers

A central issue in successfully completing the sale of your home is the buyer's financial situation. Put another way, is the buyer financially capable of buying your home?

A buyer's ability to follow through is certainly an issue you want settled before getting into the meat of arranging the sale of your home. And in fact, many buyers appreciate this and obtain suitable loan *prequalification* before they even begin their search for a new home.

But not everyone. That's why it's advantageous to develop a relationship with a lender to provide prequalification services for any buyers who may express an interest in your home. It's an important form of self-protection—even the most enthusiastic of buyers is, in the end, of little value to you if it turns out no lender will provide them with the necessary financing to buy your home.

Just what's involved in prequalifying? Basically, it involves comparing a buyer's income with the various elements that go into the financial obligation of owning a home, including the mortgage payment itself, taxes, and insurance. Generally, not counting credit cards and other forms of debt, most lenders do not want a buyer's home buying financial obligation to exceed 28 percent of their gross income (36 to 40 percent if other kinds of debt are included).

To illustrate: if your gross income is $50,000 a year, most lenders will want to see no more than roughly $1600 in overall monthly debt to qualify for a loan.

To get a further feel for the sorts of issues raised in the prequalification process, here's a sample prequalification form.

Buyer Pre-Qualification Form

Information Supplied by Buyer
A. Gross Annual Income (Pretax) $_____

B. Monthly Long Term Obligations:
   Automobile $_____
   Child Support $_____
   Student Loans $_____
   Credit Card Debts $_____
   Other $_____
                        TOTAL $_____

Calculations Based on Information Provided Above
C. Gross Monthly Income $_____
                                             (Line A ÷ 12)

D. Monthly Allowable Housing
   Expense plus Long Term Obligations $_____
                                             (Line C ×.36)

E. Monthly Allowable Housing Expense
   E1. Line D − Line B (TOTAL) $_____
   E2. Line C × .28 $_____
   E3. Lesser of Lines E1 or E2 $_____

F. Monthly Principal and Interest $_____
                                             (Line E3 × .8)

G. Estimated 30-Year Mortgage Amount $_____
                                             (Line F ÷ Interest Rate Factor)

Interest Rate	Factor		
6.0%	.0060	7.5%	.0070
6.5%	.0063	8.0%	.0074
7.0%	.0067	8.5%	.0077

H. Estimated Affordable Price Range $_____
                                             (Line G ÷ Down Payment % Factor)

Down Payment % Factor	
3%	.97
5%	.95
10%	.90
15%	.85
20%	.80

A sample prequalification form.

Of course, as the seller, you can prequalify buyers yourself. We offer a few websites at the end of this chapter that can help you do just that. The preceding prequalification form gives you an idea of the sorts of issues that need to be addressed. But given the importance of prequalifying buyers—identifying qualified buyers and weeding out others who, however interested, just won't be able to get the deal done—it's never a bad idea to defer the responsibility to a pro. If nothing else, that frees time up for you to concentrate on other responsibilities in the FSBO process. It can also prove advantageous to a buyer who, if they follow through on buying your home, has a lender already in place with whom they're prequalified.

Prepare a Financial Breakdown Sheet

A solid lender on your team can also assist in marketing your home. Other issues aside, it's inevitably important that you attract buyers who are financially capable of buying your home, and letting them know in complete terms just what those financial requirements might be.

That's where the importance of a financial breakdown sheet comes in. A breakdown sheet can be provided to anyone who visits your home during the sales process, and it specifies in the most concrete terms possible the various financial requirements involved in buying your home, including necessary down payments, monthly mortgage payments, and other monetary issues.

A lender can prove to be of invaluable help in identifying and calculating what you need to include in a financial breakdown document. Not only can the breakdown sheet prove important in clearly identifying who's capable of buying your home and who is not, but it can also be an effective marketing tool. A buyer who likes the look of your house and, with a quick glance at the breakdown sheet, can recognize it's within her financial means receives a great deal of positive news in a short timeframe—good news that may prompt her to move quickly to take her interest to the next level.

Sales Snafu

Don't confuse the financial breakdown sheet with other sorts of buyer handouts. A financial breakdown sheet addresses the various numbers associated with a home, nothing more. Other sorts of handouts highlight the actual features of the home, such as number of bedrooms, kitchen features, and other issues. Taken together, they provide buyers with a quick, yet comprehensive overview of your home.

Help with Your Next Home

Obviously, what homesellers do after their home is sold differs according to individual circumstances. Many may relocate, others may move into retirement communities and other like facilities, while still others may opt for a type of housing that's completely different from the one they just left, such as a former single-family homeowner choosing the easy maintenance of a condominium.

But no matter the route you choose, chances are good you may need a lender sometime in the future—perhaps immediately after selling your old home. That can make the presence of a lender particularly convenient. Rather than having to search for a new lender—a task that can dilute the time and effort you put into selling your home—partnering with a lender at the outset of the process gives you one less thing to worry about. And when it comes to selling a home and mapping out where to go from there, that's an advantage that's dearly worth seeking out.

Lender Checklist

As with anyone with whom you partner in your FSBO odyssey, it's always important to know the right questions to ask to ensure that you're partnering with someone suited to your needs and goals. Here's a sampling of issues to raise with any prospective lender:

- ◆ How experienced are they in working with a FSBO?
- ◆ How available will they be to answer questions and, if need be, prequalify prospective buyers?
- ◆ What sorts of loan programs do they offer?
- ◆ Can they assist you in drawing up a financial breakdown sheet?
- ◆ Will they be available to help identify elements of loan programs that may affect you as the seller?
- ◆ Can they provide you with samples or prototypes of loans that would be consistent with a home in your price range?

Legal Leverage—The Role of an Attorney

A solid attorney is as critical a member of your FSBO team as anyone with whom you may work. While many other partners will focus on one specific element of your home selling strategy—such as the lender sticking to the financial end of things—an attorney can help you in any number of areas. That means it's essential to know what attorneys do, how they can help, and how you can find one that suits your needs and goals.

Sales Snafu

Is it absolutely required that an attorney work with you on the sale of your home? No. A number of sources exist where you can get boilerplate legal documents; on top of that, you can always do whatever legal research may be necessary. Is it a good idea to work with an attorney anyway? Almost always, the answer is "yes." Legal pitfalls are everywhere in real estate; tack on the guidance and feedback of a trusted advisor, and an attorney's services prove to be well worth the money you spend.

Although an attorney's work with FSBO will likely differ considerably between clients, the following provides just a sampling of some of the issues and responsibilities with which an attorney can prove of invaluable help:

♦ Supply you with all necessary legal documentation.

♦ Tailor documents and advice to conform with specific local requirements and laws.

♦ Review any documents which you may draft, such as flyers and disclosure material, to ensure that they're legally compliant.

♦ Offer general feedback on strategy, marketing, and other aspects of the sale.

♦ Participate in or head up any negotiations that may be necessary.

Selling Smarts

It's always best to bring an attorney on board as early in the process as possible. That way, she becomes part of your team and can help direct your efforts as efficiently as possible. Early participation can also help identify and head off problems before they blow up in your face.

That's a pretty hefty list, one that makes a pretty compelling case for partnering with a suitable attorney. Particularly important is the last item on our list—the attorney's role in negotiating various terms of the sale. To be blunt, many of us don't enjoy or aren't particularly good at the art of negotiation. If you're one of them, an attorney willing to take on any negotiating that may be necessary will be worth his weight in gold.

This makes finding the right attorney an early priority. For some, that's an easy responsibility to fulfill because they may already work with an attorney who they like and trust. If that's not the case, it's always a good idea to ask for recommendations from colleagues and friends. Ask them how they have worked with their attorney. In particular, have them discuss any sort of real estate transactions in which their attorney was involved. Get a sense for how their attorney was to work with, how responsive she was, and what level of involvement and contact seemed the most appropriate.

If no one you know can suggest an attorney, contact your state bar association and ask for several local recommendations (see the figure that follows). Additionally, ask around your town or city's tax department or any other sort of governmental agency that may have something to do with real estate. Because they work in the field, chances are good they know of several qualified attorneys who may be able to meet your needs.

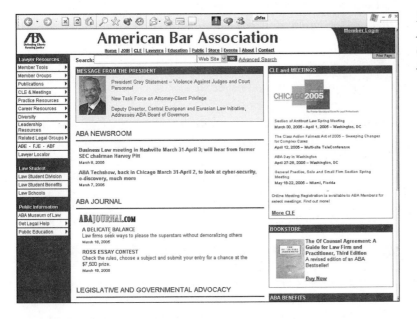

Legal websites such as the American Bar Association often have lawyer referral search engines.

Checklist of Attorney Questions

When looking for an attorney to work with on selling your home, there are a number of questions that you may wish to address. Here's a rundown:

◆ Do you have any experience or training specific to real estate? (It's not an absolute requirement, but experience or a professional background in real estate certainly is a plus.)

◆ How involved would you like to be in the process? (Some attorneys prefer ongoing contact, while others may only offer their services when they're asked. Ask, too, how they maintain contact—telephone, mail, or email.)

◆ How knowledgeable are you about local real estate market conditions?

◆ Would you be willing to take part in negotiations related to the sale of the house?

◆ What are your fees? (Because it's a fairly laid out process, lawyers often charge a flat fee to help with the sale of a home. Expect to pay anywhere in the range of $500 to $1000 for an attorney's services.)

◆ When do you expect your fees to be paid? (It's best not to pay the entire fee before the sale is finalized—that way, you don't have to pull out the checkbook until you're satisfied that everything has been taken care of. Better to pay a portion upfront and the balance when all is done.)

◆ Would you consider adjusting your fee if you represent me in the purchase of my next home? (Attorneys' rates are often subject to negotiation and a possible discount if more than one job is packaged together.)

It's usually a good idea to interview at least three attorneys before choosing one you like. That way, you get a sense of the various ways they may approach a relationship with you, their personal style, fee structure, and other considerations. Also ask about those parts of the sales process where they may not have to be involved. That can save you some money. It's ideal if the attorney also has a title company practice. Not only can that make the process go more smoothly, it may cost less in the long.

FSBO Facts

Although attorneys' fees will differ according to the individual practice, the local standard rate, and other issues, don't be surprised if you pay a bit more for an attorney's work with a FSBO. Because there's no agent involved on your end, there may be more work for the attorney to handle, such as any negotiations you involve him or her in—hence, a potentially bigger price tag.

Online Sources for Real Estate Laws

Because understanding real estate law is such an essential element to a successful FSBO—one that warrants some special treatment—here are a few websites that will prove helpful in fining solid legal advice and guidance:

- ◆ LawGuru.com (www.lawguru.com). An extensive resource of questions and answers on legal issues of all sorts, including real estate.

- ◆ ForSalebyOwner.com (www.forsalebyowner.com/servicedir.html). ForSalebyOwner.com provides a referral database for leads to real estate attorneys in your area.

- ◆ Legal organizations' websites, such as the American Bar Association (www.abanet.org). These also provide referral services for people trying to partner with a suitable attorney.

- ◆ Real Estate Lawyers.com (www.realestatelawyers.com). As the name suggests, a substantial source of information about real estate and the law. The site also provides a referral service.

The Title Company—What It Does

Our discussion of selecting an attorney naturally leads to the issue of the title company. Like an attorney, title companies are an important part of the home sale process and one which will work very closely with you and your attorney to see the job through to completion.

In a nutshell, a title company works to certify that you, as the seller, have the legal rights and authority to sell the property to a buyer. This is known as a *"clear title."* And whether you use a real estate agent or sell your home yourself, you'll need to pay for title services.

But a title company also provides a significant psychological boost to any FSBO. Paperwork for a closing on a home can be intimidating—that's what a title company does. In that sense, it's reassuring that you have someone on your team whose specialty is that very unnerving responsibility.

 Tools of the Trade _____

The term **title** refers to the legal ownership of a piece of property. You'll see this term cited in a number of instances throughout the sale process. A **lien** refers to any sort of legal claim that must be paid off when the property is sold. A lien can take in everything from an existing mortgage to a legal judgment against the property owner which has yet to be paid off. A **title policy** is basically a legal guarantee of the buyer's ownership of the property. It's essential in case someone in the future files a legal challenge to the ownership of the property.

A title company also works on the buyer's end. Here, the company works to make certain that the buyer has the legal right to obtain any sort of mortgage related to the purchase of the property.

One of a title company's primary responsibilities is to conduct a title search. This process, which can take upwards of three days or so to complete, involves reviewing records in your local County Clerk's office. The first task of the title search is to determine definitively who owns the property. The title search also aims to uncover whether there are any *liens* against your property.

The title company's search is rather thorough. The company will also contact local officials to make certain that all property taxes, sewer and water bills, if they apply, are paid and up to date. The overall idea is to make certain that you can legally sell the property and that there are no financial hurdles that can crop up later.

After the title company has completed its search and is satisfied that you have the legal right to sell it and no liens exist, it issues a type of insurance coverage known as a *title policy* to the buyer.

From there, a title company handles instructions and documents related to the closing on the sale of your home. It also prepares a final settlement statement. Also known as a HUD-1 statement, the settlement statement itemizes all funds that are payable at the closing. The totals identify what you as the seller will receive as well as what the buyer has to pay at the closing. The title company is also responsible for collecting and subsequently distributing all money involved in the sale.

Obviously, a title company will charge for whatever services it provides. These can differ according to individual companies and where you happen to live. However, some good news, a title company with whom you recently worked to buy the home will often offer you a discount. The same holds true for title companies with whom you do repeat business.

Home Inspectors

This is a specialist whose presence on a FSBO team may be a surprise to some. If you've taken part in the sale or purchase of a home, you know that a savvy buyer usually makes the final purchase contingent on a home inspection. Moreover, it's usually the buyer who pays for the service.

Why a home inspector for the seller? Naturally, no one can reasonably expect any home to be completely free of flaws. But the fewer problems a buyer uncovers, the greater your chance of a sale (and, possibly, at a better price as well). That's why it's a good idea to consider a home inspection proactively—to uncover significant problems and issues and, if need be, address them before a buyer ever steps through your front door.

What It Involves (And What It Doesn't)

A home inspection involves a careful review of various parts of your home, including the roof, electrical, heating, and plumbing systems, foundation, and other elements. The inspector looks for problems and then summarizes his findings in a written report (an example of a Sample Home Inspection Report is in Appendix C).

It's important to recognize that a conventional home inspection, while designed to be reasonably thorough, isn't necessarily exhaustive. For instance, while many inspectors will try to do so, insurance limitations may keep some from physically climbing onto your roof for the closest examination possible. Instead, they may just climb to the top of a ladder and look around.

A regular home inspection also may not cover certain specialty items and issues. These can range from pools to in-lawn sprinkler systems, fireplaces and chimneys, septic systems, and other features. These may mandate additional fees.

Depending on where you live, termites, radon, and other environmental issues can be of particular concern. In fact, local regulation may mandate checking these issues as part of any home inspection. Check with your local government to see if any of these additional issues should be of concern to you.

Sales Snafu

If your roof is of concern, you should ask a home inspector whether he makes it a practice to actually get on the roof during his inspection. If he doesn't, you may want to search for an inspector who will. Another option is finding a roofing contractor for a quick inspection.

What to Look For

To find a home inspector, ask for referrals from friends or colleagues who have been satisfied with their inspector's work. Your mortgage lender or attorney may also be able to recommend someone. A third option is contacting the American Society of Home Inspectors, which offers a referral service (www.ashi.org).

Ask any home inspector you're considering working with how many years experience they have. In particular, ask them about local experience, as the homes in your area may have issues specific to them. See if they are members of the American Society of Home Inspectors or some other professional organization. These groups have standards of practice that all members must follow.

Sales Snafu

As of this writing, not every state has legislation on the books that outline home inspection licensure and standards of practice. Additionally, what laws have been passed differ quite a bit from one state to the next. Visit the American Society of Home Inspectors' website to see if your state has enacted any laws that regulate home inspections.

The final issue is what you should expect to pay for a competent and comprehensive home inspection. Rates vary according to location and the size of the home—not to mention any add-on tests and inspections that may be necessary—but a reasonable ballpark estimate would be somewhere between $300 and $400 for a home in the neighborhood of 1,800 square feet.

Bear in mind that any problems of note that a home inspection identifies doesn't automatically mandate a cash outlay to address the issue. If you don't think it may adversely affect your chances of selling your home, let any buyers know about it and adjust your asking price accordingly.

Others on Your Team

There are still others you can recruit to be on your FSBO team. Unlike an attorney or the title company, any additional help is just that, but others can provide a valuable contribution to your overall home selling strategy and effort.

The Neighbors (Both Good and Bad)

Neighbors are like family members—as a rule, you don't get to choose who they happen to be. And as we know all too well, that can result in something of a mixed bag. There will be neighbors you get along with famously, while there will be others who rank alongside root canal work on the pleasant-to-experience scale.

Neighbors can pose some unique challenges when you're selling your home. Remember, you're not just selling your house, you're also selling its surroundings. Not only do you want to downplay those aspects of your neighborhood that may be less than utterly appealing, you also want to enlist your neighbors in your home selling effort as much as possible. Like any other aspect of your team, the more competent players you have on your side, the better your chances for eventual success.

Start by making sure all your neighbors know that you're trying to sell your home. After you have any marketing materials in hand, pass them along to any willing neighbors. See if they have any friends or acquaintances in mind who are on the hunt for a new home. This accomplishes two things: First, you recruit people who may be eager to help you out in any way possible. And, in so doing, it's a subtle way of asking them to keep their own property reasonably neat to boost the appearance of the neighborhood as a whole. This is a lot more subtle and diplomatic than asking them to take their empty trash cans away from the curb.

Believe it or not, telling neighbors you don't get along with about your FSBO can actually work in your favor. After all, if the guy across the street can't stand you, wouldn't it stand to reason that he'd like to see you move yesterday? Not to mention replacing you with a friend? Negative motivation, but powerful nonetheless.

From there, give some thought to a "neighbors only" open house where guests are encouraged to bring an interested friend. Put out a spread, mix some drinks, and let both neighbors and prospective buyers check out your home in detail.

Give some thought to hosting the neighbors-only open house before any other more general open house. The reason: if someone comes to an open house and knows that she may be one of the first prospective buyers to look at a house, she feels she has an inside track. That can lead to quick action if a buyer is genuinely interested.

Another strategy is to offer incentives. Let your neighbors know that anyone who refers the eventual buyer to you will win some sort of prize or reward. It may be a night on the town, 10 free movie rentals, or some other treat. But whatever you choose, make it clear that you appreciate any effort they may expend on your behalf.

Finally, let your neighbors know that their participation in the sale of your home doesn't just benefit you, the seller. By having a hand in looking for and referring suitable buyers, they can help craft the sort of neighborhood they enjoy and value. If, for instance, the street is stocked with young children, they can look for interested families. Older, empty nesters? Keep an eye peeled for buyers who fit that bill. Whatever characteristic or value they think important, taking an active role in helping you sell your home successfully gives them an opportunity to build the sort of neighborhood they like best.

 Sales Snafu

Unless you're Donald Trump or have several oil wells in your backyard, try not to go overboard with the perk or gift you choose. Granted, it's nice to be generous, but keep the reward reasonable so that it encourages a fun atmosphere rather than some sort of break-neck competition among your neighbors.

Real Estate Agents—How They Can Help

Seeking a real estate agent's help with a FSBO may seem like asking a brain surgeon for tips on how to hold the scalpel. But, unlikely or not, there are ways to solicit help and information from real estate agents to help your FSBO move along. As often as not, it just comes down to how you ask.

One way to leverage the resources available to real estate agents is to contact one and request a comparative market analysis. A comparative market analysis basically compares your home with other similar recently sold homes to establish a target price range. The formula takes in the size of the home, location, number of bedrooms, and other amenities.

The obvious benefit to you is that you get a real sense of what sort of price your home may be able to command. But it's also essential to be as upfront and honest as possible. Any agent who performs a comparative market analysis hopes to eventually list your home. Don't lead them on or sign anything that commits you to any sort of listing relationship. Rather, tell them that you're considering various selling options and would be grateful for any specifics that a market analysis might provide.

Sales Snafu

Not every agent is going to be willing to take the time and effort to perform a comparative market analysis without a clear commitment from you to list your home. If one agent turns you down, keep shopping around. An alternative is to tell the agent that you're trying to sell your home on your own. Say you'll consider placing the listing with him if you can't do the deal yourself.

If you do develop a relationship with an agent by way of a market analysis, now's the time to solicit whatever feedback you can get. Ask what he thinks of your home, ways you can improve its marketability, and how long similar homes are taking on the market. But tread lightly—agents can be highly zoned in on homeowners who are trying to do little more than pump them for whatever information they can get.

Online Resources for Lenders, Attorneys, and Others

The following is a list of a few websites that can help you locate partners to build your FSBO team:

- Yourloanhelper.com (www.yourloanhelper.com). A nationwide discount mortgage broker service that can help with prequalifying buyers and preparing financial breakdowns.

- Fidelity Title Company (www.fidelitytitlecompany.com/fsbo.htm). This title company offers a nice page of sample FSBO documents as well as information about the functions of a title company.

- The American Society of Home Inspectors (www.ashi.org). The website for the largest professional home inspectors organization in North America. Information on inspection services, referral services, and other helpful material.

The Least You Need to Know

- Establish a relationship with a mortgage lender to help prequalify buyers and provide other valuable services.

- It's a good idea to partner with an attorney early in the selling process—not just to provide paperwork, but to serve as a source of feedback and guidance.

- Be creative in involving your neighbors in your efforts. Host a neighbors-only open house and encourage them to refer interested buyers.

- See if a real estate agent would be willing to provide a comparative market analysis. But don't mislead them about your interest in having them list your home.

Chapter 4

The Price Is Right

In This Chapter

- How to target the right price
- Putting a strategy into place
- Appraisers aren't just for buyers
- Know market factors and other considerations

Bob Barker has, indeed, had it right all these years. No matter what you're selling or buying, the price has to be right. Otherwise, either party involved in the transaction may simply walk away.

Given the price tag of many homes, this is particularly true with selling a home—and even more so when you're doing it on your own. As is the case with so many other elements and issues, it's up to you to perform the necessary legwork, research, and other steps to arrive at a price that's both enticing to prospective buyers and reasonably profitable for you. In this chapter, we offer concrete steps and guidance on how to do precisely that.

Basic Market Research—First Steps to the Right Price

There's no way around it—setting the right asking price for your home is the first step to a successful FSBO. If your price is too high, you'll only discourage potential buyers. And that can lead to one of the least desirable after effects—the home that just languishes there, unloved and unwanted.

The other side of the coin is no more appealing. Here, you price your home too low. You may sell it quicker than you expected—and, on the surface, that can be great—only to discover later that you merely shortchanged yourself. If profit lost is worth the speed, fine. But as often as not, sellers kick themselves for not getting top dollar for their property.

Selling Smarts

Don't overlook the importance of seeing other homes for yourself. Visit open houses and compare those properties and their asking prices with your own home. Note specific features and how they stack up against the ones in your home.

One of the reasons it can be so challenging to find just the right price for your home is that there are so many factors involved in the process. Some of them are rather straightforward, including the size of the house, number of bedrooms and other amenities, condition of the property, location, and other factors. Some are a bit more unpredictable, including local market conditions, the time of year, prevailing interest rates, and others which, boiled down, really have no direct connection to your home at all. But they can still affect what asking price works best.

Resources—Online and Elsewhere

Another powerful factor that dictates what price works and what doesn't is the price of other homes in your local market—more specifically, other homes that have recently sold. To get a sense of what other homes have gone for, it's necessary to perform a comparative market analysis. A comparative market analysis estimates the value of your property based on recent sales prices of comparable pieces of property.

Doing a comparative market analysis the old fashioned way—without an agent, as we mention in Chapter 3—takes a bit of legwork. First, you need to keep track of similar homes nearby that have been sold recently. Stick to homes that sold within the past six months. The closer their location to yours, the better. Then, contact your local assessor's office and ask for the name of the owner of record. You then need to look up the applicable deed for the property. That should tell you the home's most recent selling price.

It's also possible to obtain comparative market analyses online. Sites include www.pricehomeonline.com and www.valuemyhouse.com (see the following figure), among others. The system usually requires you to enter information about your home and emails you back an estimated value (often, many such sites are connected to a real estate agency with an agent in tow, so be prepared to say something to the effect that you were just doing some preliminary research.)

Sales Snafu _____

One drawback to using your local government offices for a comparative market analysis is that you can only obtain sales prices. It doesn't provide other details that may also impact your own strategy, such as special features, particularly attractive location and other elements that may impact price.

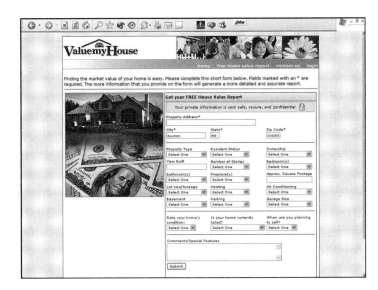

This page at valuemyhouse. com gives you an idea of the information you enter to obtain market information.

Another option that's a good deal more comprehensive takes in features and details other than just the price of the home. This is known as a *comparable*.

Tools of the Trade _____

Comparables, which is short for "comparable properties" or "comps," are pretty much what the term implies. These are homes that have recently been sold and are very much like yours in terms of size, location, and features. In effect, they set the pricing parameters for your home by having preceded you in the marketplace.

It really makes sense. All other things being equal, your home's asking price is closely tied with other similar properties that have recently been sold. The added advantage to a comparable versus a comparative market analysis is that it's just not a matter of price—individual features and specifics are also examined as well.

What are you looking for in a comparable home? Among other issues are the following: square footage, age of the home, condition of the home, style (cape, ranch, and so forth), number of bedrooms and bathrooms, property size, special features (pool, central air, and the like), landscaping, location (proximity to shopping, recreation, and school district, for example).

Thanks to the Internet, going online greatly streamlines the necessary steps to obtaining comprehensive comparable information. For instance, Forsalebyowner.com provides a service that automates comparables research. Ranging in price from $9.90 and up, homeowners can obtain information about comparable sales in the area, including sales trends, demographics, and other information pertaining to target price research.

Selling Smarts _____

Other websites that offer information on recent comparable sales and other information that can help identify a suitable asking price include www.domania.com and www.homeradar.com.

No matter the method you choose to get comparables in your area, it's helpful to draw up a checklist of features and other relevant information to make side-by-side comparisons as easy and useful as possible. To give you an idea of format and the sort of information that's important to include, here's a sample comparables report from Forsalebyowner.com that provides an overview of some elements to consider.

Location Information

Legal Description:	GREAT BERRY ESTATES 3-B LT 90
County:	PALM BEACHAPN: 12-43-46-07-16-000-0900
Census Tract:	0066.03 Subdivision: 0900

Township Range Section

Map Reference 1:	335
Legal Book/Page:	41-124
Map Reference 2:	
Legal Lot:	0900
School District:	
Legal Block:	000
Township Name:	DELRAY BEACH

Last Market Sale Information

Sale Price:	$160,000
1st Mortgage Amount:	
Recording Date:	06/22/2004
1st Mortgage Int. Rate:	
Sale Date:	05/15/2004
1st Mortgage Int. Rate Type:	
Document Number:	13918-1935
2nd Mortgage Int. Rate:	
Deed Type:	WARRANTY DEED
2nd Mortgage Int. Rate Type:	
Transfer Doc Number:	
Price Per SqFt:	$88
Title Company:	ATTORNEY ONLY
Seller Name:	SHINE JOHN R

Property Characteristics

Living Area:	1,825	Parking Type:	GARAGE
Total Rooms:	3	View:	
Number of Units:	Garage Area:	441	
Bedrooms:	3	Garage Capacity:	
Bath (F/H):	3	Number of Stories:	2
Year Built:	1982	Basement Area:	
Pool:	N	Finished Basement Area:	
Air Conditioning:	N	Roof Type:	
Fireplace:	N	Roof Material:	ASPHALT

Site Information

Land Use:	SFR	Acres:	.25
Flood Zone:	AE	Lot Area:	10890
Flood Panel:	1251020002D	Lot Width/Depth:	/
Flood Panel Date:	19890105	Zoning:	PRD4

Tax Information

Assessed Value:	$126,644	Tax Exemption:	HOMESTEAD
Land Value:	$44,000	Property Tax:	$2,345
Improvement Value:	$82,644	Tax Area:	
Assessed Year:	2002	Tax Year:	2002

Comparables Properties Expanded Information

Comparable 1

Address:	1825 10TH ST, DELRAY BEACH, FL 33115
Distance:	0.01 miles
Living Area:	1,737 sq ft
Sales Price:	$125,000
Rooms/Bdrms:	2
Rec Date:	12/27/2003
APN:	12-43-46-07-16-000-0800
Air Condition:	N
Prior Sale Price:	
Lot Area:	5,662.8 sq ft
Baths(F/H):	0
Prior Rec Date:	
Year Built:	1982
Fireplace:	N
Loan Amount:	
Stories:	1
Pool:	Y
Total Assessed:	$135,851

Comparable 2

Address:	1835 10TH ST, DELRAY BEACH, FL 33115
Distance:	0.01 miles
Living Area:	1,654 sq ft
Sales Price:	$214,000
Rooms/Bdrms:	2
Rec Date:	05/31/2004
APN:	12-43-46-07-16-000-0790
Air Condition:	N
Prior Sale Price:	$108,000
Lot Area:	5,662.8 sq ft
Baths(F/H):	0
Prior Rec Date:	03/00/1985
Year Built:	1980

Fireplace:	N
Loan Amount:	
Stories:	1
Pool:	N
Total Assessed:	$118,723

Comparable 3

Address:	1845 10TH ST, DELRAY BEACH, FL 33115
Distance:	0.02 miles
Living Area:	1,825 sq ft
Sales Price:	$129,000
Rooms/Bdrms:	3
Rec Date:	10/24/2003
APN:	12-43-46-07-16-000-0780
Air Condition:	N
Prior Sale Price:	$89,900
Lot Area:	5,662.8 sq ft
Baths(F/H):	0
Prior Rec Date:	03/00/1984
Year Built:	1982
Fireplace:	N
Loan Amount:	
Stories:	2
Pool:	N
Total Assessed:	$126,644

Total sales price is only one useful tool in setting the price of your home. Another way to use comparables to calculate the price for your own home is to break each down into dollar per square foot. For instance, in the three comparable houses cited, the price per square foot would break down as follows:

- ◆ Comparable Number One: $71.96 per square foot.

- ◆ Comparable Number Two: $129.38 per square foot.

- ◆ Comparable Number Three: $70.68 per square foot.

As you can see, there's quite a bit of difference between the first and third homes and the second. That suggests something that may make the second home irrelevant to setting the price of your own home. Maybe there was one specific feature that a buyer simply couldn't live without or some other unusual circumstance that drove the per square cost up so considerably. In any case, a difference of more than $50 per square foot is substantial enough to drop that from your calculations.

But the other two are close enough in per square foot value to suggest a possible target range for your home. And, the more comparables you can get that happen to fall within this general range, the greater your confidence that you're zeroing in on a suitable price.

To calculate what sort of price your own home might command, simply take the average per square foot price of appropriate comparables and multiply by the square footage of your house. Let's say you find a per square foot average of $71. Here are some sample prices based on different sized homes:

- 1,700 Square foot home—Estimated price—$120,700.

- 2,000 Square foot home—Estimated price—$142,000.

- 2,250 Square foot home—Estimated price—$159,750.

Strike a Balance

You're likely getting the sense by now that pricing your home effectively isn't just grabbing some number out of the thin air in hopes of getting the biggest payoff. Sure, everyone selling their home wants to pocket the biggest profit possible, but the overriding objective is to sell the home—hopefully, for the best price that it can command.

Tools of the Trade

Fair market value refers to the price that a buyer—any buyer—will agree to pay for your home. As we've seen—and will continue to discuss—there are a variety of factors that determine fair market value.

Of course, one of the advantages of selling your home yourself is that, because you don't have to factor in the cost of a real estate agent's commission to the price, you can afford to lower the asking price slightly, potentially making your home even more attractive to buyers.

To arrive at a suitable asking price, it's essential to balance two considerations—pricing your home to sell and making a reasonable profit. This illustrates the importance of arriving at the *fair market value* for your home.

Because fair market value depends on a number of influences—some within your control, others outside of it—it's important to make the most of those that you can influence. That's why it's so critical to consider both your need to sell your home and your desire to make the most money you can—as we cited in the beginning of this section. When setting the asking price, you need to keep in mind a price that will sell, not merely the price with the biggest payoff for you.

Here's an example. Let's say you've done a bit of market research and found several comparables in your area that sold for approximately $150,000. But, you think, your home has so much more going for it than those (what that happens to be, you're not entirely sure, but your feeling is no less compelling.) So, you price your home at $160,000, determined to wring an extra 10 grand in profit from the sale.

Unfortunately, you see nothing more than a stream of prospective buyers who look around, smile politely, and hightail it out the door. Then, that highly unpleasant phenomenon occurs that we mentioned earlier in this chapter—the ever-dreaded house that languishes without selling.

And it languishes. And languishes some more. Troubled, you cut the price. Still more languishing. You drop the price a second time. Nothing. Finally, a third price cut does the trick. The only trouble is, you accept an offer for $143,000—some $7,000 less than other comparables commanded.

FSBO Facts

One of the first questions that buyers ask about a home is how long it has been on the market. That question comes with good reason—the longer a house goes unsold, the greater the leverage to the buyer, who can make a relatively low offer in hopes that the seller is discouraged or desperate enough to accept it. It's also a form of leverage that grows more powerful with time. The longer a house stays on the market, the more likely it becomes that an owner will consider a lower offer.

The preceding illustration is a typical example of a home that was initially priced beyond its fair market value. In the end, the payoff was considerably less than it would have been had the owner simply put more stock in the influence of comparables.

Balancing the need to sell and a reasonable price also plays into how quickly you'll likely be able to sell your home. In the prior example, not only was the eventual price disappointing, the home simply floundered on the market for a needlessly long period of time. Priced at fair market value, a home will not only provide a reasonable profit, chances are good that it will also turn over relatively quickly.

Strategic Planning

Finding the right price for your home isn't merely a matter of compiling research and letting that speak for itself. Calculating just the right price at which point your home will sell both quickly and profitably mandates strategic planning. And that involves a mix of various issues and concerns, some of which are external, others derive from you and your understanding of the overall FSBO process.

Understand Your Marketplace

A central concern of effective strategic planning is coming to know your local real estate market as thoroughly as possible. In one sense, you've already started to get a handle on that by obtaining comparables sales information. This offers critical information about your local market—what sorts of homes are selling, at what price, how long the process is taking, and other elements that will affect your own sales efforts.

Tools of the Trade

As the names suggest, a **buyer's market** is generally favorable to those shopping for a home, while a **seller's market** favors those trying to sell a home they already own.

But it's also important to understand your marketplace in a more global sense. Individual homes may sell more or less quickly depending on their features, but prevailing conditions also play a hand in how fast homes turn over. So, it's important to study your overall market and, if need be, adjust your strategic planning accordingly.

Two terms you have likely heard in connection with real estate are a *buyer's market* and a *seller's market.*

Just what causes these two rather global market trends varies considerably. For instance, a downturn in the local economy—say a major local employer shuts its doors or lays off scads of workers—can push a lot of homes onto the market quickly as people look to relocate. That creates a glut and prices fall, which results in a buyer's market. There's a lot to choose from and sellers are highly motivated.

By contrast, a seller's market can develop if an area becomes particularly popular—the local economy takes an upturn or a city or area is mentioned in the media as being a particularly desirable place to live. As a result, homes are harder to find, buyers are fighting tooth and nail for those that are on the market, and prices go up.

Also know that there are variations within this seller/buyer seesaw. For instance, many markets are balanced, favoring neither buyer nor seller. In some cases, particular parts of a town or city may experience a boom or bust, making neighborhoods and sometimes individual streets hot and cold.

The reason this is important to you is that prevailing trends influence what you can expect to receive for your home and how quickly. Even an exceedingly desirable home in a down market may sit unsold for weeks and even months. By the same token, a home that's nothing to write home about (pardon the pun) may get snapped up if a seller's market exists and there aren't that many homes from which to choose.

That, in turn, influences the sort of price you should consider. A solid home in a seller's market may be in a position to be a bit more aggressive in starting out at a slightly larger asking price. On the other hand, if things are slow, adjusting your expectations downward a bit may be the most realistic course.

 Selling Smarts

How do you know what sort of a market you're in? Stay on top of the local news. Keep an eye on other homes for sale and how long it takes before the yard sign changes to "sold." Call a few local real estate offices and try to establish a consensus on what their take is on the local market. If you know someone who just sold their home, ask them how it went.

Taking a FSBO Into Account When Setting Prices

One of the advantages we've been stressing about selling your home on your own is the substantial real estate agent commission you stand to save. And as we've pointed out, at a going rate of about 6 percent of the sale price, that can be quite a tidy sum.

But the absence of a commission proves advantageous in other ways. It can actually help you sell your home faster and at a greater profit. Why? Because you can afford to set your asking price lower than you would have had you used an agent while still coming out ahead in the end.

Here's an example. Let's say, after all your legwork with comparables, price per average square calculations, and the like, you figure your home can sell for $200,000. Drop an agent into the mix. At 6 percent commission, you pocket $188,000 ($12,000 lost in commission.)

But now let's assume that you're in a hurry to sell your home, so you set the price at $195,000—$5,000 less than the going average. A true bargain in sight, buyers beat your door down and the sale goes through quickly. And even though you set the price $5,000 lower than you possibly could have, your profit is $7,000 greater.

So in its own way, a FSBO unto itself can go against the temptation to be too greedy. Instead, trim your price just a bit, sell your home faster, and haul your extra profit straight to the bank.

Selling Smarts

One way to take a FSBO into account when setting the price is to split the commission savings between yourself and the buyer. For instance, in the previous example, your home can sell for $200,000, but you would only get $188,000 after an agent's 6% take. Consider setting your home's selling price at 194,000. This is the market price minus half the agent's commission, or 3%. You set up a bargain for buyers, but one that still earns you a handsome profit.

Appraising the Appraiser—What They Do, How to Choose

Up until now, we're assuming that, like so many FSBOs, you're a real self-sufficient do-it-yourselfer. Terrific! Every task you can handle on your own not only saves you money, it also furthers your understanding and overall appreciation of the FSBO experience.

But determining the absolute best price for your FSBO may be one of those instances where it's the better part of valor to defer to a professional. That means it may be well worth your time and your pocketbook to give some thought to hiring an *appraiser*.

As you can see, an appraiser does what you would do in establishing comparably priced homes. Why bother to use an appraiser? It's a matter of objectivity and substance. A professional appraisal provides comprehensive evidence to substantiate the asking price for your home. Rather than simply taking your word for it, a professional appraisal provides prospective buyers with clear-cut information that shows the asking price is, indeed, fair.

Tools of the Trade

An **appraiser** is professionally trained to estimate what your home is worth. An appraiser goes through your home in some detail, noting various features and the condition of the home, then compares your property with others of similar features.

Another plus to using an appraiser is that he or she will be trained to take differences between homes into account and make necessary adjustments in their respective values. That means they look at size, location, condition of the home, special features and other elements and calculate respective values depending on how one home may differ from another.

If the idea of using an appraiser seems to make sense, be sure to do a bit of shopping and research. Ask them about the training and other forms of necessary certification. When asking about experience, be sure to have them specify how much local experience they have, as markets differ enough to make experience in some other part of the country somewhat irrelevant. Of course, ask how much they charge—expect to pay in the neighborhood of several hundred dollars for a thorough home appraisal.

 Sales Snafu

Currently, no uniform federal regulations exist for licensing and certifying appraisers. That's up to the individual states. There are, however, several professional groups (listed at the end of this chapter) that enforce certain standards for training and practice. When looking for an appraiser, be sure to ask for referrals from your local bank or government housing agency. Chances are excellent they've worked with several in the past they would recommend with confidence.

Other Pricing Considerations

You have several final issues to consider in setting the price of your FSBO. They are not as central as some of the topics we've covered in earlier sections of this chapter, but they can matter, often in quite a substantial way.

Every Dollar Matters

Have you ever noticed that most retail stores price items in what, on the surface, may seem like a needlessly complicated manner? For instance, a DVD player isn't $100; it's $99.50. Likewise, the DVD that goes into that machine isn't $10; it goes for $9.95.

If you break things down, the differences in those prices are rather modest—just a matter of a few cents. But, the way a prospective buyer sees those prices is decidedly different. Even though $100 and $99.50 is only a difference of fifty cents, from a psychological standpoint, it's substantial. By buying a DVD player for $99.50, you're not cracking the $100 mark. And, substantial or not, buyers find that comforting and appealing.

 Selling Smarts

Pricing your home in this fashion can also matter if you list your home on an online listing service. Because many buyers specify a price range when beginning their search, dropping your price just below a certain level can tuck it into more moderately priced searches.

Consider that same approach in pricing your home. If you think you can get $300,000 for your property, price it at $299,000. That's only a difference of $1000, but to a prospective buyer who has it in her head not to exceed $300,000 for a home, that relatively modest difference can, in the end, make all the difference in what you get for your home and how quickly you're able to finalize a sale.

A Sweeter Transaction

Unto itself, many sellers might assume the asking price is the only pertinent financial information that goes into setting the right price. But there are other elements having to do with the overall sale that may, in fact, boost the asking price that works for you.

♦ First, consider how quickly you're willing to close on the deal. If you make it clear to prospective buyers that you're willing to move things along as fast as they need them to go, that can attract buyers who are in a particular rush to close a deal and move in. And that can mean a slightly greater asking price in return.

♦ Almost everyone these days finances a home purchase. Many of those buyers—often first timers and others of more limited financial means—find it a challenge to obtain conventional financing. If you're willing to offer even a modest amount of owner financing, that, too, may command a slightly larger asking price than what you would ask for under more usual circumstances. More about this in Chapter 14.

♦ With regard to first time homebuyers, anything you can provide in the way of more generous terms can mandate a larger asking price. For instance, a rent-to-own option offers buyers with modest resources an opportunity to get their foot in the home buying door—and, you as the seller, with an opportunity to trade that generosity for a slightly larger price tag. This, too, is addressed in Chapter 14.

The bottom line here is, the broader the financial options you're willing to consider, the greater number of buyers you'll likely attract. Not only might that result in a faster, less hassle-ridden sale, it may increase your profit margin at the same time.

Other Online Pricing Resources

We've already mentioned a few, but here are a few additional websites that will help you research and determine the absolute best price for your FSBO:

- Quicken Loans (www.quickenloans.com/refinance/refinance_calculators/ home_value_calculator.html?lid=772). This is a quick and easy way to get a ball-park figure of what your home might be worth.

- For SaleByOwner.com (www.ForSalebyOwner.com/homesales/prices). This displays a list of recent sold homes in a specified area. Going to www. ForSalebyOwner.com/Appraisals takes this information one step further and offers an estimated value of your home.

There are also a number of professional appraisers' organizations. The following are worth having a look at:

- The American Society of Appraisers (www.appraisers.org)

- The Appraisal Foundation (www.appraisalfoundation.org)

- The Appraisal Institute (www.appraisalinstitute.org)

The Least You Need to Know

- Focus on pricing your home to sell, not merely for the biggest profit possible.

- A comparative market analysis is one way to get a quick estimate of what a suitable selling price for your home might be.

- Comparables—which can be obtained online—offer a comprehensive comparison of homes similar to yours that have recently sold. They offer a more specific idea of a target price.

- Remember, because you're selling your home without having to pay a commission, you can price your home lower than you would have with an agent and still make a good profit.

- Consider hiring an appraiser to identify comparable homes. An appraiser's report is essential in justifying the asking price for your home.

- Be open to financing options for buyers. You may command a slightly larger price for your home if you do.

Part 2

Let the Selling Begin!

Okay, we've got a bunch of basics under our belts. In this part, we start putting things into action. Specifically, we'll cover targeted advertising strategies, the ins and outs of crafting an effective listing, and a comprehensive examination of the open house. We'll also tackle other ways to attract prospective buyers, including strategies for home tours that show your house in the best light, attracting out-of-town buyers, and ways to cope with the unexpected, such as would-be buyers who just show up at your front door. Last, we'll look at the Internet and ways you can incorporate that into your overall sales effort.

5

It Pays to Advertise

In This Chapter

- Getting the word out
- Essential marketing tools
- Describing your domain
- Disclosure do's and don'ts

Chances are excellent there is a buyer out there for your home—maybe even more than one. Your challenge is finding them and enticing them to your doorstep. That means you need to get the word out to everyone you know that your home is available. The most successful sellers—those who sell their homes fastest for a good price—are the ones who use several different marketing tools to attract potential buyers.

Putting up a lawn sign and calling it a day won't cut it. Not unless you're in a highly desirable neighborhood with few other homes currently for sale. Because most of us aren't in that situation, you may want to explore all the ways to advertise your home is for sale.

The Killer Newspaper Classified Ad

According to the 2003 National Association of REALTORS (NAR) "Profile of Homebuyers and Sellers," the most common marketing methods FSBOs use include:

- Yard sign   72%

- Newspaper ad   61%

- Open house   41%

- Friends/neighbors   27%

- Internet   20%

Yard signs, which we'll cover in a minute, are great for folks who happen to visit your neighborhood. But for people who don't live near you but would like to, other marketing tools are more effective.

Selling Smarts

After your home is officially on the market, such as after you put up your sign, change your voicemail or answering machine message to let callers know your home is for sale. An outgoing message as simple as: "Thanks for calling. If you're calling about the house, yes it's for sale. We'd love to show it to you, so leave your name and phone number and we'll call you back to make an appointment.

Most, if not all, daily U.S. newspapers have a special real estate section each week profiling area homes for sale. As NAR's list suggests, that's a powerful outlet for promoting your home. Or, if there are smaller community newspapers, you may opt to buy an ad there for less. But don't ignore newspaper advertising.

Buying a classified ad in the newspapers published in your immediate area is an excellent way to alert buyers to your home. Classified ads are relatively inexpensive and powerful, getting your home's information in front of people looking to buy one. To make the most of your advertising space, you'll want to follow some general rules of advertising and copywriting.

Power Words to Include

The best newspaper classified ads cite home features buyers are looking for. Some universal elements most people would like to have in a home include:

- Attractive inside and out

- Spacious

- ◆ Comfortable
- ◆ Move-in ready
- ◆ Quiet locale
- ◆ In a desirable neighborhood
- ◆ Convenient location

When drafting your newspaper classified, you'll want to include the following information, at a minimum:

- ◆ For Sale By Owner
- ◆ Location
- ◆ Price
- ◆ Square footage
- ◆ Number of bedrooms/bathrooms
- ◆ Best features
- ◆ Financing assistance, if available
- ◆ Contact information

Start the process of writing your ad by listing every possible *feature* and *benefit* of your home. Anything that comes to mind, write it down.

After you have a list of words to describe your home, pick out the most compelling features and biggest benefits. Because you're charged for your classified based on the amount of space it takes up in the paper, you'll want to provide enough information to entice buyers to call without breaking the bank. Keep your description short, sweet, and specific.

Tools of the Trade

A **feature** is a word that describes some facet of your home. A backyard pool is a feature, for instance, as is 2,100 square feet of space. A **benefit** is what you enjoy as a result of those features, such as room-to-grow or access to a better school system.

Look at ads in your real estate section for tips on how to describe your place.

> **Stunning!** Immaculate contemporary colonial in desirable Greenville location. Custom built, 4 bdrm, 3 bath on 1.2 acres in a secluded wood setting. Cathedral ceilings, wood fireplace, hardwoods throughout. Finished basement with gas fireplace. Move-in condition. Call 222-333-4444 for more information or visit www.forsalebyowner.com for a virtual tour.

Words to Avoid

Now make sure your descriptors all pack a powerful punch. Trade less powerful words for stronger, positive ones, such as:

- House or apartment—home
- Small—cozy, charming, appealing
- Casual—inviting, welcoming, comfortable
- Big—roomy, spacious, luxurious
- Different—distinctive, breathtaking
- Upscale—exclusive, executive
- Close to local amenities—convenient, accessible

Words that have a negative connotation should be avoided. Phrases that suggest a buyer will quickly outgrow the home, will spend lots of time cleaning or repairing it, or won't like some aspect should be replaced with words that emphasize the home's advantages.

Terms that suggest more than you may intend, and should be avoided, are:

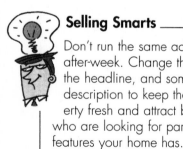

Selling Smarts

Don't run the same ad week-after-week. Change the photo, the headline, and some of the description to keep the property fresh and attract buyers who are looking for particular features your home has.

- Needs repairs/needs TLC—suggests that the whole house may need to be razed in order to be livable
- Quiet—generally means dark
- Bright—faces the street
- Soundproof windows—the noise is deafening when you open them
- Old World—means the home is worn and needs to be renovated and updated

- Unique—"What were they thinking when they came up with that layout?"
- White glove—very expensive with space for staff
- Virtual doorman—implies an intercom system with a large camera monitoring the door

*These terms provided compliments of C.B. Whyte, vice president of Stribling & Associates in New York, which specializes in the sale of Manhattan apartments over $3 million.

Other Sales Tools

While newspaper ads are one way to alert potential buyers to your home's availability, it's not the only way. There are several other ways to get the word out, too.

Signs

The most popular marketing method on the list of tools used, signs are probably the easiest way to market your home. Whether you stake them in your front yard—or back—or place a colorful sign in your front window, signs are an excellent way to communicate that your home is on the market. Anyone who travels through your neighborhood or is scoping out potential homes will immediately see that your home is available.

You'll find a variety of yard signs available. Choose the one that will be easiest to read from the road.

The most important information to have on your sign, in large enough letters to be seen from the road, is "FOR SALE BY OWNER." The second-most important information is your phone number, in large point type.

If you decide to set up a website with information about your home, it would be smart to list the website address as well so prospective buyers can go home and check it out before calling to schedule a walk-through. You can also list your home on one of the For Sale By Owner websites, such as ForSaleByOwner.com and Owners.com, thereby eliminating the need for you to do everything yourself.

> ### FSBO Facts
>
> Yard signs are the second most popular information source for buyers, according to the National Association of REALTORS, used by 69% of the buying public. The top information source was real estate agents, which were cited by 86% of those surveyed.

Some advertising packages sold by FSBO websites offer you the option to purchase a professionally created yard sign. You can also call a local sign company and investigate the cost to prepare one. The more durable and professional your sign, the better the image buyers will have of you and your home.

Choose a background color for your sign that is not white and will stand out against the colors in your yard. White signs get lost in yards with snow, for instance, and signs with green or black backgrounds can be overlooked when placed in a grassy or shaded area.

In addition to placing a sign by your home, also place one at the entrance to your development, if you're in one, or at your closest major intersection, to drive traffic by your place. Ask businesses in your area if you can place directional "Home For Sale" signs pointing toward your home on the front of their property. Anyone driving or walking in the area may want to swing by and check out your home's exterior.

Talking Ads

A new twist on the traditional yard sign is the new talking sign, which provides pre-recorded messages about a home that can be heard by cars driving by. Using a low power AM radio transmitter, the Talking House system broadcasts recorded information about a home's size, interior, and features to a specific radio frequency. Homebuyers are instructed to tune into a specific station listed on the Talking House yard sign. Once there, they will hear up to five minutes of information about the home.

Because buyers may be frustrated by not being able to immediately schedule an appointment to tour your home, the Talking House system moves the buying process along by giving home shoppers more information about your home.

The transmitter is easy to set up in your home, or in a garage or attic, and has a 300-foot reach. Recording a message about your home is also simple, much like recording a voicemail or answering machine message. At a minimum, you'll want to be sure to include the following in your recording:

- Total square footage
- Size of the lot, including the back yard
- Number of bedrooms and bathrooms
- Types of flooring, such as hardwood
- Any fireplaces
- Size of the master suite
- Upgrades, such as a Viking range
- Kitchen description
- Mention of recent improvements
- Asking price

> **FSBO Facts**
>
> More than 65 percent of all homebuyers begin their search by driving through neighborhoods they like, reports *Real Estate Business* magazine.

The only downside of the system is the price. It costs around $650 to buy a transmitter, which you probably don't want to do because you'll only be using it for a few weeks. They were designed for use by real estate agents, who can turn around and use them in different houses they have listed. You, however, want to rent one.

Many agents currently using the Talking House technology rent their transmitter units to FSBOs at a price of about $1 to $2 a day, reports Scott Hagerman of Talking House (www.talkinghouse.com).

To find an agent in your area currently using Talking House, Hagerman suggests using a Google search with "Talking House" as the keyword. After you find an agent in your locale that has the system, make contact and ask about renting it. Some agents will even include help writing a script and recording it as part of the fee. At a cost of $30 to $60 per month, Talking House is a fairly economical advertising vehicle.

Flyers

In addition to attention-getting yard signs of the traditional and high-tech variety, you'll also want to create an advertising flyer that visually showcases your home's best features (see the following figure). The purpose of a flyer, like the talking ad, is to give prospective buyers more information about your home to help them decide if they should make an appointment to tour it.

On a flyer, which is typically an 8.5"×11" sheet of heavy white paper, you should have a photo—color, preferably—of the front of your home.

Flyers are a great way to attract potential buyers.

At the top of the flyer, put your home's street address, in bold type. Below the photo, have a bulleted list of your home's key features and benefits. The difference between this list and the one you prepared for the newspaper classified is space. You have plenty of space to include more features and to be more descriptive. Elaborate a little.

Instead of stating that you have a master suite, you can call it "deluxe " or "spacious." Describe the back yard, the garage, the basement, as well as the living space. Highlight the biggest selling points with the goal of encouraging the buyer to come take a look inside.

Selling Smarts

Attach an information box on the side of your yard sign, or buy a separate little plastic box on a stake, and fill it with flyers about your home. As potential buyers drive by, they can stop and pick up a printed flyer to tell them all about it. It's also smart to laminate one of the flyers and attach it firmly to the interior or exterior of the box so that if all the flyers are taken, buyers can at least scan the material on the box.

Think about all the different places you can display your flyer. Some common ones include:

- Library bulletin boards
- Restaurant bulletin boards
- College/university housing offices
- Military installations
- Hospitals
- Doctors offices
- Churches and synagogues
- Banks

You should also consider mailing some out to area real estate agents, who may be trying to find a home in your neighborhood for a client, as well as corporate real estate and relocation offices, which are responsible for helping executives find housing. Note on the flyer: "Brokers welcome" to alert them that you are prepared to pay them 3% for bringing a buyer.

The Importance of Professionalism

Some buyers think that because you haven't hired a real estate professional to handle the sale of your home, you're going to be willing to accept less to sell it. And unless you make every effort to be as professional as the agents, that may be the case. You need to prove otherwise.

Sales Snafu

Make appointments by telephone to see your home, rather than letting people walk in off the street at their convenience. Treating the meeting professionally shows you mean business and that you're not interested in wasting your time with people who aren't serious about buying.

Your marketing and advertising, the appearance of your home, and your demeanor when dealing with prospective buyers sends a signal about your expectations. The more professional you are, the more you demonstrate that this is a business transaction and you expect to be paid fairly.

The Information Sheet

While your flyer is a promotional tool designed to give buyers a hint of the treasure they'll find once they're in your home, the information sheet is an all-encompassing list of your home's features.

Although you certainly want to describe your home in the best possible light, you need to be factual when creating an information sheet. In addition to the year the home was built and the town and school district it is in, you'll also want to list:

◆ Room dimensions

◆ Type of flooring in various parts of the home

◆ Special amenities, such as a fireplace, ceiling fan, or hand-painted mural

◆ Appliance brands and age

◆ Window treatments

◆ Built-in fixtures, such as bookcases or kitchen banquette

◆ Recent upgrades or improvements

◆ Recent repairs

◆ Annual taxes

◆ Monthly utility estimate

Have a stack of information sheets available for anyone who tours your home, requests more information, or for attendees at any open houses you schedule.

Marketing and advertising force you to focus on all the positives your home has to offer, but you need to be aware that when push comes to shove, you can't lie about any home defects or problems. In nearly every state, homesellers are now required to disclose any and all defects to prospective buyers. And if you fail to disclose something that the buyer believes is important, they can sue you later and force you to take back the home. It doesn't happen often, but it has happened.

Selling Smarts

After you and the buyer agree on a purchase price, you'll both want sign a disclosure statement indicating the defects that were disclosed. Without it, you have no protection from a buyer who later claims they were never told about certain defects, which you know you disclosed up front.

To protect yourself from a disclosure disagreement, be up front about any problems you're aware of. Whether it's a minor leak in the second floor bathroom or a chimney that smokes, you must tell the buyer.

And because you can also be held liable for defects you didn't even know about, you'll want to take steps to uncover any problems. The easiest way to do this is to pay for your own home inspection. Yes, buyers generally ask for one themselves, but you can have one done yourself to make sure everything is in order. You can also simply wait, let the buyers pay for the inspection, and see what the inspector spots. If a defect is discovered, you can either opt to repair it immediately or offer to reduce your purchase price to cover part of the repair cost. But making repairs isn't always necessary. In some hot markets, buyers are agreeing to take the home as-is.

Become a Marketing Machine

All the marketing materials in the world won't work unless you use them to communicate with potential buyers and people who know them. After you've designed and installed a yard sign and created flyers and an information sheet, make sure they are seen! Marketing only works when you communicate with potential buyers.

Informal Marketing with Friends and Colleagues

Because more than 6.6 million existing homes sold in the United States in 2004, it's likely you'll come in contact with someone in the market for a home this year—that's approximately one for every 36 people in the country who are in the market for a new place to live. So why limit yourself to your own circle of contacts? The more people you tell about your home, the more likely you'll find potential buyers. And although it takes just one buyer to make a sale, the more interested parties there are, the higher your selling price can go.

To involve family, friends, neighbors, and co-workers in your quest to sell your home quickly for the best possible price, make sure you tell them you're selling your house. But don't just tell them that your home is for sale, tell them where it is and describe it a little. And ask for their help in locating a buyer.

Make sure you always have flyers with you ready to hand out to someone who may know someone who is looking. Put them on the cafeteria bulletin board and note that you'd appreciate help in finding a buyer. People like to help others, so specifically asking for help in selling your home will encourage others to think of anyone they know who is in the market for a new home.

Mention your situation to folks you see at church or synagogue, at PTA meetings, at the grocery store, at Little League games, or dance practice. The more people you tell about your home, the better your odds of finding a buyer sooner rather than later. You may even want to offer a finder's fee or reward to the person who sends you a buyer, just as you would pay a broker their commission. Any type of incentive is likely to get people thinking of likely prospects.

Don't Forget Real Estate Agents

Along the way, in your journey to sell your home yourself, you'll inevitably come in contact with real estate agents and *brokers*. They'll probably introduce themselves to you and offer to assist you, should you decide you're not cut out to sell your home yourself. That's good information to have, certainly, but you should also ask for their help in selling your home to their clients.

Tools of the Trade

A buyer's **broker** is an agent hired by a buyer to help them find a home. Without such an agreement, agents are bound to represent the seller first and foremost. With a buyer's broker, the buyer pays half the commission in exchange for the knowledge that the agent is working on their behalf, not the seller's.

Just because an agent hasn't listed your property doesn't mean they can't help sell it. Granted, they would only earn a possible 3 percent, versus 6 percent if they had both listed and sold it, but 3 percent is 3 percent. And if they've been retained as a buyer's broker, the buyer is responsible for paying that fee anyway, not you.

Take the time to send out information sheets to agents in your area, to let them know it's available, and to ask their help in finding a buyer. We've seen bulletin boards in real estate agencies with FSBO information sheets on them, so agents certainly do pay attention. Agents can be your allies, even if you're not their client. And, who knows, down the line you may decide you want to use an agent, either to buy a home or to sell one.

Online Ad Resources

For more information about topics covered in this chapter, check out the following websites:

- www.fsboadvertisingservice.com. Sells FSBO yard signs and flyer holders.

- www.fiftystatesfsbo.com/for-sale-by-owner-yard-sign.htm. Another source for durable yard signs.

- www.uslegalforms.com/real-estate-forms.htm. For $12.00, you can buy and download a state-specific seller's disclosure form.

- www.TalkingHouse.com. Information on how talking ads work and what it takes to get one up-and-running in your front yard.

The Least You Need to Know

- When written well, newspaper classified ads alert a large number of potential buyers that your home is for sale.

- Selling tools like yard signs, information boxes, talking ads, and flyers are an effective way to get the word out about your home.

- Although you want to sing your home's praises, don't try to hide its bad side. You're legally required to disclose any defects and can be sued if you don't.

- Perhaps as important as preparing professional-looking marketing tools is the number of people you tell about your home. Network with everyone you can think of, alerting them that your home is for sale and that you'd appreciate their help in finding a buyer.

- Behaving professionally at all times conveys the impression that you are serious about selling your home, and that you expect to receive a fair price.

Chapter 6

Listing Your Home

In This Chapter

- ◆ MLS plusses
- ◆ Other online options
- ◆ Listing sheet how-tos
- ◆ Advertising your home's availability

In addition to putting out yard signs and holding an open house to attract buyers, you may want to consider including your home in the Multiple Listing Service (MLS) for your area. The MLS is a virtual bulletin board of the hundreds or thousands of homes being sold by local real estate agents. Formerly printed in hard copy form and distributed to area real estate offices each week, MLS is now online and available to search by both agents and the buying public.

Some studies suggest that being listed in a local MLS can increase the speed with which a home is sold. Although how much more quickly is unclear, a listing in the MLS will surely increase the number of buyers who see your home is for sale. For that reason, it is an excellent marketing tool.

Real estate associations nationwide manage the MLS for their area, controlling which properties qualify to be included. Only properties being sold by member agents may be listed—a requirement designed to put FSBOs at a disadvantage and to increase the value of an agent. However, there are ways to get around this.

The Multiple Listing Service

The MLS's biggest advantage is its reach—anyone shopping for a home in your area can find information about your home through a search on your local MLS if it's listed there. Thousands of area real estate agents will also take note of your home if it meets the needs of one of their clients and is in the system. But getting listed in the system can be quite a challenge for FSBOs, unless they sign on with a site like www.forsalebyowner.com, where they have the option to be listed on an MLS for a flat fee.

Some sellers may argue that an ad in the newspaper accomplishes the same objective, but unless you run continuous ads, you may be at a disadvantage—out-of-town buyers, for instance, may not subscribe to the local paper, but they can easily go online and check for listings. MLS listings are available online 24-hours-a-day, generally for at least six months, or for as long as it is represented by an agent.

Major cities and regions across the nation have their own MLS, which makes it easier for homebuyer and sellers to connect (see the following figure).

Home buyers in Northern Colorado will likely head to this website, at www. coloproperty.com, to take a look at many homes in the area currently on the market. It's an example of a local MLS site specific to Colorado.

Check out your local MLS by doing a search on the web using the keyword "MLS" and your city or town name. On your local MLS website, you'll find a wealth of information about your area and virtually all the houses, condos, townhouses, mobile homes, and vacant lots now on the market.

With just a few keystrokes, you can identify homes in your zip code or on your street that are currently available. Frequently such listings also include photos of the exterior and interior of the home, helping buyers rule in or rule out homes even before they take a live tour. Detailed information about the home's layout and its features is also presented on the MLS site, in addition to photos.

Use of the MLS also effectively screens out disinterested buyers before they ever arrive at your door—they've already seen photos of most of the rooms, and now they're interested in seeing it in person.

Putting aside all the advantages of inclusion in the MLS system, the one con is the cost. Most MLS systems require that you agree to *co-op* an agent if they are responsible for finding you a buyer, which can increase your costs by thousands of dollars, potentially. There are strict rules for which homes can be listed in the MLS, the most important of which is that the home must be represented by a real estate agent who will be paid a commission for their services. Which means you may have to agree to pay 2 to 3 percent of the home's sale price in exchange for inclusion in your local MLS. In almost every market, it's virtually impossible to be included in the MLS unless an agent posts the listing there. However, there are also agents willing to get your home listed for a flat fee of a few hundred dollars. Do a search on some of the FSBO websites to locate these agents. Signing up for a help-you-sell FSBO service, such as America's Choice, is another way to get access to your local MLS; for an additional fee of a few hundred dollars, services like America's Choice will represent you as your agent and get you listed.

On www.forsalebyowner.com, you also have an MLS option where affiliated agents list homes but do not charge a commission to the seller. The only agent left to pay is the buyer's agent, if they have one.

Tools of the Trade _____

The traditional real estate commission of around 6 percent is split between the selling and buying agent. If you agree to **co-op** an agent, you are agreeing to give them their "cut" or their half of the commission (3 percent), if they end up selling your home. Make sure to add this information to your listing if you do agree to a co-op; it will significantly increase agents' interest level. "Brokers welcome" is the standard lingo.

And the truth is that you still have an excellent chance of selling your home without an MLS listing if you are using a combination of other marketing methods. Your yard sign, for instance, is possibly the most important, and most effective, marketing tool—even more effective than the MLS where local buyers are concerned. Although the Internet is a very popular search tool for home buyers, drive-bys are used even more frequently early on in the process, to help them scope out particular neighborhoods; a well-placed yard sign can prove more useful than an online listing. Open houses, neighborhood networking, newspaper advertising, and direct marketing to relocation professionals can all pay off just as well or better than an MLS listing.

For this reason, an attractive, legible sign can make a big difference. In fact, between 10 and 20 percent of the calls about your home will be based on your sign, according to ForSaleByOwner.com. A cheap, unattractive sign will detract from your home's appearance and may make buyers leery about going inside.

An MLS listing is no guarantee of success—it simply guarantees that thousands of agents and home buyers will have access to information about your home.

Alternative Listing Options

If you like the enhanced exposure that online listings offer but don't want to commit to coughing up thousands of dollars in commissions, there are a number of other real estate listing services to consider. Many offer advertising packages costing less than $1,000 that include setting up a website or preparing an online description, while others specialize in getting you into your local MLS for a few hundred dollars up front. Some of those flat fee MLS services require you agree to cover an agent's 2 to 3 percent commission, while others don't.

Check out the Internet Real Estate Digest at www.ired.com for a list of home selling links, including FSBO sites, mortgage lenders, and market data (see the following figure).

Check out several different sites before you commit to advertising on any—some do a better job than others of marketing themselves. Do a search for a property in your area and see how many homes are listed, both to see what kinds of properties they currently represent, and to get an idea of how aggressive the site is at attracting buyers. Having an online presence can be a big plus, but only if buyers can find you electronically. Otherwise, it's a waste of money.

The Internet Real Estate Digest is a useful resource for buyers and sellers.

No matter which service you decide to sign with, make sure your advertising fee includes assistance in preparing and uploading a web page for your home. Some sites may give a template and instructions for you to follow while others may provide a list of information needed, which they use to create the page for you.

Information you'll want to be sure is available online at your property's homepage includes:

- Color exterior photo(s) of your home, taken straight on

- Asking price

- Address

- One paragraph description of your home's best features

- Number of bedrooms and baths

- Total square footage

- List of features from listing sheet

- Your contact information, so buyers can ask questions or make an appointment to see it

Tools of the Trade

Websites today often give visitors the option to visually tour a home by clicking on individual photos of a home. This series of photos, which effectively leads you through the home, is called a **virtual tour**.

Additional photos of the interior of your home, perhaps available in a pop-up window, or a *virtual tour*, are also extremely desirable features to have in your advertising contract (see the following figure). Again, buyers who have already seen such photos and ask for a tour are that much closer to buying your home.

Many homes advertised online feature a "virtual tour" or "photo tour" button that gives a slideshow of the inside and outside of the home.

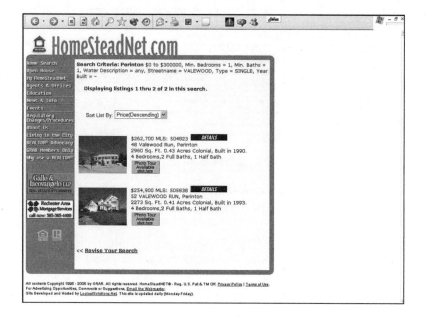

Whether part of the MLS or not, making information about your home available electronically, on the Internet, greatly increases the number of people likely to hear about its availability.

An Intro to Online FSBO Listings

If you decide to forgo an MLS listing, that doesn't mean you should skip the Internet altogether. In addition to local MLS websites, there are probably hundreds of websites devoted to FSBO listings. For less than it generally costs to get an MLS listing, you can have your home profiled online at a FSBO-focused website. Some of the top sites include:

- forsalebyowner.com
- homesalediy.com
- owners.com

- fsbofriend.com

- fsbo.com

- onlinerealtysales.com

- propertysites.com

- homesalewizard.com

- fsboadvertisingservice.com

- fiftystatefsbo.com

 Sales Snafu _____

Beware of real estate websites that offer a terrific price to advertise your property—sometimes you do get what you pay for. Make sure for that low, low price, you're still going to get all the services you need, as well as access to a decent number of prospective buyers. A website that has only a handful of properties, or none in your area, may not be in the best position to help you sell your home.

Some websites have a geographic specialty, which focus on FSBOs in certain areas. Some examples of localized FSBO sites include:

- fsbofriend.com—FSBOs in the Denver, CO area

- fsbomadison.com—for sellers in the Madison, WI area

- chicagofsbo.net—for Chicago, IL area homes

- bigdfsbo.com—FSBOs in Dallas, TX

- losangelesfsbo.com—Los Angeles, CA-based FSBO properties

- floridaguide.com/classifieds—FSBOs in Florida

- bostonfsbo.net—Boston, MA FSBOs

- picketfence-vt-fsbo.com—FSBOs in VT, MA, and NH

- philadelphiafsbo.com—Philadelphia area FSBOs

 Tools of the Trade _____

Websites count the number of people who visit their site and report it as **traffic**, or the number of potential buyers who stopped by to take a look. Ask websites about the number of "unique visitors" they see in a week or a month to get a sense of the number of buyers likely to see your listing.

If you live in or just outside a metropolitan area, see if there are local FSBO sites with decent web *traffic*. If you live in a rural area, it may be tougher to find a local or regionalized FSBO site, but you can still investigate searchable national FSBO websites.

A Primer on Online Alternatives

Inclusion in an established website visited regularly by potential buyers is a smart goal, but what if you don't find such a website in your area? Or at a price you're comfortable paying? Then build your own website. Because your home's information is not included in a database of properties, it won't come up in any real estate searches, but there is still value in listing a web page on your yard sign, in your flyers, and in your newspaper classified.

> **FSBO Facts**
>
> Properties included in local MLS systems are frequently picked up by national websites like Realtor.com, Yahoo! Real Estate, and MSN HomeAdvisor. Some MLSs go so far as to provide their whole database to such websites as a means of increasing their clients' exposure to potential buyers.

Websites that will help you build and host your own website, some for free, include:

- buildfree.org
- buildwebsite4u.com
- cityslide.com
- handzon.com

You can also invest in a web design package that provides templates to lead you through the process of building your own web page. Some package names include:

- Web Studio—available for download at www.webstudio.com
- Easy Web Editor—downloadable at www.easywebeditor.com
- DIY Web Kit—available at www.diywebkit.com
- Yahoo SiteBuilder—free software to create a personal web page

Although saving money by creating your own web page sounds like a great option, keep in mind that unless you're very familiar with the Internet and web design, it may take you many hours to set up a web page the way you want it. Depending on how much time you have available to commit to this process, you might want to select an online advertising package that includes web page design. For just a few more dollars, you could save countless hours in front of the computer.

Design a Listing Sheet

A web page advertising your home for sale is essentially an electronic version of a listing sheet, which is an essential real estate document. A listing sheet can be a starting point for a web page, or a standalone marketing tool.

A listing sheet is a property fact sheet used to market your home. In addition to serving as a handout during home tours, a listing sheet can also help you organize your thoughts for a web page.

Information you'll want to be sure is on your listing sheet includes:

◆ Your home's address

◆ Your asking price

◆ The lot size

◆ Number of bedrooms and bathrooms

◆ Room dimensions

◆ Features, such as hardwood floors, fireplace, enclosed porch

◆ Amenities, such as central air or central vacuum

◆ Appliances that will remain with the home, such as washer/dryer and refrigerator

◆ Recent upgrades or repairs, such as roof, furnace, windows

◆ School district

◆ Town or city amenities, such as pool, recreation facility, and parks

◆ Garage or parking information

◆ Basement size and description, especially if finished

◆ Distances to major roadways or public transportation

◆ Tax information

◆ Annual utility costs

◆ Condos and co-ops should also state monthly fees and recent or upcoming assessments, as well as access to amenities like a health facility or sundeck.

◆ Any restrictions regarding showing the property, such as if you work 9-to-5 and can only show it before or after those hours, or before 9:00 P.M. because you have young children to put to bed.

♦ Any restrictions regarding a move date. One family we know was building a new home but decided to put their current home on the market in April, before the new house was ready. Because they didn't want to move twice, they alerted buyers that they didn't want to move until their new place was ready in August.

A listing sheet aims to answer 95 percent of all basic questions buyers may have about a home's location and features to help the buyer determine up front whether it meets their needs. And if you've done a good job of writing the listing sheet, prospective buyers will want to check out your home to have the remaining 5 percent of their questions answered in person.

Important Facts and Figures

When a buyer is interested in your home, they want specifics. Specific square footage measurements, specific lot size details, and specific feature details—specifics about what they will get if they purchase your home.

But buyers are also concerned with what it will cost, in total, to own it. That means you need to provide last year's total taxes—property, school, city, and so forth. You should also pull out, or call your utility company and request, a total figure for what you paid last year for your utilities—gas, electric, and oil, if applicable. Because higher winter heating costs raise gas bills for part of the year in the northeast, you should also divide that total by 12 to provide an average monthly utility bill—that's much better than telling a buyer that their utilities will set them back $80 a month in the summer and $380 in the winter.

Another number, or percentage, you'll want to provide is the typical home appreciation for your area. If housing prices in your neck of the woods have been rising steadily by 5 or 10 percent a year, point that out to buyers. Or if your area's prices have held steady in a declining market, that would be a big plus for your home. Don't assume buyers know these statistics, especially if they're moving to the area. Dazzle them with numbers that suggest your home is a great buy.

To look at home appreciation reports for 320 different U.S. cities, visit http://netscape.homestore.com/Finance/HousePriceIndex/default.asp?poe=homestore (see the following figure).

Check out how much homes in your area have appreciated.

Why a Photo Is Important

You've undoubtedly heard the adage: "A picture is worth a thousand words." That statement applies perfectly here, with listing sheets.

No matter how long your list of features, or how appealing your description of your home, in the end, buyers want to see a picture of it. On paper, a contemporary home with cathedral ceilings and hardwood floors may sound perfect to a buyer, but after having a look at the exterior, he or she may decide it's not quite their style. Likewise, a cozy three-bedroom cottage with built-in charm may sound too small for buyers set on a home with room to grow, but a picture of the home tells a different story, and they're hooked. Home sales can be made or broken based on a home's photos.

While interior photos are great to have, a buyer has to like the exterior before he or she will even consider looking inside. So make sure your exterior shot is as good as it can be.

Condition

When it comes to homes, buyers often want properties with charm and character—qualities frequently found in older homes. But they don't want to be saddled with huge repairs or maintenance costs. How well you've maintained, or even upgraded, the property while you've owned it can be a big selling point. The more you've done to improve the home's condition, the less potential buyers will worry about what kinds of work they may be required to do.

So, if you've done any of the following while you've lived in your home, be sure to include it on your listing sheet:

- Replaced the roof
- Replaced the furnace, or any major appliance
- Replaced windows and doors
- Refinished hardwood floors or added tile
- Purchased new kitchen appliances
- Replaced bathroom fixtures
- Finished the basement
- Painted the exterior
- Added additional space, with a room or enlargement
- Resurfaced driveway
- Added home security system
- Added pet containment system, such as Invisible Fence or PetSafe

Do all you can to give an image of an up-to-date, well-maintained home. The less work buyers expect to have to do, the higher the price they may be willing to pay.

Location Advantages

Buyers are also willing to pay more for a home in an area that has valuable amenities and years of price appreciation. Play up your home's location to the hilt whenever you can by raving about its convenience, community resources, great school system, low crime rate, reasonable property taxes, or proximity to desirable attractions, such as a park or lake. Add to your listing sheet whatever location benefits you can come up with, keeping in mind the wide range of buyers who may be looking at your place.

Young professionals may be more concerned about how quickly they can get to work than whether the school district has won any awards. Families with young children may be more interested in how close parks are than how many bars and clubs there are in the area. And safety and price appreciation may be top-of-mind for older couples.

Because you just never know what buyers will be attracted to, try to mention a range of your location's advantages to appeal to a broad cross-section of buyers.

Where to Place Them

Listing sheets should be made available to anyone who tours your home by placing them in plain sight on the kitchen table or front hall table. They should also be passed around to others who may come into contact with buyers, such as agents, brokers, headhunters, mortgage lenders, and whoever else you can think of.

Community bulletin boards are also a good idea, especially if the boards are read frequently. But don't limit yourself here—place them anywhere and everywhere. You just never know where the right buyer will be.

The Least You Need to Know

- Listing your home in your area's multiple listing service (MLS) will increase the number of agents and buyers who see your home is for sale, but that exposure generally comes at an additional cost.

- The main requirement for inclusion in an MLS is that your home is represented by a member real estate agent. This means you may be required to agree to pay a 2 to 3 percent commission if a member agent sees your listing on the MLS and brings you a buyer.

- Alternatives to your local MLS are national home selling websites and FSBO-focused sites.

- You can also choose to create your own website or home page to show off your home. There are websites and software packages with templates available to help you with the task.

- A web page is, effectively, an electronic listing sheet. Listing sheets are one- to two-page documents where you list every home feature you can come up with.

Chapter 7

Open Up! Hosting an Open House

In This Chapter

- The do or don't dilemma
- Best time to hold
- Open house preparation checklist
- Success secrets

Hosting an open house is one way to entice potential buyers inside to check out your home's best features. An open house can also help get the word out about your home—the more people who have seen it, the more word-of-mouth exposure you can earn. But they can also be a two-hour waste of time. This chapter will help you determine whether open houses are for you.

Agents frequently host open houses not so much in the hopes of landing a buyer for the home being shown, but to meet folks who may not already have an agent representing them. Because you're only interested in selling your home, you'll need to consider whether opening your house to the masses is worth the effort.

Prepare Yourself

Buyers love open houses because it's an opportunity for them to visit homes on their own, without the formality of an agent tagging along or the inconvenience of scheduling a specific appointment. They can visit as many open houses as they like, coming and going at their own pace.

Selling Smarts

Before scheduling your open house, spend an afternoon or two attending other open houses in your neighborhood. You'll get a feel for what's currently on the market and how those homes compare with yours, as well as experience first-hand how an open house works. You'll be better educated and more relaxed when it's your turn.

From the buyer's perspective, there's a lot to like about open houses. From the seller's perspective, there are both pros and cons.

Open House—Yay or Nay?

The biggest advantage of an open house is being able to show the home to several prospective buyers at once, rather than having to schedule separate tours. You save on clean-up and prep time, as well as host time. But you also get guests who have no real business being there.

FSBO Facts

Although 28 percent of all buyers attend open houses, says the National Association of Realtors, just 2 percent first learned of the house they bought through an open house.

Approximately 20 percent of open house attendees are friends and neighbors just dropping by to get a peek at your place, reports *The Washington Times*. On the other hand, your friends and neighbors are also your best sales agents, so having them visit may not be such a bad idea.

With condos and co-ops, be sure to investigate any rules regarding when and how units can be shown. You may be required to give ample notice to the condo board of your intention to hold an open house. There may also be rules about timing, length, and staffing. Requirements vary by building, so pull out your condo association guidelines before announcing your open house.

Holding an open house shortly after putting your home on the market is more likely to attract crowds than waiting a few weeks because there is generally more interest in a new listing than an older one. So as you plan to put your home up for sale, get ready to hold an open house shortly thereafter for maximum impact.

When to Schedule

Traditionally, open houses are scheduled on weekend afternoons, typically on Sunday between 1:00 P.M. and 4:00 P.M., when people are thought to have more free time and are focused on finding a new place to live.

However, workers in the process of being transferred to a new job may come into town during the week to find a place. Holding an open house mid-week during the evening might attract more buyers who are on a tight timeline.

Before settling on an open house date, double-check schedules for holidays, major sporting events, community festivals, or other obligations that would keep buyers from attending. No matter how attractive your home is, you'll see fewer buyers if you decide to hold it the weekend after Thanksgiving or on Super Bowl Sunday, for instance.

Sales Snafu

> For safety's sake, consider having two or three "hosts" in your home during an open house rather than tackling it yourself. Being alone in your home with strangers is not a smart move, especially if you're holding the open house in the evening. Having another person there will also help you attend to all the visitors' questions when several buyers are around.

You may also want to host a neighbors-only open house, where families in your area are invited to stop by for coffee and dessert one evening. Showing your neighbors all the features you've enjoyed, just as you will potential buyers who tour your home, will help you practice your spiel and get your neighbors thinking about who they know who may be in the market for a home in their neighborhood.

After you decide on the day and time for your upcoming open house, announce it far and wide to make the most of your time. Place a classified ad during the week before the date, making sure it gets into the weekly real estate section of your local paper by buying a small classified ad. You'll also want to have it appear in print the day of the open house, in case someone suddenly decides that is the day to begin looking.

Preparing Your Home

To show your home at its best, run through the following checklist before the event:

❑ Have the grass cut the day of the open house and sweep away any clippings or debris.

❑ Hide any valuables from sight (you won't be able to watch all of your visitors at once, so be safe).

❑ Put out "Open House" signs at major intersections near the home, as well as one out front with the hours listed.

❑ Park your car, or cars, in the driveway to make your home look occupied and popular.

❑ Open all the curtains or drapes and turn on all the lights in the home.

❑ Give your toilets a good swish with a disinfectant-smelling cleanser, to impress buyers with their cleanliness, and close the lids.

❑ Light a fire in the fireplace.

❑ Put some potpourri on the stove, or a scented candle in the kitchen to provide a pleasant scent without overwhelming visitors.

❑ Turn some soft music on for background noise and to make your home more cozy.

❑ Do a final run-through to clear off clutter that has appeared on surfaces and to wipe down sinks and mirrors.

❑ Have a sheet or guest book out for visitors to sign.

❑ Put out information sheets for buyers to review.

When Kids and Pets Should Be Gone

Up to half of all buyers are either allergic to, afraid of, or don't like pets, say the authors of *Dress Your House for Success*, giving you plenty of reason to take your furry friends and their paraphernalia off-site during any open houses. Yes, your pet may be anything but scary, but if prospective buyers simply don't like dogs, cats, birds, pigs, or ferrets, for example, no amount of convincing is going to get them to tour your home if an animal is nearby.

Instead, ask a neighbor or family member to watch over Fluffy during the open house to avoid any negative reaction to your home. If you fear it will be difficult to arrange for last minute petsitting, you may want to look into boarding your pet at a kennel or animal hospital for the day. It may be less stressful for your pet to be in an unfamiliar place than to be home and watching strangers wandering through their space.

Although children are generally less scary to buyers than pets, it's probably a good idea to have them off-site as well. Your attention needs to be on meeting and greeting potential buyers, which is tough to do if your toddler is on the loose or your teenager's still in bed. Perhaps your spouse can entertain them elsewhere while you manage the open house, or hire a babysitter to keep an eye on them at their house. It will be less stressful for you to know they are being watched so you can focus on showing off your home.

Protecting Valuables

Most buyers coming to check out your home are there for the right reason, but once in a while someone who is more interested in your home's contents will also stop by. To prevent the loss of any items of real or sentimental value, tuck them away out of sight before anyone arrives. We're mainly concerned here with small items, such as money, prescription medication, and collectibles, which can be easily placed in a coat pocket or purse while your back is turned.

While you're at it, you may want to roll up any special rugs gracing your floor. It's unlikely someone would be so bold as to walk off with one, but you can protect it from lots of dirty shoes by pulling it up before visitors arrive. Some homeowners put down plastic sheets near doorways or in traffic patterns to further protect floors and carpeting from open house wear and tear.

The Open House Itself

An open house isn't very different from the personal tours you give potential buyers, except you may have several buyers inside at the same time.

Fielding Questions

Many visitors will walk quietly through the rooms in your home, perhaps pointing out something to others in their group or whispering amongst themselves.

Selling Smarts _____

Having visitors sign a guest book makes later follow-up possible, which is smart, but it also provides a measure of security by knowing who has been in your home. Ask potential buyers to jot down their name, address, phone number, and e-mail. You could also ask how they learned of the open house, so you know which marketing methods are working best.

Selling Smarts _____

When asked why you are moving, try not to give an answer that points out a glaring negative of your home, such as its size, location, or lack of a garage, for example. Instead, mention that you want to move closer to work or to family—giving a reason other than some deficiency with your current home as the reason.

If you're leading a room-by-room tour, try to offer useful observations. By all means, don't state the obvious, such as "Here's the dining room," unless it's unclear that the room was designed to function as such. That would be the case for instance, if you're currently using it as a home office or kid's playroom.

A better approach is to point out each room's best features, such as the brick fireplace in the living room, the massive amount of countertop space in the kitchen, or the skylight in the master bedroom. Talk about how much you've appreciated certain amenities, such as the Jacuzzi, the backyard lined with tall trees, or the walk-out basement.

Some people, generally the more interested buyers, will ask questions about the home and the area. Be prepared to answer them truthfully. You may need to brush up on your home's history to do that, such as by checking old blueprints or pull out a year's worth of gas and electric bills to calculate your average monthly expenditure, but any question left unanswered may prevent someone from continuing to consider buying your home. If you don't know the answer, certainly say so, but if you could get the answer, offer to do that and ask for the individual's phone number so you can reach them later with a response.

If you're asked questions about living in your home, such as whether your neighbors are nice or the schools are good, answer those honestly, too, but always emphasize the positive. For example, the wood stove in the house will require you stock up on wood each fall, but it will also cut your heating bill by half, or whatever the percentage is you've seen. Your home may not currently have a deck on the back, so the new owners will have the opportunity to design and build exactly what they'd like.

Preparing to Talk with Potential Buyers

Before your open house, try to anticipate what buyers may want to know about your home and neighborhood and have answers ready. For instance, how long does it take to get into the city from your place? If you don't know, take a drive and find out, so you can confidently give an answer. Other answers to have at-the-ready include:

- ◆ What school district are you in?

- ◆ What are the taxes?

- ◆ Is there a home owners association (HOA)?

- ◆ What is the monthly association or condo fee, if there is one?

- ◆ How far are you from the nearest major roadway?

- ◆ What is your average monthly utility bill?

- ◆ What additional monthly expenses do you have, such as trash pick-up?

- ◆ Are there any restrictions on what can be done in the backyard, such as no above-ground swimming pools or laundry poles? (Your deed should state these).

Help in learning more about your area can be found at www.foresalebyowner.com/ reports (see the following figure). The link gives you profiles of cities and comparisons of school districts, demographics, crime, and weather.

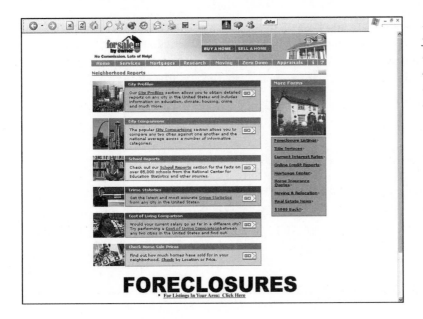

Doing your homework on your town or neighborhood before your open house will allow you to answer buyers' questions authoritatively and completely.

Handling Recreational Visitors

There will be people who stop who have nothing better to do, or because they've always wondered what your home looks like inside, or maybe because they aspire to have a home like yours and enjoy imagining what it would be like to live there. After you recognize that they're not serious, such as if they are more interested in admiring your window treatments than measuring the size of the rooms, don't waste a lot of time talking with them. Be friendly and cordial, but focus on answering the questions of other groups who appear to have a serious interest in learning more.

Among those recreational visitors will undoubtedly be some real estate agents. Some will be there to scope out the place for their clients while others will be there to scope you out.

Some ambitious agents will get in touch to offer to help you, should you decide not to continue to try to sell your home yourself. While you may want to collect this information for future reference, don't spend a lot of time with agents at the open house unless they seem to be inquiring on behalf of a client.

Watch What You Say

As you're chatting with buyers about your home and your move, don't mention personal information that could damage your negotiating effectiveness later. That is, don't reveal that you need to sell by such-and-such date in order to close on your new home, or that you start your new out-of-town job in two months and are eager to sell.

Such information may lead buyers to believe they can offer far less than your asking price and still have a shot at buying your home because you're crunched for time.

 **Selling Smarts** _____

If you're a shy person who is a little uncomfortable making small talk with strangers, make a point of skimming the morning paper the day of your open house. Read up on some of the newsworthy items that may be conversation starters, such as the 12 inches of snow predicted that night, or the local boy who won the national spelling bee. Having some ideas for conversation topics in your back pocket may reduce your uneasiness.

In talking with prospective buyers, be sure to treat all interested parties the same, regardless of their race, sex, handicap, religion, color, nationality, or familial status. The Fair Housing Act makes it illegal to treat anyone differently based on any of these statuses, for instance, telling some people the home isn't yet available (when it is), or quoting a different asking price depending on who has asked. Although you would never do this, make sure your buyers know that, too, to avoid any nasty legal action.

Tips for an Effective Open House

Now that you've set aside the time to show off your home, here is a recap of elements of a successful open house:

- **Sign-in sheets.** Either use a simple lined note pad with handwritten columns to capture visitors' names, addresses, and phone numbers, or you can create a printed one in Microsoft Word or Excel fairly easily. The key is capturing the information.

- **Snacks at the ready.** Offer guests some food and drink right away, or tell them where it is in case they want to enjoy some later. Having food on hand does two things: (1) It helps buyers relax during what is a stressful process, and (2) It encourages them to dawdle in your home. Instead of feeling like intruders who need to rush in and rush out, now, with a plate of veggies and dip and a cup of coffee or lemonade, they're friends. Maybe they'll even start to imagine entertaining their own friends in your space.

- **Flowers.** If you have time, head to the local farmer's market the morning before your open house and stock up on fresh colorful flowers. Or visit your local florist that day and buy a nice seasonal bouquet. Spread the flowers throughout the home for a nice aroma and fresh appearance.

Selling Smarts _____

Wholesale clubs, such as Sam's Club, now have florists on-site, where floral bouquets are sold for very reasonable prices. If you don't have time to hit the farmer's market, head to a discounter with a floral operation.

- **Start on time.** If your open house sign or ad lists your start time as 1:00 P.M., be ready for buyers to be on your doorstep as early as 12:45. Because this isn't a social occasion, your guests will be more likely to arrive early than fashionably late. And you need to be ready for them.

◆ **Listen carefully to questions.** Leave buyers alone to tour your home at their pace and to discuss what they like and dislike about your décor, but pay attention when they start asking questions. Their questions are your clue to what they really want in a home and allow you to elaborate on other aspects of living there they may appreciate. For example, if one couple asks about the property taxes, they may be concerned about the cost to live in your home. When responding, throw in extra information about the municipal utilities, which keep gas and electric bills extremely low, and the community resources living there those taxes pay for.

FSBO Facts

If your town or city has a lot to offer in the way of amenities, such as a new park, pool, or recreational facility, buyers will likely find that property values are steady or increasing. And if you know that is the case in your neighborhood, point it out (see Chapter 6 for more information on property value reports).

◆ **Answer questions and clarify.** As prospective buyers ask you questions, answer them, and then ask them a question to clarify why they asked. So for the family concerned about the school district, ask how many children they have and what their ages are. With that information, you can tell them about other benefits of living in the neighborhood that will be of interest to kids that age. Or if someone asks about the crime rate, fill them in, and then ask if they've had a problem where they currently live. You'll gain more information about their situation, reason for wanting to move, and the possible fit with your home.

Learning more about buyers will help you tailor your responses to emphasize features and benefits they're interested in. And the more you can convince potential buyers that your home will meet all their needs, the better your chances of getting a sale.

Other Considerations

While an open house is one way to entice potential buyers into your home, it's by no means the only way. If things don't go exactly as planned, don't beat yourself up. There are other tactics you can use to promote the sale of your home.

Keep Your Sense of Humor

Visitors to your open house will be more relaxed and comfortable if you appear to be relaxed and upbeat, rather than anxious and desperate.

Sure, you may be feeling overwhelmed and stressed, but act like you've got all the time in the world to sell your home—it's no big thing. Not only will it keep you in a strong negotiating position by suggesting you feel no pressure to jump on the first offer that comes along, but you'll endear your open house guests to you, making them feel more positively about your home.

Selling Smarts

If your neighborhood is a hot spot for kids, you may want to schedule a special child-friendly open house where your children are on-hand to fill in visitors about all the great people and activities in your neck of the woods. Encourage buyers to bring their kids along, too, and have popular children's snacks available to keep everyone happy.

Following Up

A few days after the open house, pull out your sign-in sheet and call the folks who toured your home. Ask if they are still considering it, or if they're looking at other places. If they're still considering it, ask what their concerns are, or if there were any questions they needed answered in order to seriously consider it. Be helpful and friendly, not pushy.

If they mention a particular area of concern, try to locate some additional information on that topic to send them a few days after that. Whether it's finding a low cost mortgage or the ability to add central air to the building, try to find a reason to stay in touch.

Keep checking in every few days until the buyers tell you they are no longer interested or have bought another place. Until then, you're still in the running.

Hosting, Again

Depending on how successful your open house is at attracting potential buyers, you may decide to try it again shortly thereafter. Or you may decide up front to schedule two open houses back-to-back, such as on a Saturday and Sunday. The advantage of open houses scheduled closely together are that you'll have less clean-up and preparation to do.

Having two scheduled closely together may also help put pressure on folks who come and like what they see to put an offer in ASAP. Or it may encourage buyers to come back and take a second look, which is also a step in the right direction.

Online Open House Resources

For more information about topics covered in this chapter, check out the following websites:

◆ www.usdoj.gov/crt/housing/title8.htm. For more detailed information about the Fair Housing Act, to avoid any suggestion of discrimination from buyers.

◆ www.ams.usda.gov/farmersmarkets/map.htm. Find a farmer's market in your area at this USDA website. Simply click on your state and you'll be provided with a list of area sources for fresh grown flowers and produce.

◆ www.earthcalendar.net/index.php. For a quick look at major holidays in the United States, visit this website before you finalize your open house dates.

◆ www.courier-journal.com/apps/pbcs.dll/article?AID=/20050226/BUSINESS/502260352/1003. A useful article on protecting yourself during an open house.

The Least You Need to Know

◆ Most open houses are scheduled on Sundays between 1:00 P.M. and 4:00 P.M.

◆ Check to make sure no major sporting events, community get-togethers, holidays, or family obligations fall on the day you're planning to host an open house. Scheduling an open house on Mother's Day, for example, is unlikely to attract many buyers.

◆ Arrange for someone else to watch your pets or children during the open house so they don't scare or distract buyers—many buyers are afraid of pets.

◆ Make your visitors feel at home by offering snacks and a drink when they arrive. Don't hover as they inspect your home, but keep track of where they are.

◆ Hide any money, valuable collectibles, and medication to prevent it from being stolen during the open house.

◆ Set out a sign-in sheet so buyers will note their name, address, phone number, and how they heard of the open house. Use that information to follow up later to see if they may be interested in the home.

Chapter 8

Other Attractions

In This Chapter

- Setting the stage for a sale
- Leveraging your location, location, location
- Collaborating with agents
- Remaining at-the-ready for a showing

Now that your home is on the market, the next step is to entice a buyer to snap it up. And in hot real estate markets, that can happen—overnight sales are not out of the question. But for most of the country, it can take weeks or months to find the perfect match.

During that time, you'll want to keep your home in tip-top shape, ready to be shown at a moment's notice. You'll also want to have plenty of information available to hook a buyer who's interested. And, depending on how quickly you need to sell your home, you may want to consider offering to pay an agent a partial commission for bringing you a buyer. All of these steps get you that much closer to sealing the deal.

The Home Tour—When Prospective Buyers Are on the Premises

To sell your home, you're going to need to show it (and show it, and show it …). You may get lucky and sell it to the second or third couple who comes through your door, or it may be the ninety-ninth individual. It's hard to tell who will end up being "the one"—buyer, that is.

Selling Smarts

Most home showings will take 15–20 minutes, depending on the number of rooms and special features you point out. But don't be surprised if it takes less.

Which means you need to prepare your home before each and every visitor arrives on your doorstep. Run through your checklist to be certain every room looks as large, clean, clutter-free, and bright as you can make it.

When a potential buyer arrives to tour your home, greet them warmly, give them a general description of the home's layout, and then offer to give them a tour so you can point out some of the home's best features.

Generally, you'll start by showing buyers rooms on the first floor, beginning in the entryway and moving to an adjacent room, such as the living room or dining room. Move room by room, following the natural flow of your home. After they've seen the rooms on the first floor, move to the second floor, if you have one. Typically, the master bedroom is of greatest interest, so start there and move to the other bedrooms. After you've shown the second floor, you can open the attic, if there is anything to show, and then to the basement, where you should be prepared to answer questions about the heating and cooling system and general maintenance.

Try to begin and end in a cozy room, such as the living room, where perhaps there is a fire in the fireplace, or the kitchen, where a nice snack is laid out. Buyers who are interested now have the perfect opportunity to ask you more detailed questions, such as where the nearest supermarket is or how hard it is to get into a good daycare. With comfy chairs conveniently nearby, you all can sit down and chat until their concerns have been addressed.

Selling Smarts _____

If you're feeling pressed for time and in need of a floor-to-ceiling cleaning, consider bringing in a cleaning crew the day before you put your home on the market. For a couple hundred dollars and a few hours, you can get your home in shape to show. Then, over the next few weeks, all you need to do is upkeep. Maintaining a clean appearance is much easier when the hard scrubbing has already been done (by someone else).

After you've answered their questions, it's a good idea to give your visitors some space to "talk amongst themselves." Excuse yourself to take care of some paperwork in your home office, or to do some cleaning elsewhere so the buyers have the opportunity to discuss the home alone. Let them spend all the time they need to talk about making your home their own.

Always Be Prepared

Let's face it, few of us keep our homes as clutter-free and spotless on a day-to-day basis as is required when you're selling it. But that's what buyers want to see—spic-and-span space. No mail lying on the counter, no overflowing wastebaskets, no unmade beds. No signs of everyday detritus.

To keep your home buyer-ready at a moment's notice, it's important to set up a daily routine to keep your place immaculate.

Sales Snafu _____

One of the worst selling mistakes you can make is to hover or talk too much during a home tour. Buyers are there to consider whether they'd like to live in your home, and they need time to soak in all the features and to gauge whether they feel comfortable there. A seller who refuses to give buyers some space can kill their interest instantly. And endless chatter gets in the way of the buying process. Smart sellers do more listening than talking.

Create a daily checklist that you and your family can quickly run through each morning. Take a sheet of paper and make a list of each room in your home. Then identify places in each room that need regular attention, such as wiping down the counters in the kitchen, cleaning the front of all appliances, and sweeping or mopping the floor.

In the bedrooms, you may want to be sure to make beds, open drapes, clean bathrooms, and vacuum the carpeting. After you've made your list, divide the workload so each person is responsible for the upkeep of a portion of your home.

How to Handle Unannounced Visitors

Your yard sign, classified ad, and website should all state that your home will be "Shown by Appointment." Real estate agents make appointments to show homes, and so should you. But that doesn't mean potential buyers won't show up unannounced on your doorstep in the hopes of getting a peek.

Don't be pressured into letting a potential buyer in for an impromptu showing just because they're interested. If you know them or have a personal connection and are available, you might consider it. But if they're strangers coming in off the street, use discretion. Some people will ring your doorbell in the hopes of popping in to check out your home on-the-spot.

Selling Smarts

Whether you've decided to host a neighborhood open house or not, you'll still want to enlist the help of your neighbors in selling your home. You can do that by printing up extra copies of your flyer and distributing them to everyone in your area. Attach a note asking for their help in finding a nice buyer to move into the neighborhood.

Be polite and friendly as you deliver the news that they can't see it at the moment, but for safety's sake especially, don't let anyone in unannounced. They may or may not be legitimate buyers.

Some of you may be comfortable letting people in unannounced, and that's certainly your call. Just be aware that you may be putting yourself in an unsafe situation.

If the visitors are interested in making an appointment to tour your home on the following day, take down basic contact information like their name, address, and phone number, in case you need to reach them. You could also discreetly note the make and model of their car, as well as the license plate number, as backup information for safety purposes.

How to Handle Telephone Inquiries

With your sign out front, your ad in the newspaper, and the neighbors alerted to your need for a buyer, it's likely you'll start to receive phone calls from folks looking for a home in your neighborhood. Buyers calling for the first time may have general questions for you about the home to determine whether it meets their general criteria.

As you answer their questions, try to ask about their needs. What exactly are they looking for? As you get a sense of the size, location, and specific features they are searching for, you can emphasize those same features in your home. If, say, the buyers want to be sure the home has a large back yard, you can tell them about how much space you have and how much your family enjoys it, such as by playing on the swingset that's back there, or the neighborhood barbeques you enjoy around the grill.

If you get a sense that this home may match their needs, invite them to come by and take a look. Your goal with every call should be to encourage the caller to make an appointment to see it. The only way you'll sell your home is by having people come through it. After they see all that it has to offer, you're much more likely to receive an offer to purchase. So aim for an appointment with every call.

When a prospective buyer seems very interested in seeing your home, try to get them in to see it as soon as possible. The more excited about your home the buyer sounds, the quicker you want them to get over to your place. For instance, if they want to come by that evening, do all you can to be available to show it then. The more time that elapses between their initial call and the appointment to see it, the more likely their enthusiasm will wane. They may even find another home they like in the meantime.

One family we know put their home on the market on a Monday morning. Monday afternoon they received a call from a woman who had been looking for a house in their neighborhood and had noticed their FSBO sign out front. She had basic questions about the layout, the space, how recently work had been done on the roof, and other appliance upgrades in that first call and said she would call back to make an appointment to see it. Tuesday morning, she called again, bright and early, anxious to make an appointment to see the home. "How soon would you like to come by?" the seller asked. "How about 4:00 today?" was the response. "Sounds great," the seller told her. The home was ready to be shown and the seller's objective was to get the buyer in the home as soon as possible in the hopes of landing a decent offer.

Selling the Setting—How the Neighborhood Helps

Although buyers make the decision to purchase a home based, in large part, on how well it meets their needs for living space, where the home is situated is generally an even more important decision.

Before heading out with buyers, real estate agents will typically try to zero in on what part of town the buyer wants to live in. After that has been determined, they can narrow the focus to the styles of homes that may be of interest to their client, getting as specific as floor layout, number of bedrooms, and size of garage, for example. But the neighborhood decision comes first.

Attracting Out-of-Town Buyers

Your best prospects for buying your home is someone who is ready to buy, has decided they want to live in your neighborhood, and is eager to seal the deal. That description often fits out-of-town or relocated buyers who are moving for a new job or to start over near family.

Few relocating workers have the luxury of looking for weeks on end for that perfect home; in many cases, they settle for the home in their desired neighborhood that best meets their needs, of all the ones available. Which means if your home is one of three on the market in your neighborhood, you have a 33 percent shot at a sale right off the bat. Out-of-town buyers that are under the gun to find a home and move quickly may be less price sensitive, too.

Folks who aren't familiar with your area will likely start their home search by doing some research on neighborhoods near work, school, or their relatives. You can, too, and get a leg up on how your neighborhood stacks up against those nearby.

To help you emphasize the benefits of living in your area to potential buyers, visit: http://houseandhome.msn.com/pickaplace/nf_Overview.aspx to gather statistics about your neighborhood (see the following figure).

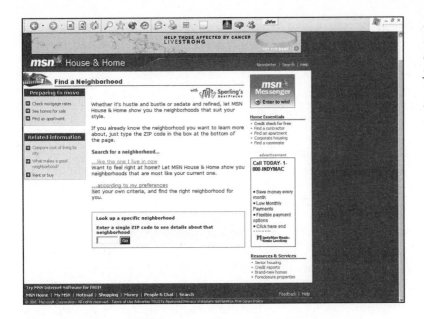

Learn about the average home selling price, median age of residents, and how your area stacks up against regional and national averages for schooling, cost of living, and more.

Working With Agents on a Sale

Despite your efforts to keep real estate agents out of the selling process, you may find they are an excellent source of prospects. Many agents are on the lookout for a particular kind of home to meet the needs of one or more buyers, which is especially true for *relos* (people relocating). If your place happens to fit a buyer's list of criteria, the agent is going to want to show it to them. Because your goal is to sell your home as quickly and for as much money as possible, you may want to consider allowing an agent to bring a buyer by.

Depending on the buyer's arrangement with the agent, the agent may already be receiving his or her commission directly from the buyer, in which case, you'd still owe the agent nothing even if they arranged the sale.

However, if the agent is expecting to be paid a commission from the seller—that would be you—you need to think long and hard about whether you're willing to pay out a 3 percent commission. One of the reasons you probably

Tools of the Trade

Buyers who are moving to a new city for work are called relocations, or **relos** (pronounced ree-lows) for short. Out-of-town buyers rely more heavily on real estate agents to find them a home from afar.

decided to sell your home yourself was to avoid writing large checks to real estate agents. Then again, if your home has been on the market for awhile, you may be willing to part with some cash to reduce the stress of the whole process.

Strategies When You're the "Amateur"

If agents offer you assistance with no strings attached, you may want to consider taking their counsel. If they offer you information on comparables, for instance, take it. If they are prepared to suggest an appropriate listing price, listen. It's all useful information you can benefit from. But why would an agent give away such useful information to a FSBO?

Many agents will pursue FSBO sellers, establishing a relationship early on so that if you decide later to hire an agent, you'll turn to them first. As a FSBO, you're a hot prospect because you've already identified yourself as a seller and you've, hopefully, already prepped your home for sale. From an agent's perspective, you've done a lot of the heavy lifting, and that makes you a desirable client.

Keep in mind that agents make their living through commissions, so be reasonable when accepting their help. Don't monopolize their time or expect them to represent you without a commitment to pay their commission—that's just not fair. But do ask questions. If you're unsure of some aspect of home selling and you have an agent willing to tutor you, ask. Or if you'd like an agent's opinion of how well your home "shows," invite them over for a quick run-through.

Special Deals You Can Negotiate

Your primary objective in selling your home yourself, without an agent, is most likely to save thousands of dollars in commissions. And agents know that. Still, they may have a buyer interested in making an offer and are concerned about being compensated for their services.

Some agents will ask you for half of the standard six percent commission for bringing you a buyer. They may also offer to assist you in putting the deal together, to justify their commission. You can take that deal, but you would be wiser to try to negotiate a better deal with the agent, such as 2 or 2.5 percent, given all the upfront marketing you've done yourself.

Many agents will be willing to come down to 3 percent because normally a 6 percent commission is shared between the buyer's and seller's agents. In this case, you're serving as your own agent and, as such, you can argue, you're entitled to half the full commission.

If, on the other hand, the buyer has hired his or her own agent as a buyer's broker, the responsibility for paying the agent's commission is in their hands anyway. To compensate for assuming that burden, the buyer may ask you to come down a little in the selling price. This is a fairly reasonable request, though you should certainly try to reduce your price by less than three percent, to avoid, effectively, paying the agent's three percent commission.

Selling Smarts _____

If a prospective buyer asks how firm your asking price is, respond that you'll consider all written offers. Your goal should be to review written offers only and not engage in verbal negotiations or possible purchase scenarios with buyers unless they are serious. Putting an offer in writing confirms they are, in fact, serious.

You'll also want to weigh this type of offer, and any other offer, with the possibility of receiving a better offer in the future. If the chance of that happening is slim to none, you should seriously consider the offer.

In the end, however, the possibility of paying a commission to an agent is secondary to the final, net price you will receive for your home. For example, let's say you have one buyer offering $150,000 for your home. And you have a second buyer represented by an agent who expects a 3 percent commission. Just because the second buyer has an agent does not mean their offer will be worse. If the second buyer offers $155,000 or more, you've got a better deal, even after paying a 3 percent commission.

Real estate agents can be an excellent resource and may very well end up bringing you the best qualified prospective buyers.

Online Marketing and Sales Resources

For more information about topics covered in this chapter, check out the following websites:

◆ www.merrymaids.com. For help getting your home in saleable shape, price out a maid service like Merry Maids, found here. Depending on how much time you have before your first showing or open house, you may find a maid service invaluable.

◆ http://houseandhome.msn.com/pickaplace/nf_Overview.aspx. You'll find a wealth of useful neighborhood statistics and comparisons at this website. From learning about your particular zip code to identifying neighborhoods that are similar (in terms of crime rate, income level, and age), this site is a great place to start.

◆ http://homefair.com/homefair/servlet/ActionServlet?pid=5&cid=gmacrealestate. This Homefair.com page lets you compare your neighborhood to others in the U.S., which can be a useful follow-up tool if you know the zip code a potential buyer lives in. Printing out a comparison to demonstrate your neighborhood's best features may help encourage a sale.

The Least You Need to Know

◆ Create a daily clean-up checklist for your family to follow each morning to help keep your home in showable condition at a moment's notice.

◆ Be amenable to showing your home whenever a buyer wants to come by—the more excited the prospect is, the more important it is to give them a tour ASAP. However, letting people walk in off the street is dangerous; requiring a phone appointment is better.

◆ Do a little research on your neighborhood to see how it stacks up against other areas, so you can point out to buyers the great community resources and the rising home values, for instance.

◆ When showing your home, plan to spend 10–15 minutes on a home tour, pointing out the best features. Then leave the buyers alone, so they can discuss the property without you nearby.

◆ Out-of-town buyers and relocated executives are some of the best buyers because they are crunched for time and may be willing to pay a little more in exchange for a quick move-in date. Make sure relocation specialists in the area know your home is for sale.

Chapter 9

Taking Your Sale Online

In This Chapter

- ◆ Selling electronically
- ◆ Website package deals
- ◆ DIY (Do-it-Yourself) websites
- ◆ Online marketing tools

Years ago, the tools used to sell a home were a yard sign, an information sheet, and an open house. Today, those traditional methods are still very effective, but they're not the only means of marketing your home. Now there is the whole realm of Internet, or online, marketing available to home sellers.

Although the high-tech nature of online selling may scare some folks off, the good news is that you don't need much in the way of computer skills to be successful here. There are plenty of services that are more than willing to handle the entire process of marketing your home on the web, for a small fee. But if you like working on the computer, you may enjoy the challenge of setting up your own web page.

A Wealth of Organizations and Options

As we've said before, 70 percent of home buyers start their search for a home on the web. That means, odds are, the person or family who ultimately buys your home is also going to turn to the Internet to find possible homes for purchase early on.

> **FSBO Facts**
>
> The web can hasten the sales cycle for some homes, reports the California Association of Realtors. Buyers who use the Internet spend slightly less than two weeks looking at homes and visiting about six properties in person. Those who don't use the Internet spend more than seven weeks and look at 15 homes, on average.

If you're not on the web, they may not find you—ever. Of course, they can still find your home through your other marketing tools, such as your yard sign and flyers, but that may only occur if they don't find a home they like during their initial search of properties online. Marketing your home online significantly increases the number of potential buyers who will hear about it.

Making information about your home available online can help get your home in front of a prospective buyer. It's that simple. Fortunately, it doesn't cost an arm and a leg, and the added exposure is generally well worth it.

If you've already made the decision to market your home online, you now have several approaches to consider:

- ◆ Sign up with a FSBO-dedicated website and receive help in creating a web page.

- ◆ Sign up with a local service that features agent-represented and FSBO homes, which may or may not provide much help in the actual construction of your page.

- ◆ Register with a website that helps you create a web page, but that is not connected with buying and selling homes.

- ◆ Create your own web page on your own and list it with search engines yourself.

Choosing the Right Service

All else being equal, it makes the most sense to work with a company, or website, that will both help you create your own site and market it to potential buyers. After your site is developed, the service's sole purpose is to market and sell your home. Of course, cost usually plays a role in the decision-making, so you'll need to take that into account as you survey your options.

The most expensive way to go may be to sign on with a FSBO program that includes a website listing as part of the service (see the following figure). Make sure you get a website listing as well as yard, directional, and open house signs as part of your package. In the long run, this can turn out to be your least expensive option, but in terms of total dollars expended up front for a web presence, it probably leads the list.

FSBO packages, like those at Forsalebyowner.com, often include a web page and listing.

The second most expensive option will usually, but not always, be a local service for FSBOs or homesellers. The amount of help in preparing your website or web page will vary, and your listing will generally be included with other homes in your area, rather than homes nationwide. But because buyers typically focus on a particular locale for their search, this shouldn't be a deterrent.

Using a company or service that helps you create and host your own site can cost as little as $30 or $40 up front, which is great as long as you can get help in making the site visible to buyers looking for a home. That $40, plus hosting fees of a few dollars a month, will go to waste if you create a site that no one ever sees.

Creating your own site using software and templates available online may cost you nothing out-of-pocket, but your challenge of alerting buyers to the existence of your site is even greater. You may need to do some research to identify local home selling websites to link to, which may cost you some cash.

Going Solo—Building Your Own Sales Website

Setting up your own website may save you a little money if you use a free web template and free web hosting service, but you'll still want to have your home page look like a lot of the other homepages that feature homes for sale.

A few of the better-known websites for free or low cost web design and hosting are:

◆ bravenet.com. Provides free templates and online accessories to help build your site.

◆ buildfree.org. A free three-step approach to setting up a basic website.

◆ www.freeservers.com. You can build a site for free here that has ads on it, or you can pay up to $7.99 a month for one with no ads.

◆ geocities.yahoo.com. Offers a limited free website or two other options that cost either $4.95 or $8.95 a month, much like freeservers.com.

◆ www.ivillage.com/ivillage/memberwebsites. Members can build personal websites for free at this site, which is geared mainly toward women (but that doesn't mean men can't visit and use the site). See the following figure.

Major websites like iVillage and Yahoo! offer free and low cost processes for setting up your own site.

Sales Snafu _____

Some websites that advertise "free websites" or "free hosting" provide neither. Although they may advertise freebies, with a little searching, you may find they charge for use of their template, or they charge a large monthly fee to host the site, neither of which is free in our book. There are some legitimate sites out there, just be sure you know what you're committing to when you click on the registration button.

When building and designing your site (see the following figure), some of the basic information you'll want to be sure you feature front and center includes:

♦ Photo of the front of your home (preferably taken straight on, rather than at an angle)

♦ Your name and contact information

♦ Asking price

♦ Address

♦ Total square footage

♦ Lot size

♦ Year constructed

♦ Number of bedrooms

♦ Number of bathrooms

♦ Type of property (single family, duplex, ranch)

♦ Type of construction (brick, stucco, log)

♦ Type of foundation (typically slab)

♦ Siding (wood, aluminum)

♦ Roofing material

♦ Heat source (gas, electric)

♦ Heat type (forced air, radiant)

♦ Sewer (public, septic)

♦ Water source (public or well)

- ◆ Cooling system

- ◆ Property taxes annually

- ◆ Homeowner association/Co-op/Condo fees

- ◆ Room dimensions

- ◆ Flooring (carpeting, tile, hardwood, linoleum)

- ◆ Fireplace

- ◆ Locations of bedrooms (number on each floor)

- ◆ Parking (attached garage, on-street, detached garage)

- ◆ School district (and names of specific schools in your district)

- ◆ Amenities (access to swimming pool, municipal electricity, convenient location)

This web page features all the basic information home buyers are looking for, as well as interior photos to peruse.

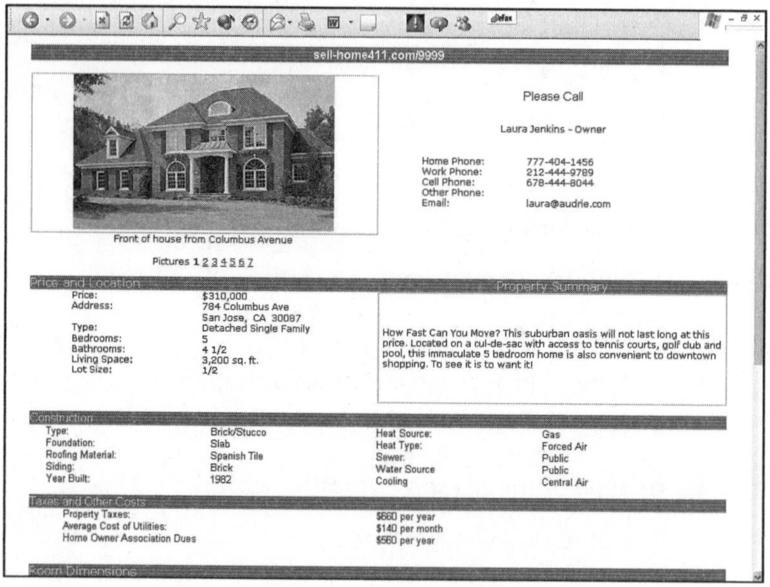

Other information you may want to mention, if you have the capability, includes:

- ◆ Floorplans for the home

- ◆ Mapping ability, such as a link to Mapquest.com, to show the home's proximity to area landmarks (see the following figure)

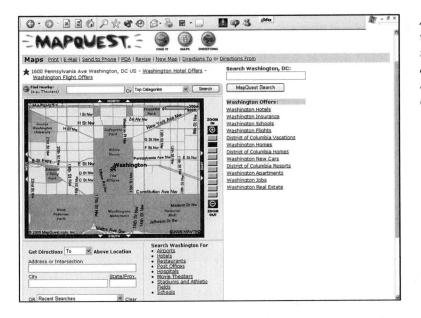

A link to an online map allow visitors to pinpoint your location relative to nearby amenities, which is especially helpful for out-of-town buyers unfamiliar with the area.

- Virtual tour or additional interior and exterior photos

- Links to online lenders, to get the process started

- Mortgage amortization calculator, to help buyers determine whether they can afford your home

- Any awards your town has earned, such as "Safest Community in the United States"

If you decide you don't have the interest or inclination to set up your own website to market your home, there are still some web-based services that can help you make a sale.

For those of you who want to check out some of the larger, national sites, here are some biggies to visit:

- www.forsalebyowner.com

- www.choiceofhomes.com

- www.homes.com

- www.househunt.com

- www.luxuryrealestate.com

- realestate.yahoo.com (see the following figure)

♦ www.realestate.com

♦ www.realestate4.com

Like many other national real estate websites, Yahoo! real estate listings are reviewed by thousands of buyers.

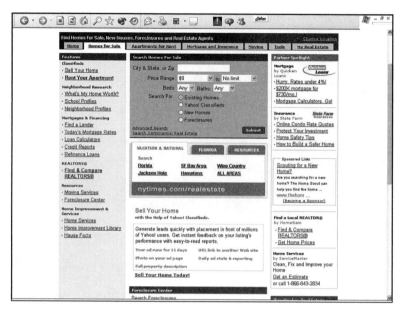

Virtual Home Tours

Many MLS systems now offer homesellers the opportunity to add a "virtual home tour" to their listing, which provides potential buyers with several photos of the home's interior. These tours generally consist of several exterior and interior photographs of a home to give potential buyers a clearer picture of what's inside and around the back.

Fortunately, it isn't necessary to have an MLS listing to set up a virtual tour of your home. There are a number of services more than willing to give you the tools to create one, or to do the work for you, for around $100.

Some of the providers currently on the market are:

♦ www.tourfactory.com. For as little as $49.95, and using your own photographic equipment, you can set up your own panoramic virtual tour with TourFactory. Or you can bring in the pros, starting at $109.95. The more help you get, the higher the cost, however.

◆ www.tournow.net. Sign up for a no-cost agent account at this website, and for $24.95, you can create your own virtual tour with as many scenes of your home as you want (instead of being limited to four shots, for example). You take the still photos using a digital camera, upload them to your computer, and type a description and title of each room. You can also add audio comments if you'd like. (See the following figure.)

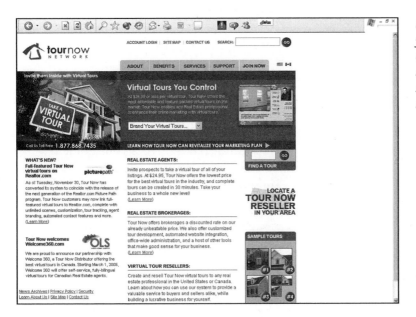

Setting up a virtual tour of your home on your web page or website generally costs around $100, but there are services that will help you for as little as $24.95.

◆ www.realtourvision.com/contact.asp. For $80–100, a Real Tour Vision dealer will handle all the work associated with creating a 360 degree panoramic home tour. Simply complete the form requesting more information, and you'll receive a list of dealers in your area who can create a virtual home tour for you. If you really want to do it yourself, you can buy a virtual tour kit from Real Tour Vision for $299.

◆ www.360house.com. For around $100, you can have four panoramic shots and 10–15 professional still shots taken by a pro. However, not all dealers offer FSBO packages. Call 800-sayobeo to request the name of your local dealer and to find out if they offer a FSBO package.

If a buyer likes the looks of the front of your home, being able to immediately see attractive photos of the inside can move the buying process along quickly. They may love the brick exterior of your place, and when they see the fireplace, large kitchen, and beautiful backyard, they'll really be sold. But without additional online photos, buyers need to schedule an appointment for an in-person tour, which may take a few days to coordinate and schedule—days during which they may be looking at other homes.

Virtual tours provide more information instantaneously, which is a big plus in the information age.

E-mail Campaigns

E-mail can be a very effective marketing tool, as long as you don't *spam* anyone.

You can approach e-mail marketing in a number of ways. The first step is to decide what information is most interesting, or relevant, for buyers. Does your home have an unusual architectural feature, such as leaded glass windows? Or does it sport a very private backyard? Is it in a very popular neighborhood or school district?

Tools of the Trade

Spam is the electronic equivalent of junk mail. Email messages that come into your inbox uninvited and unwelcome are considered spam. Those messages about online prescription drugs or hot stock tips you never asked for are prime examples of the category you don't want your email to fall into.

After you've decided what single piece of information is likely to catch the attention of potential buyers in your area, you should start to write up a brief subject header to lead off your message. Then draft an e-mail message introducing yourself and alerting the recipients to the fact that your home is for sale. Strive to get all the information to fit on one computer screen, so readers don't have to scroll down for more information, but hit on several of your home's advantages here, within the body of the message.

And then include a link to your home's web page or listing on a website, so recipients can immediately check it out.

Your next task is to determine the most effective source for names of buyers. In many cases, you won't be able to get the e-mail addresses of all the people currently in the market for a home in your area, so you have to broaden your search a bit and seek people who may have contact with such buyers.

Some of the people you may want to contact via e-mail with this information include:

◆ People who visited your open house

◆ People who have called to ask for information

◆ Local bankers

◆ Local mortgage brokers

◆ Local real estate agents

◆ Local home inspectors

◆ Local home appraisers

◆ Local employers—the human resource department, specifically

◆ All your neighbors

◆ People at your church, temple, or mosque

◆ All your friends

Like mailing out your flyers, e-mail is one more way to let people know that your home is for sale. And where they may throw out a lot of their printed mail, they may open your e-mail—or vice versa.

If you've already done a mailing of your flyers, you can also use e-mail as a follow-up mechanism to remind people the home is still available and to point out something you didn't mention in your earlier message—like the fact that taxes are lowest in the region, or your kitchen has all new appliances, for instance.

Specific Geographic Internet Sites

In addition to national real estate websites, there are many websites that specialize in a particular geographic area, which is helpful both to buyers and sellers who may not want to wade through thousands of listings to find those specifically in Memphis, Tennessee, for example.

Although national websites can be useful because they often get more traffic, the local sites generally cost less to advertise on and will appeal more to the people who are looking in and around your zip code.

A few of the localized websites you may want to investigate are:

- Charleston, SC. www.sciway.net/reloc/chasres.html
- Dallas, TX. www.dallasnews.com/classifieds/homecenter
- Los Angeles, CA. www.latimes.com/classified/realestate
- Maine. www.mainerealty.net/fsbocat.asp?category=Residential
- Michigan. www.mlive.com/realestate
- New Jersey. www.nj.com/homesforsale/index.ssf
- Oregon. www.oregonlive.com/homesforsale/index.ssf (see the figure that follows)
- Pittsburgh, PA. www.tribrealestate.com
- Sacramento, CA. www.sacbee.com/content/homes/sell

In addition to these localized sites, there are also websites like www.craigslist.org that are not real estate-specific, but function more like an online community bulletin board. People can search for items they want to buy, such as a house in a particular town, or a computer, or a used car, as well as listing items they want to sell. The traffic at this site is huge.

Many local real estate websites are affiliated with the area newspaper. So if you've already paid for a newspaper classified, it may not cost you much extra—if anything—to add an online listing, too.

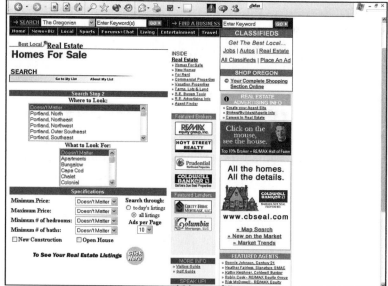

The reality is that the best website program for you will vary depending on where you live. You can use a number of companies or websites to prepare a web page with information about your home, but where you post that information will differ by region of the country.

Some areas have excellent local or regional FSBO sites, others don't. You may have access to local real estate sites in conjunction with your newspaper in some parts of the country, but not in all. In some places, the free alternative newsweeklies and community pennysavers have corresponding websites that are less expensive, but just as popular, as the major daily newspaper, and are worth exploring as an online marketing tool. And in some locales, networking via e-mail may be a better bet than uploading information about your home.

However, no matter where you live, you can be virtually guaranteed that buyers will go to the web for information about homes available in your neighborhood.

The Least You Need to Know

- ◆ It's possible to create a website for your home yourself, at little or no cost, but it may take a few hours, and you will need to get the site included in home selling search engines and databases to make the site worth it.

- ◆ FSBO websites frequently include a web page or website as part of their marketing package, which can be a good value.

- ◆ Including your home's information on a web page or within a home selling website can significantly boost the number of buyers who will find out about your home.

- ◆ Virtual tours are a smart way to provide prospective buyers with more information about your home without having to schedule a lot of in-person tours.

- ◆ Carefully compare national real estate websites with local ones to determine where you'll get the best bang for your buck—that is, the most traffic from qualified buyers.

Part 3

Setting Up the Deal

Now the fun really begins. You're starting to attract offers, so you're going to need to know what goes into them and how to handle them intelligently. Got you covered. From there, we'll move onto negotiation strategies and the various ways you can work out a deal to everyone's satisfaction. Then, financial nuts and bolts, including the basics of a mortgage and the various types of loans your buyer may pursue. Finally, we address some alternatives to consider that may help you close the deal, including owner financing, rent to own, and other options.

Chapter 10

Fielding Offers

In This Chapter

- ◆ Here comes the offer!
- ◆ Breaking down the basics of an offer
- ◆ Know every last detail
- ◆ Contingencies, remedies, and other factors

We're starting to get down to crunch time. You've done all the necessary steps, from advertising to hosting an open house to doing an absolute stellar job of putting your house in the best light when buyers come to call.

Now, someone is about to put in an offer to buy it. And as Sally Field once declared after having won an Academy Award: "You like me! You really like me!"

Because someone is poised to make an offer to buy your home, you need to know what that offer is going to contain and be ready to respond.

That's exactly what we cover in this chapter. We address the nuts and bolts of what a properly presented offer should include and how each offer can impact your ultimate goal—selling your home.

The Mechanics of an Offer—What to Expect

The moment has finally arrived. A prospective buyer has notified you that he intends to forward an offer to you.

Fantastic! Uhhh ... now what happens?

The first rule of thumb is to keep doing what you've been doing, at least for the time being. Just because someone says they plan to place an offer on your home doesn't necessarily mean they'll follow through. A lot can happen—they may change their minds or, by chance, come across another home that they prefer. You need to have a written offer in hand to know for certain whether their intent is genuine.

The Essentials of an Offer

Sales Snafu

From a legal standpoint, an oral offer isn't worth much. If, for instance, you agree orally on a price, who's to say otherwise if the buyer submits a written offer that's a good deal less? Never accept anything but written offers. If a buyer asks if you'll accept a certain offer, say you'll be glad to consider it— when it's on paper.

Initial offers can be as varied as the people who make them. Some you see may be rather thorough in their scope while others are quite a bit more basic. A buyer can use a preformatted document or simply type up something on their own (be sure to have your attorney review both). But a valid offer is always comprised of a completed real estate agreement known as an Offer to Purchase. Depending on the format used, the offer will specify a purchase price, the necessity of a home inspection, and, as we discuss later, a satisfactory *Purchase and Sale Agreement*. A valid offer also always includes an *earnest money* check.

Tools of the Trade

The **earnest money** deposit, in effect, means what it says. By including a check with an offer, a buyer is indicating that she is in earnest in her desire to buy your home. More on this in the next section. A **Purchase and Sale Agreement** is drawn up to cover every single term and condition that applies to the sale of a home. Depending on where you live, the document may go by a slightly different name.

Offers can be delivered by the buyers themselves or, if they're working with one, their real estate agent. Now keep in mind that any offer you receive to buy your home will never be open ended in terms of how long you have to respond. The time can range from anywhere between "upon presentation" (meaning you have to yay or nay on the spot) to the more common timeframe of 48 hours. But two can play the time game as well—if you counter a buyer's offer, you also specify just how long you're going to give him to decide what he wants to do next.

Here's a way to save yourself some real headaches. If a buyer lets you know she's going to present an offer, ask her to attach a letter to her Offer to Purchase from a lender saying she's been approved for at least the sales price of your home. That can save you the headache of waiting for a buyer to prequalify for a loan if their offer is worth considering.

The Purchase and Sale Agreement

As we mentioned earlier, initial Offers to Purchase will vary in their content and, to a certain degree, format. But, no matter their makeup, signing them commits you to a legally binding contract. And that moves you into a second, more comprehensive sales agreement, which must be drawn up and agreed to by both parties. This contract goes by various names depending on where you live. For our purposes, we'll use "The Purchase and Sale Agreement."

Where you can obtain suitable Purchase and Sale documentation depends on just how autonomous you want to be in selling your home. There are a number of websites—several of which are cited at the conclusion of this chapter—where you can download Purchase and Sale Agreement forms. Depending on the site, you may also be able to obtain documents that conform to any local real estate laws that may apply.

 Selling Smarts

Independence is all well and good, but it's never a bad idea to have your attorney draw up Purchase and Sale Agreement contracts. Not only can she address any local real estate legal issues, she'll be in on the ground floor should any hurdles or problems come up later.

As we've said before, the Purchase and Sale Agreement you consider is likely going to be vary somewhat between buyers. But, boiled down somewhat, the agreements do share a number of common (and significant) features. It pays to know just what those are and how they may impact your sale.

If you're wondering why we're hitting on the makeup of a sales contract before we cover counteroffers, negotiation, and finalizing financial details, the reason is simple: the better you know the ultimate makeup of your sales contract, the better you'll be positioned to negotiate effectively. First things first! Because agreements vary, bear in mind that our advice for the treatment of a Purchase and Sale Agreement may not apply uniformly to all the agreements you may work with. Be smart and direct any questions or concerns to your attorney.

Here are some common elements of a Purchase and Sale Agreement:

- **The purchase price, including other financial details such as earnest money.**

- **Date when the contract goes into effect.** This happens when both the buyer and seller sign the contract.

- **Include the full legal names of buyers and sellers and whether they are single or married.** Usually, the buyer's legal address is also included. Note: It doesn't come up all that often, but it never hurts to make certain that the buyer listed in the Purchase and Sale Agreement is of legal age—usually 18. If they're not, that may ultimately kill the contract. This can happen when, for instance, a family buys a college student a home to live in while he's attending school.

- **Description of the home.** This portion describes the property. It usually includes the address and an approximate square footage of the lot where the home is located. The description will also include a legal description, which is information about the property that is looked up when the sale is recorded at the local registry of deeds.

- **Purchase price.** First and foremost, this identifies the purchase price upon which both the buyer and seller have agreed. This section also addresses how the buyer will pay at the time of closing. Options include cash, banker's check, certified check, and other methods of payment. This portion should also address terms of any necessary financing, including down payment, the type of loan the buyer plans to use, and other relevant details.

- **Earnest money.** The section on purchase price will also include the earnest money deposit and who holds the earnest money deposit. The earnest money deposit is also called the good faith deposit. As we mentioned earlier, this represents a serious intention on the buyer's part to do his utmost to complete the sale. The general rule of thumb is that the earnest money deposit should be at least $1000 or at least 1 percent of the purchase price. From there, this figure increases the more expensive the home. Bear in mind that this is not a fee but a deposit that eventually goes toward the purchase price. After certain inspections have been completed and all forms of disclosure have been given to the buyer, the earnest money is generally deposited into an *escrow* account with a real estate attorney or escrow company.

Always try to get a reasonable earnest money deposit—as we suggest above, 1 percent of the purchase price. While you want a fair commitment from the buyer in return for taking your home off the market, you don't want to demand too large a deposit—they may just walk. One good way to strike a balance is to know the buyer's credit rating—the better the score, the less risk you can take on with a lower earnest money deposit.

Tools of the Trade

Escrow refers to something of value—in this case, the earnest money deposit—that's held by a third party. Escrow agreements instruct the holder to distribute the funds after the sale is finalized.

The earnest money section in the Purchase and Sale Agreement may also address what happens to the funds if the deal falls apart. Depending on the circumstances, they may be returned to the buyer, retained by the seller, or divvied up between the two. Deals can fall apart due to an unsatisfactory inspection, failure to obtain a loan, prohibitive liens on a home, or a buyer simply changing his mind. Each will effect just how the earnest money will be divvied up.

Of course, we're all wonderfully trusting human beings, particularly when it comes to selling real estate. But no buyer is going to let you, the seller, hold the earnest money while the deal goes through. So the contract will specify who keeps the money safe and sound. It will go into an escrow account.

Selling Smarts

As a solid form of protection, have your attorney work language into the contract that directs the escrow agent to hold all escrow funds in the event of some dispute until both the buyer and seller agree that they can be released. That can help stop a buyer from walking away from a deal unnecessarily soon.

A deal that falls apart is one good reason to try to obtain as large an earnest money deposit as you can. If the sale doesn't pan out, and you've lost days and even weeks with your home off the market, it's often the only compensation you may be able to obtain.

Who holds the earnest money can vary. Often, it's one of the attorneys involved in the sale. There are also escrow companies who specialize in safeguarding escrow funds.

♦ **Deadlines.** Having things happen when they should is as essential an element as any on the Purchase and Sale Agreement. Look for items such as these:

Financing timeframe. This spells out how quickly the buyer has to get any necessary financing in order. Usually, this begins with a preapproval letter with a credit check within five to seven days after the contract is signed (unless, of course, the buyer was already preapproved when they presented the purchase agreement to you). If he's not, you can always have any lender with whom you may be working do the job for you—refer back to our discussion in Chapter 3 for additional details. After that's out of the way, a formal loan application follows. Complete loan approval should be obtained within 30 to 45 days from the date you sign the contract offer.

Deadline if a loan is denied. If the loan is denied after the date specified here, the buyers should forfeit their earnest money deposit. This may seem unnecessary, particularly with buyers who are preapproved, but things can go wrong, so it's a valuable bit of protection.

Inspection and disclosure timeframes. This spells out the timeframe for inspections and any action to correct any identified problems with the house. Inspections and delivery of any disclosures should be completed within five to seven days after the contract is signed. The buyer usually then has two to three days to let you know—in writing, by the way—any problems discovered in the inspection or disclosures. You then have two to three days to determine what you want to do. You can agree to fix the problems at your own expense, propose that you split the cost, or simply refuse to do anything. Like the buyer, you have to respond in writing.

Deadline for appraisal. If the buyer—or, by chance, the loan company—insists on a fresh appraisal, this specifies when that has to be completed.

Termite inspection timeframe. This is generally done any time before the closing takes place. Most lenders require a clear termite inspection within 30 days before you close. That ensures the termite inspection is up to date.

Date and location of settlement. This is also called the *closing*. You should also agree with the seller on a timeframe for closing the sale. If the details of the loan approval permit it, it's often a good idea to aim for as quick a closing as you can.

Not only do you get your money faster, but a tight deadline can help keep things moving forward as they should.

Tools of the Trade

The **closing** is the point at which real estate formally changes ownership. You sign a variety of documents and also settle up on various related charges and fees. We cover the closing in exhaustive detail in Chapter 16. **Broom clean condition** means more than a quick sweep. State guidelines vary, but most apply the term to mean a rather thorough cleaning—countertops washed, bathrooms cleaned, and all garbage and remnants removed and hauled away. It's not just complying with contrac-

Date property is vacant and property condition. This spells out when you will be out of the home and the shape the property is in at that time. With regard to property condition, many contracts specify that the home be left in what is known as *broom clean condition*. The buyer may require a walk-through of the house on the day before or day of settlement to ensure it is in good condition.

It's always a good bet to get out on or before the day of closing if possible. Of course, that's not always possible. Some sellers will need to stay in the house after closing. If it's more than two or three days, you may have to pay the buyer a pro-rated "rent back." This amount is usually the daily cost to the buyer for their entire mortgage payment, including taxes and insurance.

To protect against any claim of damage or complaint that the property is not suitably clean, keep your homeowner's insurance in effect until the sale has been completed.

◆ **List of items included in the sale.** This is a list of what will stay with the house after the sale, including appliances, lighting fixtures, window treatments, and other features. We address this in some detail in the Chapter 11 on negotiation strategies, but know for now that you can try to bring certain elements of your home with you after you move—even such things as outdoor trees and shrubs, if they have a certain sentimental value.

◆ **Payment of *closing costs*.** This is a biggie. The contract should stipulate who will pay the buyer's and seller's closing costs as well as the various transfer and recording fees that localities and states charge when property is transferred.

Who pays these costs is almost always negotiable between buyer and seller, but there are usually common local practices. Check with your attorney to see what's expected and what may be somewhat unusual.

We will tackle the issue of closing costs and other related expenses and fees in Chapter 12, but it's important to recognize that these issues will be raised in a sales contract. For instance, depending on the circumstances of the sale, it's not unusual for a buyer to ask the seller to pay some of their closing costs, such as transfer and document recording expenses. It's also a good idea to check with your attorney on this because which party pays what can also be influenced by what's normally done in the area where you live.

- **Payment of commission.** If you and the buyer have agreed to work with a real estate agent in some manner, the contract should spell out the amount of commission due, to whom it's due, and who pays it.

- **Proration of expenses.** This spells out how real estate taxes, rent, fuel, water bills, and utilities should be adjusted (prorated) between buyer and seller. This usually depends on the time of month in which the closing takes place.

- **Type of *deed*.** This portion of the contract specifies what sort of deed will apply to the sale. A deed, in essence, is proof of ownership of a particular piece of property. There are two sorts of deeds—a *warranty deed* and a *quitclaim deed*. On the surface, this may seem a headache in the making, as some buyers may insist on only a warranty deed. But the truth is local real estate regulations usually specify what sort of deed is used in a particular location.

- **Quality of title.** Because title means ownership of a property, quality of title refers to just how solid that ownership happens to be. Generally, contracts will include the term "clear record and marketable title" to specify the best title possible. However, the sale can fall apart if certain problems are discovered that may affect the quality of the title. These can include outstanding mortgages, court judgments, tax liens, and other snafus that muddy just who has clear title to the property. Obviously, title problems can prove to be a real deal killer. Do what research you can proactively to identify any problems and, in the case of issues such as tax liens, have them taken care of.

- **Offer *contingencies*.** This can prove to be a broad list. We've already touched on some of them earlier in this chapter, but any sales contract is likely to contain a broad number of contingencies.

Tools of the Trade

Closing costs are various costs, fees, and other expenses connected to the final closing on a property. A **deed** is the formal, legal document that conveys title to a property. The difference between the two deeds is largely one of guarantees. A **warranty deed** guarantees, in effect, that ownership of the property is absolutely free and clear. A **quitclaim deed**, on the other hand, lets a new owner take possession of the property but makes no warranty that the title is free and clear. **Contingencies** in a sales contract are clauses inserted or added that make the offer subject to something taking place. They establish certain conditions that must be fulfilled for the sale to proceed as planned.

Contingencies

As we noted, you've already seen some contingencies, such as obtaining suitable financing and having certain inspections and appraisals performed. The mechanics of those are simple. Say, for instance, if the buyer isn't happy with the termite inspection, the contingency gives him a right to pull out of the deal. By the same token, if the buyer is unable to obtain suitable financing in a timely fashion, that particular contingency lets the seller walk away and put the house back on the market.

But there are other possible contingencies that may appear in a sales contract. Here are a few to consider, some of which protect the buyer, while others are built to address the seller's interests:

♦ **Additional inspections.** Not every buyer will stick to a conventional home inspection. Others will insist on certain additional tests, including radon, water quality (particularly if the home is on a well system), lead in the home's paint, and other issues.

It's never a good idea to balk if a prospective buyer wants to perform any of these additional tests. If you hesitate, the buyer may become suspicious and back out of the deal.

♦ **Third party approval.** This can apply to the home or details of the sales contract. In either case, it inserts a contingency that some third party—perhaps an attorney or a relative who knows home construction—has to lend their approval to the deal.

- **Subject to buyer's sale of current home.** This is fairly common, as many buyers simply can't afford to buy a new home until their current house is sold.

A buyer having to sell her home first may be common, but consider this contingency carefully before you approve it. First, check out their home as best you can to determine if its chances of selling quickly are good. And, as we mentioned before, get as large an earnest deposit as you can to protect yourself in case things go slowly (or not at all).

Selling Smarts

Legal issues can be particularly tricky if you're trying to sell a condominium. Condo associations can have all sorts of specific rules, such as having the right to step in and buy your condo even if you've found a buyer. Have your attorney check if anything applies and, if need be, attach an appropriate contingency.

- **Subject to seller's purchase of new home.** This contingency cuts both ways. You can try to protect yourself by making the deal contingent on closing on your new home.

- **Other legal contingencies.** Sometimes it happens that other legal constraints are placed on the sale of a home. For instance, if a home is part of an estate that has yet to be legally closed, you may have to insert a contingency to obtain a suitable court order to sell the property.

This page at ForSalebyOwner.com offers a wide range of downloadable legal forms and materials.

One way to keep track of progress through the various contingencies is to formally remove them from the contract with an appropriate addendum. You can either use prototype-like addendum forms to complete and add to the contract or you can direct your attorney to keep the contract up-to-date with current addendums. The following figure gives you an idea of the various sorts of forms that you'll need to keep track of.

Prescribing a Remedy (If You Have To)

Until now, we've covered a number of circumstances and events that, in effect, represent a buyer or seller's inability to fulfill certain parts of the contract. If that happens, the contract should also specify what either the buyer or the seller may be entitled to in terms of compensation. These are referred to as remedies.

Remedies, like seemingly everything else in the fluid world of home selling, can differ. For you as the seller, one remedy we've already discussed is hanging onto the earnest money deposit. Depending on the size of the deposit in question, that can prove substantial, not to mention serving as a powerful motivator for the buyer to fulfill her end of the contract. It's a good idea to have your attorney work specific language to that effect into the contract.

There is a second remedy, one for the buyer, known as *specific performance*. This, in effect, involves a court ordering the parties to complete the deal regardless of the problems they have experienced to date.

Specific performance may also be used on the buyer's side. The contract obligates the seller to sell the home to the buyer under the conditions and within the specified timeframe. Most contracts specify that sellers must make a reasonable effort to solve whatever problems may be holding up the sale.

Tools of the Trade

Specific performance is a holdover from old English law. It was developed when land was the most powerful commodity there was. The thinking was that monetary damages were inadequate to compensate someone for the loss of land. Hence, the legal mandate that the sale be concluded as planned was established.

If, however, there are no problems—or those that are present are not addressed by the seller—the seller is then legally obligated to proceed with the sale. If he chooses not to, the buyer then has the option of asking a court to introduce specific performance to proceed with the sale.

Why would a seller knowingly fail to follow through on a sale that was ready to go? Often as not, the reason is money. It's possible—particularly in active markets—that another buyer has presented an offer that's more attractive than the one under contract. The seller hopes that the buyer simply gives up and leaves him free to pursue the more lucrative option.

When to Involve Your Attorney

If all the various terms that can apply to a Purchase and Sale Agreement seem a bit intimidating, it's because they are. You wouldn't be the first FSBO to go cross-eyed trying to work your way through the various elements and requirements of an appropriate and legally suitable sales contract.

That's why it's an awfully good idea to involve your attorney as early in the process as possible. For one thing, it's prudent to have her review anything—and that means everything, from the most substantial document to the most innocent-seeming note—before you sign. Anything short of that could be courting disaster.

Selling Smarts

Another plus to involving an attorney in the contract process is peace of mind—both for the seller as well as the buyer. Rather than hoping a layperson will be able to construct the best sales contract possible, which is certainly doable, the presence of an attorney lets everyone know that a pro is on the job. And that can help things proceed more smoothly.

As we've mentioned, an attorney can also prove invaluable in drafting sales documents that are not only geared to meeting all parties' needs, but are also legally suited to the area in which you live. Even if you obtain perfectly legal prototypes, chances are good they may have to be modified—often substantially.

As we've also pointed out, having an attorney ready can be exceedingly valuable from a negotiation standpoint, particularly for buyers who are a bit gun shy about any give and take. If nothing else, an attorney is not going to be as emotionally involved as you are in the process. And that can be a real stumbling block to even the best intentioned of sellers.

Online Resources

Here are a few online resources that can provide prototypes of contracts covering offers, purchase and sales agreements, and other related documents. (Even if you go with an attorney to draw up the paperwork, these offer an inexpensive way of familiarizing yourself with what goes into them.

 ◆ ForSaleByOwner.com (www.forsalebyowner.com/real-estate-forms.html) offers downloadable real estate forms, including Offer to Purchase and other sales-related documents.

 ◆ FindLegalForms (www.FindLegalForms.com) is another online resource for real estate documents.

 ◆ Two additional websites that offer a variety of real estate sales forms are www.urgentbusinessforms.com and www.LawDepot.com.

The Least You Need to Know

 ◆ Never even consider a verbal offer to buy your house. Insist that it's in written form.

 ◆ An earnest money deposit that accompanies an offer shows the buyer is genuine in her interest. Try to obtain as large a deposit as possible.

 ◆ The Purchase and Sale Agreement outlines every detail and responsibility that must be addressed before you can close the sale of your home.

 ◆ Consider any contingency attached to the Purchase and Sale Agreement carefully. Have your attorney review them to make sure none are unnecessarily problematic.

 ◆ Involve your attorney in the contract phase as much as possible. It's an inexpensive form of protection to make certain your interests are addressed.

Chapter 11

Negotiating to Win

In This Chapter

- ◆ Knowing when and how to counteroffer
- ◆ Understanding negotiation basics
- ◆ Overcoming objections
- ◆ The joy of multiple offers

Now that we have a solid handle on the nuts and bolts of a substantive offer, we can move on to another bit of reality.

Chances are exceedingly strong that, at this point, you and your buyer don't see eye to eye on everything.

First, relax. That is very much the nature of the real estate beast. What matters now is knowing effective ways to proceed, including negotiation strategies, counteroffers, and the overriding importance of knowing precisely what you want and how you can best get there.

"I'll See Your Offer ..." Effective Negotiation and Counteroffers

Okay, so you've got this offer to buy in your sweaty hand (it's natural to feel ecstatic; getting an offer can be a heady time, so enjoy the moment completely).

Now, the question jumps up. What do you do next?

Relax, you have plenty of options. The first thing to do, of course, is review the offer in exhaustive detail. Go over it item by item to determine what you like and what you don't. In Chapter 10, we walked you through the substance of what an offer contains. To be particularly thorough, you may want to have your attorney review it and have her highlight what's good and what's lacking.

Sales Snafu _____

It's a natural and justifiable reaction to pay overwhelming attention to the price the buyer is willing to pay. After all, that's why you're selling your house in the first place. But don't short change other elements of the offer. Perhaps the buyer wants to close the deal faster than you're comfortable with; maybe they want you to leave that pool table you're not about to part with for anything in the world. Pay attention to everything and you'll be that much more satisfied in the end.

At this point, you effectively have three choices:

Option 1: Every single thing in the buyer's offer—price, closing costs, time to close the deal, you name it—is A-plus perfect. You sign the offer and proceed from there.

Option 2: The offer is absurd. Maybe the price they offer is simply way too low for you to consider or they want to take six months or more before they close. Whatever the reason, you reject the offer outright. Offers often come with boxes that simply let you check that you reject the offer completely. No comment, no feedback—just a simple no.

But simply saying no outright, unless the terms of the offer are ridiculous, isn't the most productive way to proceed. In many cases, some of the provisions of an offer are appealing, while others are less so.

That means it's time to prepare a counteroffer.

Option 3: For some, the idea of negotiating may seem like an unpleasant chore to perform. But take our word for it—negotiation and give and take are as old as real estate itself. A bit of back and forth—quite often, a heck of a lot of back and forth—is expected, so it's in your best interest to sharpen your negotiation skills.

The first step is to compile a comprehensive list of everything contained in the offer with which you disagree. Then, identify what you would be willing to accept on each and every one of those particular points. Then, all you have to do is compile them in an addendum or on a counteroffer sheet, list each item and what you'd be happy to agree to, and sign it. Then, give them a timeframe in which to respond and send it on back to the buyers.

In its essence, a counteroffer is simple. But there are individual elements that comprise the overall deal, so it's important to examine.

> **FSBO Facts**
>
> If you reject a very low offer just as your home comes on the market, don't be shocked if the buyer reappears later with a more reasonable proposal. Many buyers float a low offer just to see if you'll take the bait—if you don't, they know that they're going to have to do better for you to take them seriously.

First, naturally enough, is the purchase price. Calculate just how much the offer will give you when all elements are taken into consideration. Take the overall purchase price and subtract any expenses, closing costs, and other fees the buyer has proposed that you meet. Then, calculate out what you would pocket as things stand as they are now.

> **FSBO Facts**
>
> Here's an area where the biggest price doesn't necessarily mean the biggest profit possible. Consider the following two scenarios:
>
> In the first example, the buyer proposes a purchase price of $200,000. He also asks that you pay closing costs and other expenses totaling $6,000. You net: $194,000.
>
> In the second, the purchase price is $198,000, but the buyer is happy to only saddle you with $1,000 in expenses. Net: $197,000.
>
> The lesson here is to take everything into account to make sure that, when all is signed and done, you pocket the most cash that you can. An inflated purchase price can be misleading if other costs and expenses cut into what seems to be a significant profit.

The timeline of the closing is another important element. Unless your situation dictates otherwise, it's generally a good idea to pursue the fastest closing schedule you

can. If the buyers are proposing what seems to you to be an unnecessarily long closing schedule, counteroffer with a tighter timeframe.

It's always possible to push for a faster closing with a buyer who's already lined up all
the necessary financing. If a loan is already a given, you can point out, why slow things
down? If they're not preapproved, however, this argument can lose a bit of steam.

Other negotiated items can include closing costs and even those fixtures and features
that go with the house. With regard to closing costs, who pays what can depend on
the circumstances of the sale. For instance, if you're in a buyer's market where homes
are moving rather slowly, you may be amenable to paying some of the closing costs
that would normally be assumed by the buyer, such as a portion of the loan fees. On
the other hand, a seller in a hot market has leverage to insist that a buyer take their
full share of closing costs—if they balk, an active market will likely produce a new
buyer in short order.

Closing costs illustrate the importance of knowing overall market conditions when
counter offering and negotiating. The more conditions favor you, the seller, the more
aggressive you can afford to be. But even in the most buyer-friendly environment, it's
not a bottomless pit. Generally, a lender will not allow a seller to contribute more
money than the buyer can actually spend in closing costs. Put another way: the buyer
cannot take cash away from the settlement. More in detail about this in Chapter 12.

Things such as drapes, lighting fixtures, appliances, and even items like power tools
and lawn furniture can come up in negotiations and counteroffers. Don't overlook
these. Some sellers can be very attached to some of their home's features, and you
may be too. In fact, in some countries, it's traditional to clean the house out almost
completely after it's sold, leaving little more than the bare structure itself.

One way to approach a home's amenities is to offer to replace something that you
want to bring with you. For instance, if a buyer asks for the antique chandelier in
your dining room, counter by saying that you want to hang onto it but offer to buy a
comparable replacement.

These are just some basic items that can crop up in the counteroffer process. Put
another way, many of the issues included in a contract can appear in a counteroffer
and often do. Keep in mind that the counteroffer dance can go on for some time,
with each party sticking to major points and compromising on less essential ones as
they move toward a mutually acceptable contract.

Getting What You Want

Everyone selling their home on their own thinks they know what they want, be it the best possible price, the fastest possible closing, or some other outcome. But the importance of knowing what you want—moreover, knowing precisely what you want—is a bit more involved than that. And knowing just what you want from the sale is essential in reaching that goal as best you can.

That means you must map out precisely what you want to get out of the sale of your home and in what order of priority those things line up.

The best—and most natural—place to start is the price. Determine the absolute lowest purchase price you would be willing to accept. (Don't forget to take into account what your net will be after expenses, as we illustrated earlier in this chapter.) How you come to that figure will depend. You may be in a particular rush to move on with your life, so you target a price that's rather modest. On the other hand, you may feel you've priced your home fairly and you're in no breakneck hurry to move, so you set your minimum somewhat higher.

You may know of formulas that supposedly help you target the minimum price you should be willing to take—say, 10 or 15 percent below your asking price. That's much too simplistic. Instead, take into account every financial factor—including things such as how large a mortgage you have to pay off, expenses, and other costs. Think about how much you absolutely have to receive, bottom line. Think about how much you want to receive for all the effort you're expending. That's the only realistic way to arrive at a minimum.

However unpleasant it may be to think about consider this question, "What, under the worst circumstances, would I take for my home?" Addressing this early on can make everything a whole lot easier going forward. To illustrate, if an offer comes in that's well below your minimum, you can say no thanks with a clear sense of direction, and move on. However, if it's at your minimum target price or a bit higher, there may be room for further discussion. Setting a minimum really provides a clear set of guidelines that help make any further action thoughtful and consistent.

Selling Smarts

Chances are good that, during negotiations, a buyer will ask you what's the lowest price you'd accept for your home. Don't ever reveal this to a prospective buyer because that's nothing more than an easy way for him to low ball his next offer. Instead, smile and say that, like other elements of the deal, it is negotiable.

There are, of course, other elements to consider for deciding what you want to get out of a sale. They include:

♦ How soon you want to move

♦ What you want to take from the house and what can remain behind

♦ Whether you want the sale to be free and clear or if you'd be willing to help with buyer financing

♦ Other elements involved in the sale, such as a buyer's willingness to pick up most of the closing costs

That means it's important to pay attention to the purchase price but also give a reasonable amount of thought to other aspects of the sale. That way, the overall package reflects what you want—not one particular element at the undue expense of others.

Here's an easy way to keep track. Have a look at the following chart:

Issue	Essential	Important	Neutral	Unimportant	Rank
Price	❑	❑	❑	❑	#___
Closing	❑	❑	❑	❑	#___
Items	❑	❑	❑	❑	#___
Financing	❑	❑	❑	❑	#___
Other Issues:	❑	❑	❑	❑	#___
_____	❑	❑	❑	❑	#___
_____	❑	❑	❑	❑	#___

List any other items that may pertain to the sale. Now, rank each according to how important they are to you. When you're done, look at the list in a global sense. It'll be easy to see which items are most important to you, and, as a result, you'll want to emphasize these in negotiations. By the same token, you'll also get a clear sense of those issues that are simply not as critical. Eventually, those may the terms you're willing to negotiate to keep your important items intact.

Drawing up a list of issues and prioritizing them gives you an exceedingly effective negotiation tool—the ace in the hole. One powerful way to seal a deal is to hold back on certain items initially, giving the impression that you're unwilling to budge. Then, later in the process, agree to compromise on one or more of them. You can come across as suddenly rather generous—that can often sway a buyer into moving ahead.

Knowing those issues that are a bit more expendable to you can be ideal targets for the ace in the hole.

Negotiation Strategies

Effective counter offering isn't just a matter of knowing precisely what you want from a sale; it's also a matter of effective negotiation skills. And those, like so many other skills related to selling a home on your own, can be learned and polished.

One of the overriding issues to bear in mind is that a counteroffer gives the buyer an opportunity to pull out of the deal completely. Even the smallest item that you don't agree on is, from a purely technical standpoint, justification to walk away. However, if both you and the buyer are sincere and genuinely interested in completing the sale, counteroffers and negotiations will be seen as the means to a successful end, not potential deal killers.

Because negotiation does carry a degree of risk, it's essential to respect the other side's priorities. And that means a willingness to compromise. Neither the buyer nor a seller should reasonably expect to get everything they want, unless the circumstances of the sale are very unusual. Approach issues with a desire to agree rather than "win" and things stand an excellent chance of working out to everyone's satisfaction.

One simple but very effective way to counteroffer and negotiate is to split the difference whenever possible. For instance, if a buyer wants you to pay the recording fee and other related expenses, offer half. If a proposed timeframe for the sale seems too long, suggest that half the time would work effectively. If they're reasonable, who can argue against the wisdom of meeting half way?

Every negotiation will differ based on the house for sale and the needs and wishes of the buyer and seller. There are, however, a few ideas that apply to every situation that can help move things along to a successful conclusion:

- Don't move too quickly. Take your time and map out your counteroffer thoughtfully. Move in small increments rather than huge, sweeping changes and counteroffers. Not only can that save strategies such as your "ace in the hole" for later if need be, but many buyers are simply more comfortable with steady progress.

- Keep your emotions out of it. Don't take it personally if there's a particular sticking point. If you can't stay focused and unemotional, hand negotiations off to your attorney.

◆ Don't accept the first offer you get just because it's the first one you get. This is especially true if the offer is well below what you hope to get. Stay focused on the long term, not just the immediate relief of landing an offer.

◆ But don't reject first offers out of hand, either. A well-priced home in an active market can attract serious buyers very quickly. If it's what you want, go for it.

◆ Put aside the smaller stuff. If you feel you're moving ahead on the main points of an offer, table less important points of difference. After you've worked out the meat of the offer, it can seem rather easy to compromise fairly on less central aspects of the deal.

◆ Make sure you follow all state and federal fair housing laws. It's illegal to discriminate against any buyer based on their race, sex, nation of origin, familial status, or any other protected class under the law. If you're concerned, ask your attorney about these laws and be sure to take them very seriously.

◆ Watch out for—and don't engage in—*bad faith* bargaining.

Tools of the Trade

Bad faith bargaining means that someone involved in the sale is not bargaining seriously with the intention of actually completing the transaction.

Bad faith bargaining can happen in any number of ways. For instance, you put your home on the market and field offers but are still not convinced you really want to sell your home. You start to reject offers that you would consider if you were genuinely committed to selling your house. A buyer's bad faith bargaining can take the form of ridiculously low offers or someone who's simply not financially positioned to afford your home. Not only is bad faith bargaining a real time waster, it can also prompt legal action if you or someone else feels they were intentionally misled.

Solutions to overcome bad faith bargaining include:

◆ Make sure you really, truly want to sell your home. Set what you're willing to accept as an offer and pursue it.

◆ Ask low ball buyers not to bother you unless they have a serious offer to present. If you're concerned about a buyer's ability to afford your home, ask for a preapproval loan from a lender.

Overcoming Objections

One of the central challenges to successful negotiation is dealing effectively with a buyer's objections. It's important never to ignore them. Rather, listen to them, acknowledge them, and try to understand them. That's the most effective way to address them.

For instance, if a buyer tells you that they absolutely have to have your state of the art weed whacker as part of the deal, don't react as though they've asked you to throw in your first born male child as part of the deal. Instead, try repeating their comment back to them: "You absolutely have to have my weed whacker?"

Several things happen here. First, if the buyer hears that demand coming from another person's mouth, there's a reasonable chance that he's going to see how silly such a demand really sounds. He may back down. If nothing else, you'll get him thinking about it some more. Then, if he repeats the demand, you know his interest is genuine and you may want to consider it (an ideal ace in the hole here, by the way.)

But the point in negotiating in this fashion is to pinpoint what a buyer's bona fide issues are and which ones are more fleeting. That way, you can focus on the ones of real importance and overcome those that are not as significant.

Reducing Objections

Another effective negotiation technique is reducing objections—or, put another way, boiling them down to illustrate their frequent lack of significance. For instance, say a buyer feels your asking price is $5,000 more than what they think they can afford.

That may seem like a chunk of money, but that's only one way to look at it. If you assume that the buyer is taking out a 30-year mortgage at 6 percent interest, that boils down to a relatively modest $29.98 a month. And much of that is tax deductible. This breakdown of expenses into smaller, more specific figures, is known as amortization (see the following figure). It never hurts to point that out.

> **FSBO Facts**
>
> What we did with the $5000 example is known as amortization—breaking down something into scheduled payments, including the cost of interest. Mortgages, for instance, are always amortized.

Online amortization calculators, like this one at Bankrate.com, let you calculate amortization figures quickly and accurately.

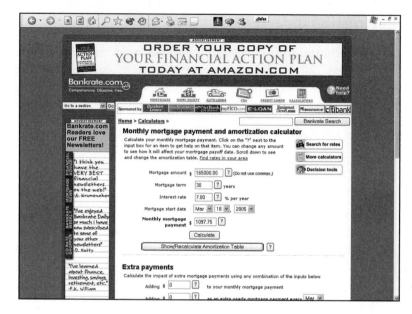

Breaking down the cost of other negotiable items works just as well. For instance, the $500 refrigerator that, over the course of 30 years, comes to $3 every month at the 6 percent interest quoted above. Not only can it prove effective in helping a buyer compromise, it can also help you as well. Seeing something in terms of a monthly expense may also prompt you to meet the buyer half way, particularly on those items that you've identified as less significant. It's a useful reminder that, in selling a home, compromise cuts both ways.

Handling Multiple Offers

Now comes the best part—multiple offers. This means more than one buyer has gone so far as to submit a formal offer for your home.

It's great, of course, to have more than one interested buyer. In hot markets where good homes are at a premium, it's not unusual for particularly attractive properties to lure two or more buyers—often to the point that buyers start bidding against one another.

But for you, the seller, it's not all smiles in the glow of all this adoration. You need to know how to handle the situation effectively and fairly. Here's a breakdown of steps to follow:

- First, let all buyers who submit an offer know there are a certain number of offers on the table and that you will consider all of them before making a decision. Set a deadline so all interested buyers have an opportunity to submit an offer—in writing, of course. Let them know when you intend to make up your mind.

- Examine all offers in detail. Choose the one you like best. If you like it, sign it and be done with it. If not, prepare a counter offer, set a deadline for the buyer to respond, and send it back.

- Now pick out the next best offer. First, let those buyers know that they're Number 2 on your list, send them a counteroffer with its own deadline. Let them also know that their offer will only apply if your first choice rejects your counteroffer. Continue adding to the list any other offers worth addressing and reject outright any that are simply out of the picture.

- Now, wait for Buyer Number 1 to respond. If they agree to your counter, deal over. If they don't agree, move on to Buyer Number 2 and so on until the most attractive deal becomes final.

Keep careful track of how the acceptance/rejection process proceeds through the offers. Make sure to finalize things with a buyer with a higher priority before moving on. If you don't, you may find yourself inadvertently accepting more than one offer. Then, you'll be forced to say no to one of the offers you inadvertently accepted, which could lead to legal action.

Online Negotiation Resources

Here are a few websites that offer further information about counteroffers and negotiation:

- A nice reference page that can lead you to several helpful pages on negotiation and relevant issues can be found at www.houseclicks.com/buying/negotiating.html.

- The federal Department of Housing and Urban Development's page on fair housing guidelines is www.hud.gov/offices/fheo/index.cfm.

- Although it's geared primarily to real estate agents, *Realty Times* has a nice archive of articles, including several very helpful pieces on effective negotiating and counteroffers. Have a look at www.realtytimes.com.

The Least You Need to Know

- ◆ Counteroffers and negotiation are an accepted—and expected—part of selling a home.

- ◆ When considering an offer, be sure to calculate what you will actually receive after factoring in closing costs and other expenses. The highest offer isn't always the best.

- ◆ With that in mind, prioritize those issues that are most important to you. Stick to those when negotiating and compromise on others.

- ◆ Don't ignore a buyer's objections and misgivings. Instead, work to overcome them through compromise and further information.

- ◆ Approach multiple offers systematically. Go for the one you like best, but order the others in case your first choice doesn't pan out.

- ◆ Above all, emphasize constructive compromise in negotiations and counteroffers. The goal is to sell your home, not beat a buyer on every single point.

Chapter 12

More Financial Details

In This Chapter

- ◆ Understanding mortgages
- ◆ Know your buyer's finances inside and out
- ◆ Know about alternative financing—FHA and VA loans
- ◆ Haggling over closing costs

You're getting closer. You've found a buyer whose offering price is suitable. You've gone back and forth on a number of items related to the sale, and you've agreed on them.

But there are a few more steps to address before you sign the Purchase and Sale Agreement and move forward toward a successful closing. Specifically, these are purely financial concerns and, as such, few things connected to the sale of your home can be more important.

In this chapter, we cover some essential financing issues, including your buyer's ability to afford your home, closing costs, and other topics.

Mortgage Basics

If the universe of home selling were perfect, every single deal would be purely cash. A buyer would arrive at your door, fall head over heels with your home, sign whatever needed to be signed, and present you with a wheelbarrow of cash.

Nice dream, but largely that. The fact is, few of us are in a financial position to pay cash for a home. In most cases, buyers have to obtain financing, particularly with expensive homes. And their ability to do that—and do so in an expedient manner—is something you as the seller need to be aware of and track as completely as possible. That's why, if you refer back to Chapter 10, suitable financing is such an important contingency to any sale.

Knowing a Buyer's Finances

We mentioned this earlier, but it bears reinforcement. The most reliable way to ensure your buyer is financially positioned to afford your home is to ask for proof of loan preapproval—ideally, when he presents his initial offer to buy your home. If the buyer can provide you with a loan from the lender verifying their financing is in place, you're golden. Move on to finalizing the deal.

Selling Smarts

If a buyer has gone to the time and effort to get preapproved for a loan, take that to the bank, so to speak. Preapproval is one of the most reliable signs that a buyer means business when she expresses interest in buying your home.

But that's not always the case. So as the seller, you need to get to know your buyer's financial particulars and, if need be, help them obtain suitable financing.

Here's where the difference between qualifying for a loan and actually being approved comes into play. Qualifying for a loan is based on a somewhat rudimentary examination of a buyer's finances. It's helpful, but not a guarantee. Approval, on the other hand, is based on a comprehensive investigation of a buyer's financial condition and is, in fact, a guarantee of a loan.

What else is involved in actually getting approved for a loan? Because you already own a home, you're probably familiar with this, but it can't hurt to brush up. If nothing else, it's important to be as informed as possible about what your buyer must do to put the necessary financing in place.

One of the first things that impacts a buyer's ability to obtain a loan is solid credit.

Good credit—often summarized by a numerical score by one of the large credit reporting bureaus—is a compilation of a person's history of handling credit. The most common name attached to this is a FICO score (named after the company that developed the system). That can include timely paying of significant bills, including mortgages and credit cards, spending habits, and other information.

The impact of credit history on someone's ability to get needed financing is easy to understand. If, for instance, a person has a solid record of meeting his financial obligations, a lender is likely to conclude they're a reasonable risk for a substantial loan. By the same token, someone with habitually late payments or, worse, a recent bankruptcy, will have a difficult time convincing a lender they're credit worthy.

FSBO Facts

A bankruptcy on a credit report may seem like a death sentence for the chance of getting a mortgage, but that's not necessarily the case. A lender may still approve an applicant who can give a satisfactory explanation for the bankruptcy. Also, having a clean credit history for several years after the bankruptcy may also help the applicant get approved.

Another element is income, a consideration we addressed earlier in the section on prequalification. Here, however, it's income as a source of funds specifically for mortgage payments. As a rule, most lenders will not want monthly housing obligations, including mortgage payments, property taxes, and insurance to exceed 33 percent of a borrower's net monthly income.

Income derived from a job isn't the only potential income source a lender might take into consideration. Income from investments, child support, alimony payments, and social security or retirement income, for instance, can be factored in as well.

And still another factor is assets. This can include stocks, bonds, real estate, and cash in bank accounts, among other sources. The thinking here is to evaluate all potential income and assets so the lender can determine whether the applicant is financially sound, even if employment income changes or is non-existent, as might be the case with independently wealthy individuals, individuals receiving spousal or child support, and retirees.

There are still other elements that can factor into the question of loan approval. Among others, they can be employment history (the longer, more stable the record of employment, the better), how long the applicants have lived in a particular place (ditto, the longer the better), and other factors.

Why are we listing these issues? Because, as a seller, you have the right to know just how financially solid your buyer happens to be. In a very real way, by negotiating with a buyer toward a Purchase and Sale Agreement to sell your home, you're trusting that your buyer is in a position to fulfill her financial obligations. You need to know that she's financially sound before you can proceed to finalize any sort of legally binding document.

How can you find out this sort of critical information that relates directly to your buyer's financial health? Well, for one thing, if you're already working with a lender—as we suggested back in Chapter 3—you can refer any buyers with an offer to them to start the approval process. If your lender approves their loan, you can be certain the buyer is, in fact, financially positioned to afford your home and proceed with the sale.

If they're just starting on their search for a mortgage, but they've put in an offer on your house, don't be shy about asking them for this sort of information. Inquire about their employment history, income, assets, and other financial information. As we discussed earlier, this isn't mere nosiness—you have the right to know if someone's interest in your home is backed up with the necessary financial means.

Finding out this sort of necessary financial information may seem similar to prequalification (addressed in Chapter 3). Well, it is, but it's more than that. Because you're moving closer to contract, you need more than the likelihood that someone will qualify for financing—you have to be absolute certain. That's why loan approval requires so much more documentation and detail.

What if a buyer balks in some manner when you ask about financial particulars? Don't necessarily take it as a warning sign—even in deals such as buying a home, many people are just very private about revealing any personal financial details. That's why it's important to know they're already involved with a lender in the approval process—like it or not, the buyers have to supply all that information to them.

If your buyer has already applied for a loan with a particular lender, ask whether they'd mind if you contacted the lender to see how likely it is that they'll be approved. If that's okay by them, ask the lender how long the process is likely to take.

The bottom line here is it's essential you know just how quickly and easily your buyer will be able to obtain whatever financing may be necessary. That way, you can move toward the closing with confidence rather than needlessly wasting your time taking your home off the market for someone who's in no position to afford it.

Selling Smarts _____

Is it an absolute must that your buyer have a loan approved before you move on to sign the Purchase and Sale Agreement? No, it's not reasonable to expect that every qualified buyer will, by definition, have all necessary financing in place. But, as the overall point of this section urges, it's essential to gather as much information as you can, before taking your home off the market, so you have a reasonably reliable sense of how likely a buyer will be able to obtain necessary financing.

The Down Payment

Another important piece of financial information that you need to address is your buyer's *down payment.*

Okay, you probably knew that already. But what you may not know is, like other pieces of your buyer's financial puzzle, it's an awfully good idea to know more than just a mere definition.

First, it's important to know that—as it has been since time memorial—20 percent of the purchase price is the acceptable minimum needed to obtain the most favorable mortgage available. On the surface, that may not seem like all that much; but, the bigger a home's overall price tag, the bigger the requisite down payment. To illustrate: a $150,000 home carries a $30,000 down payment. Push that figure to $250,000 and you're looking at a hefty $50,000.

Tools of the Trade _____

A **down payment** is a one-time payment that the buyer makes toward the purchase of your house. It reduces the amount the buyer needs to finance with a mortgage.

A down payment isn't merely a matter of numbers. The size can often tell you a good deal about your prospective buyer. For one thing, the bigger the down payment a buyer specifies in his offer, the greater you can interpret his commitment to buying your home. Unless the buyer is dishonest or intentionally misleading, a substantial down payment is a fairly safe read that a buyer is committed to investing a good chunk of his available change in a home—your home.

A substantial down payment can also indicate a buyer whose financial ducks are in a row. Not only will a lower mortgage balance better her chances for approval of the loan (we discuss that in greater detail shortly), substantial money down indicates someone who's been intelligent with her money and handled it wisely. It's not a cinch, but that, too, hints at a buyer who may be immune from some of the credit problems and other issues that can trip up a loan application.

FSBO Facts

A lot of buyers, particularly first timers, don't have the financial resources to put down 20 percent. In that case, they may have to obtain Private Mortgage Insurance (PMI), a form of coverage that's usually tacked onto their regular mortgage payment. The thinking is, the larger the loan, the greater the chance of default—hence, PMI. The going average for a median priced home is between $50 and $100 a month. FHA loans also have a similar program known as a Mortgage Insurance Premium (MIP). This ranges from 1.5 percent to 2.25 of the overall loan value, depending on when the loan was taken out.

But a good size down payment is more than a somewhat abstract character reference. It can also be a solid indicator of which offer you may wish to accept if you have more than one on the table. Think about it—if you're considering one offer for $200,000 where the buyer is putting down 20 percent and a second offer of $195,000 where the proposed down payment balloons to 35 percent, you may not wish to dismiss the lesser offer out of hand. All thing being equal, a lower mortgage amount stands a better chance of being approved and, for that matter, being approved quickly. For many sellers, that's $5000 well spent.

The down payment also lets you set up a calculation known as a loan to value ratio (or LTV).

Commonly used by lenders, the loan to value ratio is the loan amount as expressed as a percentage of the overall price of the home. For instance, in the example from the previous paragraph, the $200,000 offer would have a LTV of 80 percent. In the 195,000 offer, the LTV would be 65 percent (a $126,750 mortgage divided by an overall price of $195,000). The lower the ratio, the more attractive it is to a lender.

The size of the down payment is only one consideration. The source is also important. Ask your buyers where funds for the down payment are coming from. The best possible circumstances are sources that are safe and easily accessible, such as a checking or savings account or a Certificate of Deposit that's about to mature. Another possibility is a gift from relatives or friends. If it is a gift, check to see how long the funds are in the buyer's hands. Ideally, the buyer should have them in a safe account somewhere for about six months.

One possible source for a down payment that often leads to headaches is a loan from a friend or relative. As we all know, people change their minds about loans all the time, even for something as significant as the purchase of a home. Be very careful if the buyer tells you the down payment is coming from a loan—get more details or, even better, ask if there's an alternate source of money that may be a bit more reliable.

If your buyer has problems piecing together a suitable down payment, another alternative that's worth considering is known as third-party programs. These programs, geared in large part to first-time buyers with modest means, offers free grant money that lets buyers buy homes with no money down. Employers, community groups and others also provide cost effective loan programs that help buyers with down payments. We offer a couple of websites at the conclusion of this chapter that provide further details. Some lenders also offer 100 percent financing, addressing both the down payment and the remaining portion of the loan. However, since the risk is greater, these carry higher interest rates than more conventional loans.

Down payment assistance comes from sources other than just third-party programs. Often, cities and other local government jurisdictions provide grants and other financial assistance for first-time buyers. The programs are usually geared to specific areas or regions targeted for revitalization or some other economic goal. Two websites at the end of the chapter provide more information.

Other Types of Loans

Up until now, we've pretty much confined ourselves to discussing fairly conventional financing. The buyer has some money he can put down, he obtains a loan from a bank or other lending institution, and the deal proceeds from there.

But depending on the circumstances of the sale, a buyer may be financing the purchase of your home with something other than the cookie cutter conventional loan. Each of these types of loans may have an impact on how things proceed, so let's take a look at how they work.

FHA Loans

Offered by the Federal Housing Administration, FHA loans were created by the government to provide affordable housing to qualified borrowers who otherwise might not be able to buy a home through conventional channels. One of its major pluses is that the program only requires a 3 percent down payment. Even better, qualification guidelines are more relaxed that usual mortgages—the program is much more forgiving of bankruptcies and higher debt-to-income ratios are acceptable. Closing costs—an issue for many buyers—can be folded into the overall loan amount.

In return for all this generosity, FHA borrowers pay an upfront insurance premium equal to about 1.5 percent of the loan amount. The buyer also pays on a modest monthly premium.

> **FSBO Facts**
>
> Like Social Security, FHA loans are a byproduct of the Great Depression. The federal government introduced the program to stabilize a battered housing market. The need for affordable housing options remains to this day.

An FHA loan's biggest potential impact on you, the seller, can come at the appraisal. Because the lion's share of FHA borrowers are first timer homebuyers, FHA guidelines have stricter standards for the condition of homes it will approve loans for, and appraisals are far more protective and comprehensive than conventional appraisals. That, in turn, puts the onus on you to have your home in the best possible condition and, if necessary, pay for needed repairs to bring the house up to FHA standards.

VA Loans

This program specifically targets veterans. VA loans are made by private lenders but, if approved, the federal Veterans Administration will guarantee a portion of the loan. Like FHA loans, VAs are geared to assisting a certain portion of the home buying public with favorable terms. For one thing, a VA buyer may be able to get into a home with no down payment. Like FHA costs, the additional expense of obtaining a VA loan may be rolled into the overall loan amount.

Akin to the FHA, a VA loan also mandates that homes be in good condition to qualify for the loan. And, like an FHA, that may charge you, the seller, with seeing to certain repairs and other upgrades that a conventional appraisal might bypass completely.

Selling Smarts _____

It's important to be familiar with alternative programs, such as FHA and VA loans, for a couple of significant reasons. First, as we previously discussed, their particularly aggressive appraisal requirements may affect what you need to do so your home conforms to their guidelines. And, as we'll see in the next section, they can also impact a significant element of the negotiation process—closing costs.

Negotiating Closing Costs

As we saw earlier, putting together a down payment for conventional financing can be difficult for some buyers—for any number of reasons. Still another is the fact that buying a home can prove an expensive proposition— above and beyond the basic price tag.

Closing costs can also prove a substantial expense, both in buying and selling a home.

Unfortunately, many buyers disregard the impact of closing costs on their capacity to afford a home, choosing instead to focus exclusively on the purchase price. As we'll see from the list that follows, that can be a significant mistake (but one which you, as the seller, may be able to help them with if you so choose.)

> **FSBO Facts**
>
> Although closing costs are a significant expense in the purchase of any home, they will vary according to where you live. Local tradition and custom often dictate who pays what expenses. If you have any questions, ask your attorney for guidance.

Again, it may differ depending on where you happen to live, but here's a basic breakdown of closing costs that are associated with the sale of a home.

Buyer's Costs

Here are a few expenses that the buyer may have to meet:

◆ The down payment. As we saw in the previous section, this has to be at minimum 20 percent of the purchase price for the buyer to obtain the most favorable mortgage terms possible.

- Loan origination fees. This expense covers the lender's administrative costs in processing the loan. This is often charged based on a certain percentage of the loan and differs from one lender to the next.

- Loan discount. Also known as "points," this is a one-time charge that lets a buyer obtain a loan at a lower interest rate. Each point translates to 1 percent of the overall loan amount.

- Fees for a property appraisal, credit report, title insurance, and any inspections.

Selling Smarts

In this age of inexpensive mortgages and fast loan approval, surreptitious "preparation" and "transfer" charges are becoming more and more intolerable—and unnecessary. For future mortgage shopping reference, watch out for these things like a hawk and avoid them.

In particular, there are several costs that need to be paid by the buyer in advance of the closing itself. They include:

- Prepaid interest. Because most loans are due on the first day of the month—and chances are good that the closing will happen on another day—the buyer often has to pay prepaid interest to bring payments current to the first. For instance, if you close on Jan. 15, you will owe 16 days of prepaid interest.

- Homeowner's insurance. Buyers usually have to pay the first year's premium.

A number of additional charges may apply. For instance, depending on where the home happens to be, the buyer may have to pay a one-time flood certification fee to determine whether the house is in a flood zone.

The lender may also impose certain charges. These take a variety of guises, from document preparation charges to underwriting fees to charges for various types of transfers.

Seller's Costs

Closing costs are not exclusive to the buyer. Here are a few expenses that you, as the seller, may have to meet:

- Transfer tax. This, as the name implies, imposes a tax on the seller when ownership of a home changes hands. They're usually based on the sale price of the home. The good news is that these can differ considerably from one area to the next, so check with your local town or county clerk for specifics.

◆ Property taxes. This, like so many other aspects of the sale of your home, depends on the date when the closing takes place. Most cities and towns collect property taxes every six months; as such, depending on where your closing falls in relation to the property tax schedule, you may owe some money to ensure that your property taxes are completely up-to-date.

Many jurisdictions even collect property taxes in advance. The good news is—depending once more on when your closing takes place—you may actually be due a refund on your property taxes.

Selling Smarts

Other costs may come into play on the seller's side, including title insurance, costs related to the deed transfer, and other expenses. But, look at it this way—you're avoiding the single most prohibitive cost that saddles many home sellers—a real estate broker's commission, which can range upwards of six percent of the purchase price.

◆ Repairs. As we mentioned with regard to FHA and VA loans, you may be looking at some repairs to conform to those programs' particular appraisal guidelines. Even if the buyer is going with a more conventional form of financing, there may be problems with your house as-is that she'd like you to address.

Now that we have a fairly complete overview of possible closing costs, it's time to address the salient question: Is it possible to negotiate closing costs and, if so, what are some guidelines to follow?

The first answer is, of course, yes. Buyers and sellers have traditionally gone back and forth on closing costs. And, in many cases, a fluid approach to who pays what in closing costs has helped keep many sales together.

The first place to start is to get to know the usual guidelines that apply to where you live. As we've mentioned previously, certain parts of the country have traditional breakdowns for who pays what in closing costs. Contact your attorney to see what these are and use them as a basis from which to proceed.

From there, know that the sort of loan the buyer is using impacts what is negotiable and what is not. Here's the breakdown among conventional, FHA, and VA loans:

◆ Conventional. A buyer can only ask that a seller help pay for "non-recurring" costs, such as loan origination fees, points, inspection, appraisals, and other similar expenses. Items such as homeowner's insurance and prepaid interest are not negotiable. There are also overall limits as to how much a seller can contribute.

If the buyer is putting down 10 percent or more in a down payment, the most the seller can offer to pay in closing costs is 6 percent of the purchase price; 10 percent or less down, the ceiling comes down to three percent.

◆ FHA. Here, the guidelines are much more generous. Under FHA rules, the seller can theoretically pay for all closing costs.

◆ VA. Here, the generosity carries over. VA loans allow buyers to negotiate the seller into paying all relevant closing costs.

Selling Smarts

Know that the opposite holds true in a hot seller's market. If homes are moving fast, you can afford to be more aggressive. If a buyer asks for help with closing costs, you can stand firm, reasoning that there's always another buyer down the road.

First, take a deep breath. Unless you're in a market that's moving with the speed of erosion, and you're desperate to sell your house, it's unlikely you'll be looking at paying all the closing costs in question. In fact, with a conventional loan, that's a moot point anyway.

But bear in mind that closing costs can amount to 2 percent of the overall price—a substantial sum, particularly for first-time buyers—so it's prudent to consider some negotiation with regard to closing costs. Here are a few to consider:

◆ Boost your price. Closing costs don't exist in a vacuum. For instance, say a buyer asks you to pick up some $4,000 in closing costs, arguing they can't otherwise afford the upfront expenses. Just counter by agreeing to pay that money at closing but raise your price $4000 to compensate. The buyer can roll this amount into his loan, and chances are good he'll be able to afford that modest increase in the loan.

◆ Split the difference. As we've mentioned before, no reasonable buyer or seller is going to bolt at a 50-50 compromise. Use that as a rule of thumb, particularly for buyers who are strapped for upfront expenses. Again, offer to fold those costs into the loan, so it's not out of your pocket.

◆ Target your generosity. A willingness to negotiate over closing costs doesn't have to be a blank check. Pay attention to what seems to concern your buyer and react accordingly. For instance, if a buyer seems worried about the condition of your home, offer to pay for the inspection.

◆ Counter with something other than cash. If you want to keep your closing cost obligations to a minimum, offer other things in return. Say you'll let them have the refrigerator, a portable air conditioner, or some other item that can offset buyer expenses.

◆ Provide a warranty. If the buyer is worried about the condition of the home, address their worries with the offer of a home warranty. Check back to Chapter 2 for further details.

Online Financial Details Resources

Here are a few websites that can provide additional information about financial details:

◆ FHA Today (www.fhatoday.com) provides a nice summary of FHA loan programs and how they differ from other types of loans.

◆ You can find a handy summary of significant closing costs for buyers and sellers at: www.beachandinlandmortgage.com/closing_costs.html.

◆ Two sites that offer information about third-party down payment programs are www.thebuyersfund.com and www.getdownpayment.com.

The Least You Need to Know

◆ You have a right to know as much about your buyer's finances as possible.

◆ In particular, know the source of your buyer's down payment.

◆ Alternate financing, such as FHA and VA loans, require more stringent inspections—and, possibly, more repairs on your part.

◆ Get to know what closing costs are usually paid by the buyer and seller in your community and use that as a basis for negotiation.

◆ Keep an open mind toward negotiating closing costs. They can often keep a deal together and can be offset in other aspects of the sale.

The Path Less Taken–
Alternatives

In This Chapter

- ◆ Should you lend a financial hand?
- ◆ The rent to own option
- ◆ In the house before closing?
- ◆ Everything ready … just sign here!

The exhaustive job of seeing to every possible contingency and agreeing to every little element of the deal is near an end. The price is right, you've negotiated everything down to the doorknobs, and both you and the buyer appear committed to doing what needs done to see the deal to completion.

But still a few wrinkles remain. Unlike other topics covered in previous chapters, these may not necessarily be deal killers in and of themselves. Rather, these are options, elements to a deal that are often not a part of many conventional arrangements. But no matter how unusual, they can help a deal move forward by introducing fresh solutions to problems that can plague many deals.

Consider these alternatives as a baseball manager might consider a reliever—something to turn to if business as usual becomes a problem. Used appropriately, they can play their own roles in moving your home sale closer to completion. And, given their complexity, make sure to consult your attorney at every step along the way.

Owner Financing

As we've covered extensively in previous chapters, obtaining suitable financing—and all that requires—is often the most significant hurdle in a buyer's ability to afford your home. And, as we've discussed, there are many paths toward that ultimate goal, from alternative financing to third-party down payment assistance to private mortgage insurance.

But, sometimes, all those alternatives simply aren't enough—or, by the same token, are not attractive to the buyer for any number of reasons. And the inevitable issue crops up—would you, as the seller, be willing to consider financing a portion of the sale of your home?

Owner financing basically means that, like a bank or other lender, you're willing to agree to be paid over time, rather than receiving a lump sum of money upfront. In effect, you are making a loan to your buyer, including an interest rate and a specified period within which the overall loan amount must be paid back, including interest. Owner financing can coexist with whatever other loans a buyer may take out to buy your home.

FSBO Facts
A little historic perspective can be enlightening here. Back in the 1980s, when interest rates were well into the double digits, owner financing was as much a norm of home selling as any other aspect. One of the authors of this book took back (in other words, owner financed) a portion of a mortgage at a "bargain" interest rate of 13 percent—13 percent being a bargain because the prevailing interest rate at the time was roughly 18 percent!

Happily, as of the writing of this book, interest rates are still hovering around historical lows. That, unto itself, has helped millions of people buy homes that, under less favorable interest conditions, they would not have been able to afford.

But we're still not in real estate fantasy land. Let's face the facts. If you factor in closing costs, the burden of amassing a down payment, paying a real estate commission (if the buyer happens to be using an agent), and other expenses, obtaining a conventional mortgage to cover the purchase of a home isn't a sure thing by any means.

Selling Smarts _____

If you're reading this before getting the sale of your home into gear, it can be advantageous to mention your willingness to consider owner financing as part of your marketing plan. It can open up an entirely new pool of potential buyers—ones who may have thought your home was financially out of their reach had they been forced to limit themselves to more conventional financing.

The following list highlights some of the advantages to consider if a buyer inquires about having you help them finance the purchase of your home:

♦ It helps you sell your house by offering the buyer an alternative to regular financing. This may seem obvious, but it's no less important. If a buyer can't afford your home by any other means, owner financing can help put a sale over the top.

♦ It helps sell your house by reducing closing costs. If a portion of the purchase price is coming from home financing, that can trim the expense of obtaining the rest of the loan through conventional financing.

♦ It can help counteract a slow selling market. If conditions are sluggish, expressing a willingness to offer owner financing can help your home buck the prevailing tide.

♦ It can be an attractive investment. You can always earn a small payback through owner financing by charging a slightly higher interest fee than the going rate. That can be an attractive alternative to low paying checking and savings accounts and Certificates of Deposit. Even better, it can really add up over time, as the following table illustrates:

Payoff of Seller Financing

Amount Financed	Time Period	Total Payments Received
$30,000@ 8%	30 Years	$79,246.80
$50,000@ 8%	30 Years	$132,076.80

As you can see, if the mortgage extends for the complete 30-year term, your initial offer financing investment of $30,000 becomes $79,246—almost a $50,000 profit. The greater the loan offered, the greater the potential profit.

Not a bad bit of change, is it? Not only that, but it's a win-win situation—you pocket a nice bit of regular income while your buyer gets a home that she otherwise might not have been able to afford.

Drawbacks to Seller Financing

Of course, owner financing is not without its potential drawbacks and concerns as well. Here are a few that are well worth considering:

♦ Can you afford it? As we saw, offering owner financing can pay off nicely over the long term. Unfortunately, many sellers don't have time on their side—they need as much immediate payoff from the sale of their home to afford their next one. So consider just how much money you'll need upfront to be able to execute your next move.

♦ Do you want to play loan officer? As we'll see in a bit, offering owner financing means more than just expressing a willingness to do so. If a buyer takes you up on it, you have to be certain that the loan is a good risk. And that means conducting an exhaustive investigation into the buyer's financial particulars.

♦ Do you want to play banker? All of us take out loans with the very best of intentions. We promise to pay on time and in full, each and every month. Of course, life has a nasty habit of laying waste to even the best laid plans, including our commitment to carry out our financial obligations. So, if you provide your buyer with owner financing and the checks begin to ebb and flow in their regularity, will you be willing to do what's necessary to protect your financial interests?

♦ Can you survive a sinking ship? Taking the aforementioned issue a bit further, it's not unheard of for buyers to default completely on a loan. If that happens, are you in a position to go without that income until foreclosure proceedings move forward? And, bear in mind, should a foreclosure take place or a buyer declare bankruptcy, a bank is going to be paid off first—you with owner financing will only be paid after the bank or other lending institution gets theirs.

◆ Can you do better with the money? Our preceding example showed owner financing paying 8 percent. That's pretty good, but many stocks and mutual funds do a whole lot better than that. Are you willing to settle for a return that may not be the very best you can get?

◆ Finally, seller financing does run counter to a basic precept of investing—diversification. Seller financing puts a fair chunk of change in one basket—something that many people might find a bit uncomfortable.

Selling Smarts

Here's a quick bit of advice. If a buyer wants you to finance the entire sale, smile politely and say no. The potential problems of such an arrangement—the worst case scenario being you lose your entire investment—are far too catastrophic to warrant any serious consideration.

How to Evaluate a Buyer

The criteria for effectively evaluating a buyer for owner financing is monkey see, monkey do. If a lender—a banker, a savings and loan officer, or someone else—follows a particular regimen in sizing up a loan applicant's ability to pay back a loan, you should do precisely the same thing.

In fact, in your own way, you'll likely have to do more than some lenders because of the particulars of offering owner financing. Here are a few rules of thumb with which to start our discussion.

First, know that it is very, very unusual for a buyer to ask an owner to fund the entire purchase of a home. Under this scenario, the buyer would put down whatever payment he could muster, and the owner would agree to carry the remainder of the mortgage balance—exactly as a lending institution would. This arrangement may also be referred to as a purchase money mortgage.

If the notion of financing your home in its entirety makes the hair on the back of your neck stand up on end, trust in that response. There are a couple of overriding hurdles from the get go. First is the matter of cash. By financing the purchase of your home completely, you're foregoing a great deal of upfront funds that, as we pointed out earlier, you may need for some other use. The greater the amount financed, the less cash on hand you have for the closing. That can have some unfortunate consequences, such as forcing you to pay private mortgage insurance on a subsequent home because you didn't have enough cash from your prior sale to put down at least 20 percent.

The other concern is the onus it places on you to investigate the buyer as thoroughly as possible. With this scenario, we're not talking about a small portion of the mortgage—we're looking at the whole thing. And that makes it supremely important you do everything in your power to ensure that a loan of this significance is as safe as possible.

That makes a *second mortgage* a far more likely—and from your perspective, far more realistic—possibility with which to offer owner financing.

Tools of the Trade

A **second mortgage** is pretty much what the term implies. A second mortgage is used to supplement funding from a first mortgage whose amount is generally quite a bit larger than the second.

Here's an example of how a second mortgage may come into play. A buyer expresses an interest in buying your home for the asking price of $250,000. She's prepared to put down the requisite 20 percent down payment, which translates to $50,000. That leaves a $200,000 balance, but upon applying for a conventional mortgage, the buyer discovers the bank is only willing to approve a $180,000 loan. The buyer then approaches you about your willingness to fund the remaining $20,000.

The most compelling reason to provide owner financing is the deal that simply will fall apart without it. Perhaps your market is tight, offers have been few and far between and your providing a second mortgage is the last big step in the process. Granted, you may be leery about this—and justifiably so—if a bank has turned them down for every penny they may need. But, bear in mind that banks are purely formulaic—although the numbers and formulas may suggest otherwise, many people are, in fact, able to afford more than what the formulas dictate. Perhaps they're expecting a pay raise or an inheritance—factors that can't go into the calculations a bank makes. So, while the formulas may say no, owner financing can and does work.

With this sort of situation—or one close to it—a few ground rules are useful to follow:

♦ First, obviously enough, the smaller the amount the buyer asks you to finance, the lower your overall risk. Quite a bit different from the buyer who asks you to take on the entire loan.

♦ Find out a buyer's interest in seller financing before you negotiate a final price. That can impact what sort of overall price you'd be willing to agree to.

◆ Don't forget to examine the loss of upfront payments at the time of closing. The mortgage may be a good deal less than it might have been, but make certain that even a modest reduction in the amount of cash you carry away from the closing won't negatively impact what you plan to do next.

◆ We mentioned the influence of market conditions earlier, but it's important to evaluate them more than simply in terms of selling a home in a slow market. Pay attention to how homes are moving—if it's a seller's environment and the overall market is active, would it be a better idea to forgo the risks of owner financing in hopes of obtaining an offer down the road that doesn't require your participation?

◆ Another issue to consider with a second mortgage is that it doesn't necessarily have to be as long as the buyer's primary mortgage. While many conventional loans have 15- or 30-year terms, it's not unusual for an owner-financed second mortgage to run only five years. Bear this option in mind if you wish to collect all funds due you as soon as possible (although, given the shorter payback, what you get in overall interest earnings will be less than you would with a longer term loan).

A buyer obtaining owner financing is adding to her overall debt level—something with which a primary lender may not be comfortable. If you're thinking about owner financing, make sure your buyer provides you with a letter from the lender confirming that a second mortgage will not adversely affect their primary loan.

Playing Loan Officer

If owner financing seems a reasonable option for whatever reasons, it's time to assume the duties of loan officer. That means you need to evaluate your buyer's capacity to honor the loan terms on which you agree. Here are some step by step suggestions to make that process as systematic and reliable as possible:

◆ Have your buyer sign a loan application, just as he would with any other lending institution. That sets out a variety of information, including employment history, salary, assets and debts, and other pertinent information.

◆ Ask to review tax returns—ideally, for no less than the last three years.

◆ Request W-2s, or, if the applicant is self-employed, 1099 statements for the past several years to verify income. Ask for similar documentation from a brokerage house or other similar source if investment income comes into consideration.

◆ Ask to see as current a copy of the buyer's credit report as possible. This will outline the buyer's current credit status as well as any past financial or debt problems he may have encountered. For a handy step by step breakdown on how to read a credit report and what to look for, refer to www.credco.com/scm/read-creditreport.htm.

◆ Another important strategy is to piece all relevant financial information together to make sure that everything is consistent. Match up W-2s with income that shows up on tax returns. If a buyer's credit reports shows debt in some areas, make sure their disclosure on their loan application reflects that. Anything that doesn't reasonably match up should be accounted for and explained.

Selling Smarts _____

If all seems to be in order with your buyer's financials—and, by the same token, your financial needs are met—don't be shy about negotiating the terms of the second mortgage. For instance, if the going interest rate is 6 percent or so, don't be afraid to ask for 7 percent or even more. If you need the money relatively soon, inquire about a short payback period. If a buyer has had some credit issues, see if they can increase the size of the down payment. Remember, you're not merely doing the buyer a generous favor by providing owner financing—you may well be spelling the difference between a home that's affordable or one that's just out of reach.

If, when all is said and done, you determine your buyer is worthy of the second mortgage, talk to your attorney about drawing up all necessary paperwork related to the deal, including a note and necessary second mortgage documentation. This must be signed by the buyer at the closing and recorded alongside any other papers relevant to the sale.

The bottom line to investigating and setting up owner financing is to take the process as seriously as any other element of the sale of your home. Even if the amount is relatively modest, do your due diligence to make certain this element of the deal, however small, is carried off as reliably as any other part of the sale.

Rent to Own (Lease Option)

Occasionally, it may be your bad luck to be stuck in a home selling market that makes a garden slug appear downright dynamic by comparison. Homes, for whatever reason, are simply not moving, and even financial carrots, such as owner financing, are not adequate enough to entice interested buyers.

Happily, however dire these conditions may be, they are not without their remedies. One such option is a *lease option* or rent to own arrangement.

On the surface, this sort of an arrangement may seem to smack of desperation. That all depends on your definition of desperate. If, by chance, you're mired in a deadly housing market with nary a nibble in sight, then, yes, a rent to own setup may seem like the final straw.

Tools of the Trade

Instead of an outright purchase, a **lease option** or rent to own lets someone occupy your home without actually buying it. Rather, you and the occupant agree on a deal wherein the buyer rents your home but has the option of purchasing it some time in the future. Any rent paid can apply to the purchase price.

But there are other ways to look at it as well. For one thing, if you have to move quickly, a rent to own offers yet another possibility to, at least in part, come up with some sort of arrangement that gets you out of your home. And, it can also be advantageous from the buyer's point of view as well. Many prospective buyers who simply lack the necessary upfront cash to meet down payment or closing costs may find a rent to own a godsend.

A global issue to be aware of, though, is that a rent to own setup is not the same as a simple rental arrangement. With the latter, you pay your rent and you get to stay for 30 more days. A rent to own is more involved. For one thing, the agreement often stipulates that the renter has the option of buying the home during any time in which the agreement is in effect. A rent to own can also be more costly upfront to the renter because he generally pays a one-time fee in return for your agreeing to the rent to own arrangement.

Finally, a conventional rental payment is money paid to occupy a home and nothing else. A rent to own payment, on the other hand, can often apply—in whole or in part—toward a down payment. In effect, a rent to own allows a renter to slowly amass the funds needed to compile a down payment with which to buy the home.

Another part of a rent to own agreement is a contract to purchase. This, in effect, is part of the rental agreement and spells out the various terms and conditions if a renter opts to pursue outright purchase of the home.

The contract element of a rent to own can be a bit dicey as it can involve a fair amount of negotiation. For one thing, you need to determine what the one-time upfront fee should be as well as the monthly rent. By all accounts, there's little precedent here, so it's pretty much up to you. On top of that, you have to decide what portion of the rental payment is purely rent and what can apply toward the down payment.

Another consideration kicks in when the period in which the option to purchase expires. Because no rent to own contract goes on without end, sooner or later a buyer will have to decide whether to exercise the buy option. In many ways, the rent/down payment split that every payment represents works in your favor. If a buyer chooses not to buy, he, in effect, is giving up that portion of his payments that would have gone toward a down payment. That can provide a fair amount of leverage to convince the buyer not to throw that money away and, instead, choose to buy the house.

Selling Smarts

When figuring how large a monthly payment should be in a rent to own, a reasonable starting point is to add a certain amount of money, however modest, to what you might normally charge for rent. In that sense, the renter is obligated to begin setting aside money for a down payment.

The other unpredictable part of rent to own is the purchase price that you established when you drew up the contract. If, by chance, your house goes way up in value during that period, your renter has a bargain if she chooses to exercise the buy option. But, if prices drop, a renter exercising the buy option will pay you a price that's greater than what the home might actually be worth at the time.

Equity Sharing

Still another option for the cash-strapped buyer—not to mention a particularly aggressive seller—is equity sharing. Here, the ownership of the home is shared. The buyer may occupy the house, but you, as the seller, retain at least a portion of ownership.

Equity sharing can work out in a variety of ways. For instance, you, as the seller, may agree to provide the down payment and even the closing costs, while the buyer (kind of a loose term in this particular situation) agrees to make the monthly payments. Another alternative has the parties sharing all expenses, from down payment to closing costs to mortgage payments and property taxes.

In fact, equity sharing can consist of more than just one buyer and one seller. Additional buyers may contribute in some fashion, perhaps by helping out with mortgage payments or contributing something to upfront costs (it's very popular with parents looking to help their kids with the expense of buying a home). In fact, in some parts of the country where the cost of homes is prohibitive to many buyers, you, as the seller, may not even be in the mix at all. Cash-strapped buyers look for investors to provide upfront expenses in return for a stake in a home whose value will hopefully increase over time.

One advantage to you as the seller is that equity sharing opens up another avenue to move your home—a plus in slow markets or in circumstances where you have to move quickly. Another plus is that it positions your home as an investment without you having to assume all the risk. After all parties involved agree to sell the property outright—or one party decides to buy out the other partners—the proceeds of the sale are split. If you're in a good housing market, that can mean a tidy profit.

There are, of course, downsides to equity sharing. First, like other alternatives, it doesn't solve the problem if you need a good-size amount of cash-in-hand to buy your next home. And, as can be the case when you have someone else occupying a property in which you have a financial stake, you are putting a degree of trust into someone else. Not only do they have to meet all their financial obligations, they're also bound to keep the property in good shape.

Selling Smarts

Equity sharing may also provide certain tax advantages. Check with your accountant or tax professional to see if the particulars of your situation provide any sort of tax break.

Occupy Prior to Closing

Another circumstance that may crop up is a buyer's request to move into your home before the closing. This can happen for a variety of reasons—maybe the buyer has already moved out of her prior home and is in housing limbo (that cheapo motel is fast losing its romantic charm). Perhaps they're moving a great distance and would simply enjoy settling directly into their new home. By the same token, it may appeal to you as well. Perhaps you've already moved out and the house is just sitting there. From your perspective, it's better to have a warm body in there than just leaving it empty.

Whatever the reasons are to make it a worthwhile idea, occupying prior to closing is a fairly unusual concession in home selling—and for very good cause. The biggest and most compelling is that the buyer gets a first-hand, up close and very personal view of the home she's buying. And in this case, familiarity can cause problems. The buyer may see cracks in walls she never saw before, the hot water in the shower takes forever to kick in, and on and on with a litany of complaints. That can lead to requests for repairs and other concessions.

If all this scares you enough, just say no if a buyer requests occupancy prior to closing. Enough said. Unfortunately, there are instances where it seems unreasonable to keep your buyer in housing no man's land. If that's the case, ask your attorney to draft an occupancy agreement that covers the period prior to closing. Among other major features, the buyer must agree to accept the home "as is" at the time of occupancy; the buyer should offer some form of compensation; and the buyer should have all necessary forms of insurance in place prior to moving in.

Go for It! Executing the Agreement

Okay, the time has finally arrived. After a good deal of haggling and negotiating, you and the buyer have agreed on every last detail of the Purchase and Sale Agreement.

Time to put your John Hancock on the document. And as always, there are a few guidelines that are prudent to follow.

Selling Smarts

In truth, the document is not truly and completely final until both you and the buyer have signed off. Even as you review it during the signing, you can make changes or updates to the agreement. If you do so, make sure both you and the buyer initial any changes to make it clear that both of you approved it.

First is the number of copies. You should have at least two original copies of the Purchase and Sale Agreement—one for you and one for the buyer. Make sure these are not photocopies, but originals. You may want to make additional copies for your attorney. The buyer may want to make additional copies for his own records or, perhaps, to provide to any lender who may be financing the sale.

When possible, it's usually easier to have both buyer and seller meet to sign at the same time. Things go much faster and you, as the seller, can collect any deposit that the buyer may owe on the spot.

The logistics of the signing can depend on the circumstances. Sometimes, it's impossible for the Purchase and Sale Agreement to be signed by both parties at the same time, face to face (such as the case of an out-of-town buyer). In these cases, the buyer usually signs first, then forwards the documents to you for your signature. After you sign them, you can collect any deposit checks that may be due you.

Online Resources on Alternatives

Here are a few websites that can offer additional details on alternatives to conventional home sales:

◆ Bankrate.com (www.bankrate.com) offers a variety of easy-to-use calculators, including amortization calculators.

◆ A good page that explains how to read a credit report can be found at www. credco.com/scm/readcreditreport.htm.

◆ If the idea of letting your buyer occupy prior to the closing interests you, check out a sample occupancy agreement at: www.charlestonrealestatenews.com/ forms/370.pdf.

The Least You Need to Know

◆ Owner financing can often prove advantageous to buyers who, for one reason or another, can't afford a home through conventional financing.

◆ Don't consider owner financing if the deal leaves you with less cash at closing than you need.

◆ If you consider owner financing, act like a lender—check out your buyer's income, credit history, and other details to make sure they're a solid risk.

◆ A rent to own agreement is another option that gets a buyer into your home who may not be able to afford conventional down payments and closing costs.

◆ Equity sharing can work if you don't need a lot of cash at closing and are interested in keeping at least a portion of your home as an investment.

◆ Be cautious about letting a buyer occupy prior to closing. If it's a must, draw up a comprehensive occupancy agreement to avoid any problems.

Chapter 14

The Home Stretch

In This Chapter

- ◆ The home inspection (again?)
- ◆ More tests, more details
- ◆ The post inspection negotiation
- ◆ Let the buyer know what you know
- ◆ To extend or not extend?

Now that the Purchase and Sale Agreement is signed, it's time to start fulfilling some of the duties and responsibilities the document lays out. In fact, in some cases, what happens now may effectively repeat a step you took yourself—possibly even before you even hung out your For Sale sign.

But it's all part of the process that keeps you moving toward that happy day when pen is applied to paper and your house is sold. In this chapter, we cover the various types of inspections that may or may not take place, what you can do if a problem comes up as a result, and other necessary steps that finalize various elements contained in the Purchase and Sale Agreement.

The Home Inspection

Sound familiar? It should. We covered this back in Chapter 3, identifying a home inspector as a valuable part of your overall FSBO team. We also offered a brief overview of what a home inspection can entail and why, as a seller, it is a smart idea for you to hire an inspector proactively to uncover any significant problems.

But maybe you skipped that step, figuring you'd rather hang onto the several hundred bucks that an inspector can charge. (It's not a great idea, but don't feel too guilty—a lot of home sellers forgo a home inspection.) Maybe you just figured that any reasonably thorough buyer would insist on a home inspection anyway.

No matter the case, chances are good you may be looking at a home inspection—either the first your home has had or another one at the buyer's direction.

It is common for a buyer to order a home inspection, even though the seller had one done already. All things being equal, a lot of buyers would rather spend the extra cash to have an inspection by someone they know. And, if a fair amount of time has passed since the first inspection occurred, there's always the off chance that something has gone wrong since then that the first inspection couldn't identify.

Another reason that buyers may ask for their own inspection is some inspections are more thorough than others. Have a look back at our discussion in Chapter 3—as we mention there, some inspections may not cover roof conditions. Others may bypass parts of a home in which a buyer is particularly interested, such as a swimming pool or home sprinkler system.

The bottom line is that you should never be surprised if a buyer insists that a home inspection follow the signing of the Purchase and Sale Agreement. Most agreements stipulate a certain time frame in which the buyer may complete the inspection—say 10 days or thereabouts.

Even better—most homes have something wrong with them. If you're aware of them, let the buyer know before they come up in the home inspection. That can save some haggling over costs further in the process.

Selling Smarts _____

Even if it seems like you're watching a movie that you just saw a week ago, it's a good idea to be home when the home inspector arrives to give your house the once over. For one thing, you may be able to answer questions or explain certain elements of the home. Just as important, you get a first hand view of the inspector and his professionalism. Watch what he examines and what he might miss. Don't be afraid to ask about his credentials and qualifications. That way, if something comes up later that seems puzzling or unreasonable, you may be able to call the inspector's abilities into question rather than just the condition of your home. By the way, some inspectors would rather you not be there when they're conducting the inspection—politely insist otherwise, even if your presence has to be exceedingly low key.

Negotiating After the Inspection

After the home inspection has been completed, make sure you obtain a complete copy for you to review in detail. Go over it with a fine toothed comb to see if there are any significant issues raised in the report.

At this point, the buyer may notify you—in writing, naturally—regarding any sort of action she would like to pursue as a result of the inspection. As we've mentioned before, in certain cases, a home inspection may prompt a buyer to call the whole deal off and request all deposits be returned in full.

Just how easily a buyer can back out of a deal as a result of the home inspection can depend in large part on how the contingency is worded in the Purchase and Sale Agreement. If, for instance, the contingency says a buyer may withdraw from the deal if he is not satisfied with the inspection, he has a right to pull out. You return whatever deposit he may have given you and your house goes back on the market.

That can offer an easy out for a buyer who simply isn't all that serious or just gets a case of cold feet. By the same token, more specific wording—citing things such as significant structural or electrical defects—mandate that a buyer show specifically what he doesn't like. Check with your attorney to make sure the wording of the inspection contingency doesn't offer the buyer an easy way to bail.

The unfortunate possibility of a buyer who opts out of a deal shows the importance of keeping a tight timeframe for the inspection to take place. If by chance, things don't work out, you lose as little time as possible in beginning to work with other interested buyers.

A buyer who bails also reinforces the importance of conducting your own home inspection before putting your house on the market.

Selling Smarts ⎯⎯⎯⎯

Don't get too worried if a buyer finds something in a home inspection that he'd like to negotiate. Given the wiles of individual buyers and sellers, it's all too likely something will crop up that the buyer wants to negotiate. Roll with the punches and look to seal the deal.

Provided the contingency clause is worded appropriately, most serious buyers will have to uncover some fairly significant problems to call a deal off. Those sorts of problems can be identified and addressed long before that, thanks to a proactive home inspection.

But, if a buyer is genuinely interested in your home, chances are slim she'll simply want to call the whole thing off. Rather, she'll likely ask that the problems be addressed in some fashion. And this brings us back to the heart of home buying—negotiation. This time, we're specifically dealing with issues raised in the home inspection report.

So the buyer has presented you with a list of issues included in the home inspection that trouble him. Review the list—some may be minor and incidental, while others, such as major roof repairs, perceived plumbing problems, and other issues, may be significant and costly.

It happens on occasion that a buyer's home inspection report and a separate one obtained by the seller differ significantly on an issue of some importance—say, one finds the roof in good shape while the other likens it to a sieve. If that's the case, consider obtaining a third inspection. Find someone mutually agreeable and split the expense. Another look can often uncover a common ground and, ultimately, a solution.

Selling Smarts ⎯⎯⎯⎯

When negotiating after the home inspection, it's important to distinguish between repairs and upgrades. Repairs, as is obvious, mean something isn't working properly and needs attention, such as a dead electrical outlet. Upgrades, on the other hand, don't necessarily mean something's not working—rather, at least in the eyes of the buyer, something could stand to be improved, such as a paint job or windows which are not particularly energy efficient. Repairs are often the sole responsibility of the seller; negotiate upgrades more aggressively, as they can come more from the whim of a buyer rather than something not working as it should.

Consider the list of problems carefully. If, by chance, they're fairly minor and don't amount to much in the way of expense, the path of least resistance would be to agree to pay for them. If they're more substantial than that, ask if the buyer would be willing to share the expense in some manner.

When negotiating after a home inspection, never lose sight of your financial requirements. Selling your home may be your ultimate goal, but don't be in such a hurry you agree to pay $10,000 for a new roof and, in the end, leave you with less cash than you need to take away from the deal.

It's important to know that you, as the seller, may be obligated to make certain repairs. Certain defects may have been identified in the contract that you're obligated to address. Additionally, local and state requirements may come into play as to what a homeseller must agree to according to the law. Issues such as earthquake safety requirements, smoke detectors, and other requirements may fall under this. Check with your attorney to see if any of these happen to apply.

Keep in mind that agreeing to pay for problems raised in the home inspection is only one possible option. If you simply don't have a large supply of cash on hand, offer to adjust the sales price to compensate for the expense. That way, the buyer's concerns are addressed and you meet those obligations with as little cash out of pocket as possible.

Always keep the dynamics of your local market in mind when negotiating home inspection issues. If homes are moving slowly, it may be prudent to be rather generous in your willingness to pay for certain costs. On the other hand, an active seller's market puts the ball in your court. You can be more aggressive in turning down some of your buyer's requests, reasoning that another buyer might be less demanding.

Other Inspections

In many cases, home buyers will opt for a basic home inspection and leave it at that. However, that's not always the case. Some buyers, aware of the various, more specific issues that conventional home inspection may not address, may add on other forms of inspection. Should these pinpoint problems or other issues, these will have to be addressed the same as problems identified by a basic home inspection.

Where you live can play a big part in what additional tests, if any, a buyer may choose to pursue. In some areas of the country, drinking water is a major concern. By contrast, in neighborhoods where the homes are particularly old, lead-based paint may be an issue. As you'll see, there are three primary tests that may come into play: water, radon, and lead-based paint.

Water Tests

It goes without saying that safe, clean water is an absolute necessity, both for cooking and personal hygiene. That's why many home buyers will insist on a thorough test of a home's water supply.

Concern over the quality of water may be puzzling to some. Aren't all public water supplies routinely tested and treated for any sort of significant problems? Yes, but remember that's only at the source. Water passing through public water systems may become contaminated en route to a home. Additionally, old indoor plumbing systems—which may contain solder or lead in their network—may also impact the overall quality and safety of the water.

Water tests involve a basically simple procedure in which a sample is taken from a home's water system and examined for various characteristics, such as iron content, water hardness, and other issues. Depending on the test, issues such as chlorine, lead, bacteria, and industrial waste may be targeted by the test.

As an example, Master Water Conditioning Corp's website offers a sample water test report, outlining some of the findings such a study may include (see the following figure).

The www.masterwater.com website offers a sample water test report.

Should the test identify any problems, possible solutions range from relatively inexpensive forms of disinfection to more costly options, such as replacing or upgrading pipes or installing cleansing and disinfection systems that cover an entire home.

The decision to test a home's water is pretty much up to buyers of houses on community water systems. That's not necessarily the case with homes on individual wells. Because those do not undergo the cleansing and purification that many municipal water systems do, many lenders will require well testing to make certain no problems specific to that well exist. But know that many lenders will only insist on bacteria checks and ignore other issues.

Radon

Another common test that can be added to a home's overall inspection program is for *radon*.

Although radon can be found in any home, there are certain types of homes in certain areas where radon is of particular concern. That makes it a good idea to check out the particulars of the gas: how it occurs, the damage it can cause and what to do about it. The following guide provides that information and more. You can check out the Environmental Protection Agency's Citizen's Guide to radon online at: www.epa.gov/radon/pubs/citguide.html (see the following figure).

Tools of the Trade

Radon is a radioactive gas that has been found in homes throughout the country. Naturally produced through the breakdown of uranium in the soil, it can seep into homes through cracks in the foundation and other areas. Breathing radon in sufficient quantity has been connected with lung cancer and other illnesses.

For instance, many northern states have pockets where significant levels of radon have been identified. Older homes may be more susceptible to radon than more recently built houses. Research has also shown that radon can enter homes through well water.

But the tricky side to radon is the lack of consistency in the homes it invades. Whether well-sealed or drafty, with or without cellars or basements, almost any home can suffer from a significant amount of radon.

Although there has been some disagreement over the prevalence of radon and its potential health effects, the federal government is sufficiently convinced of the gravity of the problem. Both the Environmental Protection Agency and the U.S. Surgeon General recommend all homes be tested for radon, no matter their condition, when they were built, or the part of the country where they happen to be located.

The www.epa.gov/radon/pubs/citguide.html website offers a map of radon zones.

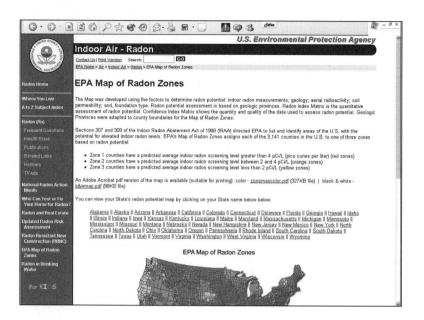

Radon tests come in two primary forms. The first, known as the short term test, can involve anything from a charcoal canister to collect radon in the air to an automatic tracking device that measures and prints out ongoing reports of air borne radon. The latter can take in as many as 90 days of readings. Although that can be far more accurate, the time involved is far too great when a home sale is involved.

The general rule of thumb is that results of 4 pCi/L or higher warrant additional testing to see whether the high levels hold up. Solutions to high radon levels can be as simple as a fan to increase circulation in certain parts of the home to more involved radon mitigation systems that can cost several thousand dollars.

Radon testing may not be limited to air in a home. Radon can also appear in a home's water supply. Contact your local water supplier if you're on a municipal system. If your home uses a well and radon is detected in that water source, the most effective solution is a point-of-entry cleansing system to purify the water before it actually enters the house.

> **FSBO Facts**
>
> Radon is generally measured in terms of picoCuries per liter of air, otherwise referred to as pCi/L. This is a measure of radioactivity, named after the famous French physicist Marie Curie. It's complicated, but one picoCurie is equal to the decay of two radioactive atoms per minute.

Lead-Based Paint

It's ironic. Lead is one of the most dangerous and toxic substances to human beings, yet its use in residential paint was only banned in the United States in the late 1970s. That's nearly three decades for the problem to pass, but the fact remains that many homes still contain significant amounts of lead-based paint.

That's a serious health issue. Prolonged exposure can lead to damage of the nervous system, particularly in young children. Other problems ranging from learning disabilities to Attention Deficit Disorder have also been connected to the presence of lead.

Although the problem of lead in paint may seem to be one of ingestion by eating, lead is far more insidious than that. Many problems result from simply breathing lead laden dust that gets into a home's air as the paint ages, deteriorates, and flakes. Even worse, everyday vacuuming doesn't address the problem because the particles are much too small to be trapped by vacuum bags.

That, in turn, may prompt some buyers to ask for a lead test. This usually involves a simple chemical test to measure the presence of lead in paint samples. Fortunately, if a lead dust problem is identified, the solution is usually simple and relatively inexpensive—either through repainting or specialized cleaning with a HEPA-filtered vacuum.

Occasionally, other environmental-related issues may crop up that can warrant further investigation or testing. These can include asbestos, formaldehyde, water contamination, and other problems. They are, however, of decided less concern than the issues we discussed earlier in this chapter.

Selling Smarts

If your home was built prior to 1978, it may be a good idea to proactively test for lead in your home's paint—a potentially poisonous substance may scare off even the most motivated of buyers, no matter how simple the remedy might be. If you want to save some money, inexpensive in-home test kits are an option.

Duty to Disclose

In the old days of home buying—whenever you happen to identify that particular timeframe—buying was not far removed from the old shell game. You paid your money and took your chances. If you got stuck with a lemon, tough luck.

Not any more. Now, as the seller of your home, it is your legal obligation to inform the buyer of information about your home—or, more specifically, any detail that may

Tools of the Trade

Duty to disclose basically refers to material facts about your home or the neighborhood that would not be evident to the buyer. In effect, it is your duty to make sure the buyer is aware of this information.

impact the buyer's decision to buy your home. It can also impact the overall purchase price upon which you had both previously agreed. This is known as *duty to disclose.*

You can see why we included duty to disclose at this juncture. Up to now in this chapter, we've been covering elements and issues relating to your home that are identified through various types of inspections. In other words, those steps the buyer takes to uncover things that can affect how much she's willing to pay for the home or, indeed, if she's willing to buy it at all.

Now the reverse is true. Instead of the buyer working to identify problems and issues that need resolution, the onus is on you to tell the truth. If you know something about the house that the buyer should know as well, it's your legal duty to let them know.

The difficulty here is that duty to disclose requirements can differ quite a bit from one state to the next. What one state mandates you tell the buyer will differ considerably from what another may require.

Check with your attorney to determine the particulars of duty to disclose where you live. Your state's housing authority will also likely be able to provide you with all pertinent guidelines. Your attorney or the state should also be able to supply you with all legally applicable documents pertaining to duty to disclose.

Even though states are different in what they require in a duty to disclose, you can expect most places to hit upon a number of common topics, including:

♦ General condition of the house. No home inspection is going to uncover every single problem. For instance, the inspector may overlook—or be unable to check—the fact that the dishwasher's rinse cycle doesn't always work. It's a very thorough inspection that uncovers bathroom blinds that don't go down all the way. Likewise, a nice sunny day during the inspection does a thorough job of hiding the fact that the rook in the garage leaks in the smallest of showers.

You get the picture. If there is a problem with anything to do with the home, you have an obligation to let the buyer know. As you can see, some of those may be significant, while others are more picayune. In either case, be sure to make your buyer aware of them.

◆ Environmental and safety issues. It's no coincidence that inspections target issues such as lead-based paint and the presence of radon. In fact, your duty to disclose goes beyond covering things such as contaminated soil and water, impact from faulty chemical storage tanks, and things of this nature. Even your home's exposure to natural disasters, such as floods and earthquakes, should be addressed.

◆ Legal issues. If you have any lawsuits in the works that may affect the property, you have an obligation to advise your buyer. This can even include covering any improvements or modifications you made to your home without obtaining the necessary building permits.

Selling Smarts

It goes without saying—if you have any legal issues that somehow tie into your home, try to get them cleaned up *before* you put your house on the market. Few buyers will want to buy a home that's dragging a legal anchor behind it.

The bottom line to duty to disclose may be unpleasant—depending, of course, on just what you have to come clean about—but it's always a good idea to err on the side of complete honesty. If you're not sure whether you need to disclose something, check with your attorney. There's a good chance you should go ahead and let the buyer know. The consequences of failing to disclose can be drastic, from lawsuits to sales that are wiped off the books because the seller failed to disclose something that affected the value or appeal of the home.

Try to look at duty to disclose as something you can use to your advantage. Rather than coming off as a seller who's looking to mask every flaw in your home, full disclosure characterizes you as an honest, forthright person who wants to sell her home with the highest integrity possible. That can only bolster a buyer's confidence in you.

Considering Buyer Extensions

Not all aspects of the process moving toward the closing puts the responsibility on you, the seller, to disclose and fix everything. Occasionally, the buyer may step into the picture with a problem that he asks your permission to address.

More specifically, this refers to a buyer's request for an extension of some sort. In certain cases, it may have to do with a home loan. The process has not gone as quickly or as smoothly as the buyer expected and the loan is not going to be in place by the time the closing is slated to occur.

When this happens, the buyer will first let you know about a hold up in the loan process. In so doing, he'll also ask to call off the deal and get his earnest money back. However, at the same time, he also requests that you grant an extension to allow additional time to obtain necessary financing.

That leaves you with one of two choices. Either grant the extension or insist that things continue to move forward according to the schedule on which you've both agreed.

That can prove a tricky decision. On the one hand, if you agree to the extension, you may be giving the buyer the time he needs to arrange all necessary financing. On the other hand, agreeing to the extension but seeing the buyer fail to get the loan he needs just needlessly ties up your home.

By the same token, refusing to grant the extension may kill the deal that otherwise could have gone through had the buyer had a little extra time. Remember, by refusing to approve the extension, you're agreeing to the end of the deal. From there, you may agree to return the earnest money deposit in its entirety. Since you also had your home off the market for a while, you may try to negotiate a split of the earnest money.

The issues to bear in mind here are, first, the buyer obviously wants to buy your home if at all possible. But, by asking for an extension, it's also obvious that the loan necessary to buy your home is in doubt. So, negotiate carefully. Find out what the holdup is with regard to the loan. If it seems imposing, you may want to agree to call the deal off.

If, on the other hand, it seems possible that the financing may go through, you have a bit of room to negotiate. First, think carefully about how long of an extension you'll agree to. If the buyer wants two weeks, counter with one. This allows you to keep the extensions going, week by week if you so choose, while keeping you from being locked into a longer-term agreement. Additionally, ask the buyer to forfeit a bit of her earnest money in return for your agreeing to the extension. That takes all the risk off you and, by all accounts, will likely be seen as more than a fair tradeoff for the extension. Moreover, should the deal eventually go though, that portion that was forfeited can be applied to the purchase as originally intended.

In other cases, a buyer may request an extension on the closing date. If that happens, follow the same procedure. Investigate the reasons for the request and, if appropriate, ask for a forfeiture of the deposit to protect you in case everything falls through.

Online Resources for the Home Stretch

For more information about topics covered in this chapter, check out the following websites:

◆ An excellent overview of environmental hazards in homes can be found at www.hsh.com/pamphlets/hazards.html.

◆ More specifically, The Environmental Protection Agency's Citizen's Guide to radon is located at www.epa.gov/radon/pubs/citguide.html.

◆ You can find a thorough overview of water quality and testing at www.inspect-ny.com/water/watrtest.htm.

The Least You Need to Know

◆ Don't be surprised or alarmed if the buyer insists on his own home inspection, even if you've already had one done.

◆ If your inspection and the buyer's differ substantially, consider obtaining a third opinion.

◆ Depending on where you live, other more specific inspections may be necessary prior to closing.

◆ If, during negotiations after inspections, you decide you don't want to lay out cash for repairs, consider dropping the sales price.

◆ Investigate guidelines on your duty to disclose. Failing to be as forthright as possible can jeopardize the sale of your home.

◆ Don't necessarily rule out a buyer's request for extensions. Instead, negotiate terms that are favorable to you that offer the best possible chance of the sale ultimately going through.

Chapter

15

Protect Yourself!

In This Chapter

- ◆ Addressing last minute misunderstandings
- ◆ The walk through
- ◆ Fixing anything the walkthrough uncovers
- ◆ Title defects and what to do about them

You're so close you can smell it.

The closing is fast approaching. Everything seems to be in order, from the loan application to all necessary inspections.

Just a few steps remain—and with them, a few last hurdles that may be necessary to overcome before you and your buyer sign on the dotted lines that transfer ownership of your home.

We cover these last few issues—and get you ready to deal with them—in this chapter. We touch on last minute misunderstandings, the final walk-through, and other problems that can rear their heads just as the closing approaches.

Dealing With Misunderstandings

It is a fact of life, not merely in real estate but in most human endeavors, that you'll run into misunderstandings. We all can have miscommunications on occasion, even in those instances where no one involved has even the slightest intention to mislead or confuse.

But misunderstandings happen—and they can happen to you as you near your closing. So as the date your house actually changes hands draws closer, it's essential to know common sources of last minute problems as well as ways to deal with them as efficiently as possible.

Disclosures, Again

One all-too usual source of miscommunication between buyer and seller is a topic we covered in Chapter 14—the duty to disclose. Ideally, necessary disclosure occurs fairly early in the sales process but, as you near the time of your closing, it's never a bad idea to double check your disclosures to make certain that nothing—and we mean nothing—may come up late in the game that a buyer could make a stink about—and, in the process, somehow kill a deal so close to completion.

As an example, an incident that occurred to one of the authors of this book reinforces the importance of duty to disclose—even as late as the day of the closing itself. A January closing was scheduled and, as luck would have it, the pipes in the home froze the very night prior to the closing. Could the owner—one of the authors—have kept that information under wraps and blithely signed the papers? Certainly. Instead, he let the buyers know about the problem, offered to pay half of the plumbing bill, and the closing went ahead without a hint of worry of what might happen after the fact.

You get the idea. The point is, with the closing looming, the last thing you want to have happen is some significant bit of information suddenly come to the buyer's attention—information that may prompt him to take action that works against you in some fashion. At this juncture, take the time to make certain you've been as thorough as possible—covering everything from run of the mill issues to more serious ones.

The issue of duty to disclose on issues that exist outside the lines of usual disclosure is, needless to say, somewhat subjective. Check with your attorney if any element of doubt exists. Chances are good she'll recommend you err on the side of caution and inform the buyer. Even if she says you're in the clear, disclosure can help put your mind at ease.

Should It Stay or Should It Go?

The second issue that can pose last minute headaches is another topic we've touched on earlier. Like duty to disclose, as the closing draws closer, it is wise to revisit the question of what stays in the house and what goes. Although we discussed this earlier, it bears a brief revisit because this issue comes up all too often as the closing nears—particularly with regard to the final walkthrough, which we will discuss shortly.

Ideally, all this has been worked out well in advance of the closing—your sales contract should be exhaustive in its discussion of what remains in the house and what you, as the seller, plan to haul off when you pull up stakes.

But it doesn't always work that way. Maybe that lovely living room clock that the buyer thought was permanently attached to the wall was anything but permanent. By the same token, the kitchen ceiling rack that the buyer was only too glad to have you take with you (and which you were all too happy to leave behind) remains, becoming an issue—to both your surprised and mutual chagrins.

In most cases, what stays and what goes would come up in the final walkthrough preceding the actual closing. But, as we'll see shortly, the final walkthrough can be rather expansive, both in what it covers and, in turn, the problems it uncovers that have to be addressed to the mutual satisfaction of both the buyer and the seller.

FSBO Facts

Want an easy way to make sure you and your buyer are on the same page with what stays and what goes—and, in the process, make the final walkthrough less of a potential headache? Schedule another walkthrough—one that occurs prior to the final walkthrough and which is specific to items and fixtures in the house. Not only can that let you solve any of those problems well before the fact of the closing, it also lessens the possibility of something significant cropping up during the final walkthrough. And, in the end, that can make the final walkthrough smoother and considerably less stressful.

The Final Walkthrough—Any Problems?

One of the final steps—no pun intended, by the way—prior to the closing on your home is the final walkthrough. In a walkthrough, the buyer and the seller walk through the home and surrounding property in as complete a fashion as possible. The idea is to make certain that everything matches what was agreed to.

The final walkthrough is a significant event in the sale of your home. So, don't skimp on the details. First, try to schedule the walkthrough at the mutual convenience of both the buyer and the seller—ideally, as close to the actual closing as possible.

It's advantageous to you, as the seller, to keep the walkthrough and the subsequent closing as close together as reasonably possible. The less time the buyer has, the fewer things he can raise as possible problems prior to the closing. But don't make it too short; if a few items need to be addressed prior to the closing, such as repairs, too little time may prove inadequate to get everything accomplished. A week or so is usually a good timeframe.

One of the first things you should do to prep your home for the walkthrough is to check and see what your legal obligations might be. These are often spelled out in the final sales agreement. For instance, the document may specify that the house be as neat as possible (good advice regardless of legal mandate). You may also have to remove most, if not all, of your personal property and, if specified, perform any necessary repairs identified and agreed to in the sales agreement.

Other pre-walkthrough tips:

- Send the kids to the movies. Now's not the time for a warm family environment. As we'll see in our walkthrough checklist, it's a cold, hard inspection. Likewise, send Spot to doggy daycare or some other temporary hang out.

- Clean, then clean some more. You may not be obligated to have your home in complete spic and span condition (identified earlier as "broom clean" condition). Still, clean up everything you possibly can. If needed, hire professional cleaners for a few hours to make sure everything is as immaculate as possible. It puts your home in the best light possible and is also respectful and courteous to your buyers.

- If you've forgotten, dust off all those old operational manuals that detail how various things work. A walkthrough doesn't limit itself to a visual once over; the buyer may have questions about how things work. Refresh your memory. Even better, set all documentation aside to pass along to the buyer—another nice bit of diplomacy that makes for good feelings all around.

Just how long a walkthrough takes will vary. Some may take a half hour or so, although a more thorough buyer will certainly earmark a good deal more time than that. It's a good idea to plan on a couple of hours. Likewise, who comes along for the ride can depend. Some buyers prefer to handle the walkthrough on their own, while others may want their real estate agent, family members, or even their attorney along.

Issues that come up during a walkthrough will also vary a great deal, depending on the individual interests of the buyer as well as the property in question. But here's a handy checklist of some things that may be included in a walkthrough as well as ways you can prepare:

- ◆ As we mentioned earlier, have all operational manuals on-hand if the buyer wants to see them.

- ◆ Likewise, gather all records of sale, warranties, and repair receipts for all the appliances and other systems.

- ◆ Expect your buyer to check the exterior of the house in great detail, paying particular attention to the roof. This is likely to be especially thorough if there's been a recent rain or snowstorm.

- ◆ If you have an in-ground sprinkler system, your buyer is likely to check it. Make sure it works as it should.

Selling Smarts

Ask your buyer who he wants to bring with him on the walk-through. If it's an agent, family member, or that knowledge-able friend who knows every-thing there is about houses, you can probably handle your walk-through on your own. But if their attorney plans on attending, it's advisable to have yours there as well.

- ◆ The buyers will undoubtedly check all interior rooms. If you made marks moving furniture out, patch them up. Make certain all windows and doors work properly. Repair any sign of water damage on ceilings. Reminder: if you think any damage falls under the issue of disclosure, pass it along to the buyer.

- ◆ Make sure countertops are clean. Clean out the interiors of all drawers, cabinets, and closets. (One of the authors had a buyer who pitched a fit that three—count them, three—wire coat hangers remained. While there's no pleasing some people, you should certainly be courteous and mindful when you do your final sweep.)

- ◆ Go through and, if needed, clean areas of the house that may have been previously inaccessible, such as crawl spaces, hard to reach storage areas, and other spots.

- ◆ Check smoke alarms, in-house intercoms, and other items typically not covered in a home inspection.

- ◆ One thing your buyer will almost surely do is check all operational systems. That includes all appliances, light switches, toilets, water systems, and other features, such as a garage door opener. Make sure they operate properly beforehand. Fill all tubs and sinks to check for leaks that can be patched proactively.

♦ Your buyer will undoubtedly venture into the basement. Be sure to clean it up, repair anything that needs it, and patch stains and signs of leakage.

Selling Smarts _____

Want to come across as an upfront seller eager to show that everything is at it should be? Carry around a couple of light bulbs during the walkthrough—if there are any bare fixtures, screw one on and proudly show your buyer that everything is in working order.

♦ Your buyer will keep an eye out for signs of pests. Spray the house with insect spray a few days beforehand. If you have mice, set up traps several days in advance to get rid of as many as you can.

♦ Clean up the attic as much as possible.

♦ Your buyer is going to want to double check any necessary repairs you may have agreed to complete prior to the walkthrough. Prepare a checklist and point out all repairs individually.

♦ Finally, let the buyer know of any changes in the condition of the property since it was inspected.

Addressing Walkthrough Issues

Okay, so you've done the walkthrough. At this point, one of two primary things can occur:

♦ The buyer finds everything acceptable. You both set your happy gaze on the closing.

♦ Not everything is as it should be. For whatever reason, the buyer is not satisfied with the condition of the home and wants something done about it prior to the closing.

In fact, problems break down into several subcategories. One is earlier problems that have yet to be addressed—perhaps the buyer pointed out the back steps off the deck needed to be replaced, and you just didn't get around to it. It may be a question of degree—maybe you thought just one of the steps needed to be replaced, while the buyer assumed you were going to have the steps replaced completely.

Another potential issue is damage. The buyer looked over your home a few weeks ago and was happy with it. Now, he says, there are dents in the wall where you moved a couch or some stains on the kitchen ceiling after a fish fry. Whatever the specifics, something's been damaged in the interim—or so he thinks.

The best way to address any problems arising from the walkthrough is to never lose sight of your ultimate goal—a successful closing. With that in mind, do your utmost to deal with problems in the most effective and efficient manner possible. Start by reviewing your list of any repairs or other steps you agreed to in the Purchase and Sale Agreement. If you overlooked something, get it done. If you can't see to the repairs, adjust your sales price.

Selling Smarts

One effective way to address walkthrough issues is to rely on your attorney. First, she's likely dealt with dozens of similar situations just like this. That will give her the perspective to advise you on what's reasonable and where you can take a stand.

Issues such as repairs can be rather clear cut. Not so with perceived damage. For one thing, one person's perception of damage will likely differ significantly from another's. Moreover, it's often easy to miss something the first time around, only to notice it later, particularly with small scratches and other minor cosmetic flaws.

There's an easy way to clear the air with regard to perceived damage that's noticed after a walkthrough. Take pictures or videotape your home early in your overall sales process. If a buyer claims recent damage after the walkthrough, take out the snapshots or pop the tape into the VCR. If things have changed, that will be evident and you can react accordingly. If things are as they have been for a while, that offers you an advantage in negotiating to a successful conclusion.

Regardless of whether it's an issue of damage, needed repairs, or some other problem, remain focused on the closing and what you need to do to get there. That doesn't mean being a cupcake who's willing to cater to your buyer's every whim—far from it. But if you approach things from a constructive perspective to solve problems to everyone's satisfaction, you'll move the process forward, rather than getting bogged down wrangling over every little meaningless issue.

Selling Smarts

One final bit of advice to keep things moving toward the closing. If minor issues come up after the walkthrough, have your attorney suggest they be addressed at the closing itself. Not many buyers simply walk away at a closing—particularly if the issues at hand are relatively minor.

Dealing With Title Defects

At some point prior to closing—maybe early in the process, maybe later—the title company you're working with will give you a preliminary title report. If you refer back to our discussion in Chapter 3, the title company is charged with doing the necessary research to ensure you have the legal right and authority to sell the property—known as "clear title." And as we mentioned in Chapter 10, some problems can be identified during a title search.

Because we're nearing the closing itself, it's time to address title issues in greater detail. Your title may be free and clear or, possibly, you received the report fairly quickly and were able to address whatever issues needed attention. But title defects can show up late in the game as well and can affect how smoothly you move toward your closing.

> **FSBO Facts**
>
> Something of a refresher—the title report identifies any liens, encumbrances, judgments, or other issues that may impact your legal capacity to transfer ownership of a piece of property.

There's virtually no limit to the sorts of title defects a report can uncover. Here, however, are a few of some of the problems you may run up against and, in turn, what you can do to solve them as efficiently as possible. And in the process, keep your closing on track:

◆ Delinquent taxes or tax liens. If you owe money to some governmental entity, now is *not* the time to protest the perceived injustices of our tax system. Pay up and move on. Likewise with any legal judgments that may affect your ability to sell the property. Ditto for any outstanding utility-related expenses. Any inequities should have been addressed prior to putting your house on the market.

◆ Mortgage-related issues. Occasionally, you refinance a loan, only the original loan somehow stays on the books, making it appear as if you have a greater loan obligation than you do. Obtain written proof from any lenders that such problems don't exist.

◆ Co-ownership. Perhaps you bought your home with someone else who has since moved thousands of miles away. Because she has to take part in the closing in some sort of legally suitable fashion, you may have to obtain power of attorney (the ability to sign on her behalf for all issues related to the sale of the home) to keep the closing on schedule. More on power of attorney in Chapter 16.

- Mistaken identity. Folks with relatively common names are often all too familiar with this problem. Occasionally, a legal judgment may exist against another person with the same last name as yours; the title report may mistakenly identify you as the guilty party. The solution is to prepare an affidavit assuring the title company that you are not the person in question. Another way this can occur is a judgment from a creditor, such as a credit card company or department store that files a claim against someone with your same name for failure to pay a bill. In these instances, an attorney from the title company may have to contact the creditor directly to resolve the confusion.

- Pending litigation. One of the more potentially serious defects has to do with pending litigation that may impact the property in some manner. Hopefully, you won't have to deal with this, but if litigation is pending that relates to ownership of the property, the legal term is known as *lis pendens*. Examples can include divorce proceedings or problems with an estate.

The problem with pending litigation is not so much that the buyers of the property are involved in the case—they're not, you are—but that they will be bound by the final resolution of the dispute. In these cases, refer the matter promptly to your attorney who, hopefully, can work out a fair—and expedient—settlement so the pending litigation is removed from the books. If necessary, ask for an extension on your closing date to allow for more time to settle the matter. Of course, as is the case with the other side of the coin, the buyer may refuse, which can effectively kill the deal.

Selling Smarts

Even though it happens, there's really no good reason for pending litigation to crop up as you head toward the closing (unless, of course, someone happens to file a lawsuit just after you sign the sales contract). If you've got legal problems, know well in advance whether they may impact your ability to sell your home and clean them up as quickly as possible. Never assume legal action doesn't involve your home—make sure. If they do, you should hold off on putting your house on the market until after you've resolved these issues.

If title defects are identified, it's up to you to clear them up. One quick and cost-effective way is if you bought owner's title insurance when you bought your home. Title insurance provides you with additional protection for title defects that occurred *prior* to you owning the property. If the title report you get when you're attempting to resell the property identifies one of these defects, just submit a claim to your title insurance company. The company should then assure the buyer that it will assume responsibility for addressing the title defect, including any sort of monetary damages.

If, however, you don't have owner title insurance or the defect occurred *after* your policy went into effect, the burden is on you to clear up the problem. As we've seen, some of these issues are relatively modest in their scope, while others are more problematic.

Just how this can impact your closing will vary. Some—if not most—title defects are minor enough that they can be addressed quickly with no effect on your closing at all. In some instances, when more time is necessary to correct defects, you may have to ask the buyer to move back the closing date. In so doing, you may also have to offer some sort of compensation to offset whatever inconvenience that may impose on the buyer.

There's an effective way to have Plan B already in place to allow for extra time for title defects. Many sales agreements build in an option for the seller to push back a scheduled closing date to deal with title defects. If you've yet to draw up a sales agreement, this is a feature well worth considering because it lets you adjust the closing date as necessary—without having to dangle a carrot in front of the buyer to get them to agree.

Selling Smarts

Last minute title defects also reinforce the importance of keeping in ongoing touch with the company or person handling your escrow. That way, should any problems arise, you'll know about them as soon as possible and be able to take fast action to correct them before they threaten your scheduled closing.

The topic of dealing with title defects as you near the closing also underscores the importance of being as proactive as possible. Granted, you may end up resolving title defects at the last minute anyway, but don't drag your feet when it comes to investigating them. The sooner you spot potential title problems in the sales process, the sooner and easier you can tackle any problems that may come up, while putting little or no impact on the eventual closing.

Online Resources for Seller Protection

Here are a few websites that can help you protect your interests as you near your closing date:

◆ You can find a list and discussion of 21 hidden potential title defects at www.invtitle.com/consumer/21-defects/index.php.

◆ Although it's directed toward newly built homes, a handy checklist of problems that can be uncovered during walkthroughs is available for download at safe.spsp.net/cgi-bin/askbuilder/BID-wlkthr.htm. Cost is $37, although that may be cheap if it saves a major headache.

◆ A great resource for title insurance information is the American Land Title Association website at www.alta.org.

The Least You Need to Know

◆ Be thorough in disclosing any issues about your home that may not be evident to the buyer.

◆ Consider having two walkthroughs—one covering what stays in the house and a second tour to address any other issues.

◆ Prepare carefully for the final walkthrough. Clean the house and make sure any repairs you agreed to have been addressed.

◆ If there are unresolved minor issues from the walkthrough, suggest that they be covered at the closing.

◆ Title defects can crop up at any time prior to the closing. Be proactive in identifying any defects and address them as quickly as possible.

Part 4

That Sweet, Sweet Closing and What Comes After

This part moves us into the final elements that precede the closing—and, of course, the closing itself, too. Here you'll walk through a home inspection, not to mention get details on the final walkthrough preceding the closing. Then, it's on to the closing … papers, more papers and, from there, some papers just to fill things out. Not that it's all fun and games, there may be tax ramifications from the sale of your home, so we wrap up with a chapter hitting on that topic.

Chapter 16

The Closing Itself

In This Chapter

- ◆ Preparing for settlement
- ◆ What all you need to sign
- ◆ What if you change your mind?
- ◆ Tips for minimizing problems

Woohoo! You've almost made it. All your hard work has paid off—you have a buyer who's agreed to purchase your home for a price that meets your needs, they've been approved for a mortgage, and you're ready to seal the deal at closing.

The closing, settlement, or close of escrow, which are different words used to describe the same event, is the final step in the sale of your home. It's where you and the buyer both sign on the dotted line—lots of them—indicating your agreement to transfer ownership of your home. Although it may have taken you weeks or months to get to this important day, the closing itself will likely take less than a couple of hours.

The focus of this chapter is to prepare you for closing and give you a behind-the-scenes look at ways to keep any problems to a minimum.

What Happens in What Order and Why

The countdown to closing begins as soon as a Purchase and Sale Agreement is signed by both you and the buyer. These signatures put into motion a lot of work that needs to be completed within the next 30 to 60 days, on average. Although a closing can be extended at the request of either the buyer or seller, it is difficult to shorten the process to less than a month—there is just too much paperwork to be shuffled.

For starters, the buyer will schedule a few inspections of the property. Depending on the type and location of the home, these can include:

- Structural inspection
- Well certification and septic inspection
- Radon testing
- Pest inspection

Depending on the results of these inspections, the buyer will either agree to the sale as planned, or he will ask that repairs and corrections be made prior to closing. And in that case, you can either agree to make the repairs or decline, in which case, the buyer will probably—but not always—decide *not* to buy.

Several reports are ordered, some by the buyer and others by the buyer's lender, such as:

- A credit report on the buyer—to qualify for the mortgage.
- Verification of the buyer's employment and assets—to qualify for the mortgage.

Sales Snafu

Make sure you bring your driver's license or passport to the closing as a form of picture identification. Some documents require a notary public to verify your signature. Unless you have proof of your identity on hand, you may not be able to close.

- Title report on your home—to confirm there are no encumbrances, or claims, to the property by outside parties.

- Appraisal of the property—to estimate the current market value as part of the mortgage approval process. The lender wants to be sure the amount of the mortgage is no more than a certain percentage of the home's value—in some cases, 80 percent is the limit, in others, as much as 90 to 95 percent. This appraisal provides that part of the equation.

The buyer's lender will also check on the current mortgage on your home, assuming you have one, and any liens against the property.

More for Your Attorney

After the buyer's financing has been officially approved, the lender will notify you or your attorney. While selling your home without an agent is a smart way to save a lot of money, you really need an attorney to oversee all the paperwork that is being generated.

Many attorneys charge a flat fee to handle a simple real estate closing for a seller, and it would be nearly impossible to avoid a major screw-up without one. Take some time to ask for referrals for a good real estate attorney to represent you. Of course, it's better if you have one lined up from the start, so the closing isn't delayed, but if you don't, take a day or two now to hire one.

Some of the best ways to find an attorney include:

◆ Asking real estate agents for some recommendations

◆ Asking your banker for suggestions

◆ Asking friends and neighbors who have recently moved

◆ Asking any attorney friends and colleagues for names

◆ Using Google to identify local real estate attorneys

After you've identified the attorney who will coordinate the closing, you can direct her to schedule needed meetings and to oversee the processing of the paperwork. The buyer's attorney and mortgage lender are doing most of the work as far as paper generation goes, but your attorney needs to check in to make sure no problems have arisen that will interfere with your planned closing date.

If you hire an attorney, it's her job to handle the number crunching. On top of the cost of your home, minus the earnest money deposit the buyer made (which is generally one percent of the purchase price), your attorney will calculate:

◆ Prorated taxes. Most likely you've only lived in your home part of the year, so you only owe taxes for that period.

◆ Prorated utilities, such as water and sewer bills

◆ Prorated condo or homeowners association fees

◆ Prorated rental income, if the property has rental units

Tools of the Trade

A **mortgage payoff** is the current amount you owe on your mortgage as of the closing date, plus any interest or administrative charges for the closing. If the closing date is close to your mortgage payment due date, you may not be required to make a payment that month. Check with your attorney to see what they advise.

- Real estate agent commissions, if any, such as if you agreed to pay the buyer's broker's fee

- Your *mortgage payoff* amount, to determine how much money you will receive at closing or how much you still owe your lender

- Transfer taxes, which counties charge when real estate is sold

- Any additional closing costs, such as your attorney's fee, the lender's attorney's fee, title fees, title insurance costs, and recording fees

Fortunately, your attorney will do 99 percent of the work required to be ready for closing.

FSBO Facts

Because property and school taxes are billed in advance, you've prepaid for the upcoming year. If you don't end up living in the home for the full year, you're entitled to a credit for that unused time, essentially. A prorated amount means you are only charged for the time you spent in the home. The buyer will effectively reimburse you for the taxes you've already paid at closing.

Where to Hold a Closing and Who Has to Be There

Although a closing can occur anywhere, it frequently takes place at the buyer's or seller's attorney's office. Other possible locations for all the paper signing are the real estate agent's office, the lender's office, the escrow company's office, or the title insurance company's office.

At a "round table closing," the buyer and seller complete their documentation simultaneously. At an "escrow closing," they sign on the dotted line at different times.

When the buyer and seller sign their documents at different times, the closing is called an escrow closing because the seller frequently does not receive a check for the proceeds of the sale on the same day. However, at a round table closing, where all parties are seated at the table for settlement, the seller receives the sales proceeds at the end of the meeting.

Although most states require the buyer attend the closing in person, the seller generally has the option to complete the required paperwork in advance. In addition to the buyer, the seller's attorney, if they have one, is also present. In some cases, the buyer's attorney will attend, as well as the real estate agent, and even the lender's attorney.

Don't be overwhelmed if you have a full house at the closing. The process is the same and it should still only take a couple of hours at most until you're done.

Power of Attorney Pluses

Anyone who is listed on your home's title and deed needs to be available to sign the closing documents—if not, the closing will have to be rescheduled and paperwork reissued.

Make sure in advance that everyone will be there at the appointed day, or make arrangements for a *Special Power of Attorney*, which permits someone to sign on the missing person's behalf. This can be an issue if you own the property with someone else, such as a parent, sibling, or ex-spouse, who doesn't live in the area.

Tools of the Trade

In cases where an individual is not available, or unable, to sign legal paperwork, a document called a **Special Power of Attorney** can be filed, which grants permission to one individual to sign on behalf of another. That permission to represent the other individual in legal dealings is limited to specific circumstances, but makes it possible for out-of-town sellers, for instance, to sign closing documents from afar and mail them in for the closing.

With a power of attorney completed and filed, you can be sunning yourself in Tahiti during the closing while your attorney or someone else representing you fills in. That's the major advantage—convenience.

And other than the hassle of filing the appropriate paperwork and having it notarized, there are few downsides. The person to whom you've given power of attorney is your substitute document signer, but nothing more. And their signatory power is limited to this particular transaction; they can't go out and buy a new car, for example, making you liable.

Grab a Pen! Documents You'll Be Signing and Why

Although every transaction is different and may require a few other documents, as the seller, the primary documents you'll be signing at closing include:

- ◆ The settlement statement

- ◆ A bill of sale for the transfer of ownership of any personal property with the real estate sale

- ◆ The contract to purchase

- ◆ The deed, which transfers the property's title from you to the buyer

- ◆ An affidavit of title, which states you have the right to sell the property

- ◆ An affidavit regarding mechanic's liens, in which you state you have not had any work done on the property that could result in a mechanic's lien, such as a major construction project, and that you are the sole person, or people, who own it

Selling Smarts

Call your utility company ahead of time to arrange having the electricity turned off on the day you move out so you're not charged when you're not living there. If it's warm enough, you can also have your gas or oil supply shut off, but if it's winter, don't—just request a final reading. Keep the heat going so the pipes don't freeze and burst.

- ◆ A certificate of occupancy, which demonstrates the home is approved for occupancy

- ◆ Any documents related to the payoff of any existing mortgage(s)

- ◆ A closing document spelling out all the various costs and fees associated with the transaction, indicating you were informed of the costs involved beforehand

- ◆ Name affidavits in which you certify that you are the owner of the home

The buyer will be signing similar documents, as well as financing-related paperwork, which includes:

- ◆ Settlement statement

- ◆ Compliance agreement

- ◆ Mortgage/Deed of Trust

- ◆ Note

- ◆ Truth in Lending statement
- ◆ Survey affidavit
- ◆ Final Good Faith Estimate
- ◆ Interest statement
- ◆ Notice of right to cancel
- ◆ Name affidavits
- ◆ Occupancy affidavit
- ◆ IRS forms

In a nutshell, your papers have to do with transferring ownership of the property, while the buyer's pile of documents involves receiving ownership and possession of the home, as well as a promise to repay any financing he has arranged.

The Deed

In exchange for the agreed-upon purchase price, you will sign over title—or ownership—of your home. This is called a deed. The deed specifies exactly what your property includes, as described by a series of measurements. For instance, the deed details how long and wide your lot is, where it is in relation to other main roads, and more, which can come in handy if you, or the buyer, ever have a dispute over property lines.

Payoff Information—the Mortgage, Note, Etc.

The buyer will be signing a note promising to repay any financing he has arranged. In some states, the buyer signs a mortgage, which is a document pledging the property as collateral for the loan; in other states, the same document is called a Deed of Trust.

In addition to the statement showing your mortgage payoff and any closing expenses you are responsible for paying, as the seller, you will also receive a statement from your attorney regarding credits you are entitled to. These may include:

- ◆ Prepaid taxes, including school, property, and any other local assessments
- ◆ Prepaid utilities, or a credit for oil left in the oil tank
- ◆ Prepaid homeowners insurance
- ◆ Prepaid condo or association fees, if you live in a co-op, townhouse, or condominium that has such charges

Be sure and check over these figures carefully to make sure you're receiving all the credits you're entitled to. Mistakes don't happen often, but they do happen.

Can You Change Your Mind?

The short answer to whether you can change your mind is, "yes." Certainly, if you are having any doubts about your interest in selling your home, speak up immediately. The sooner you reveal your misgivings, the better for everyone. In most states, you also have a three-day grace period during which you can back out of the deal, even if the paperwork has all been signed. However, keep in mind that backing out of the deal could come at a cost.

For instance, if you decide after receiving an offer that you don't want to sell, you can simply reject the offer. You may still be liable to a real estate agent for his work in locating a buyer, if you've previously agreed to pay such fees, but you won't be required to sell your home.

However, if you sign a Purchase and Sale Agreement and the closing date is fast approaching, it will be a bit more difficult—meaning costly—to back out. The buyer may also have grounds to sue you for any expenses he incurred while preparing to buy your home, as well as for the inconvenience of breaking a contract.

And if you arrive at closing and suddenly decide you don't want to sell, you may or may not be able to get out of the contract, depending on which state you are in. Even if you are permitted to cancel the contract on the spot, reimbursing the buyer for their expenses may make it cost prohibitive to walk away. At that point, they could sue for all of their closing expenses, which can be tens of thousands of dollars, as well as moving and relocation expenses they incurred. Not to mention hardship. Yes, you may be allowed to cancel the contract, but you may not be able to afford to, quite frankly.

Dealing With Snafus

With so many individual steps, and schedules needing coordination for the final closing, problems and miscommunication can sometimes arise. To reduce the chance of a delay or hiccup, stay in regular contact with your attorney to be sure everything is moving along smoothly. She is your contact with the other parties involved.

Because your paperwork is a much lighter load than the buyer's, problems are more likely to arise on their end, not yours. For instance, they may have trouble qualifying for the mortgage they need, which would slow down or cancel the contract—which is another reason to require buyers be "pre-approved" for a mortgage before you accept their offer.

Or perhaps the closing date on the sale of the buyer's home gets pushed back, forcing your closing to be rescheduled so they will have the proceeds available to afford to buy your house.

In some rare instances, problems can come up at closing, for instance, if documents have been prepared with the wrong information. If you find this, by all means, *do not sign the contracts*. Have them corrected before you agree to sign them.

In 99.9 percent of these cases, the problem can be resolved. The closing date gets rescheduled for the next day, or a couple days later. In other cases, if a closing gets pushed up so early that you're not ready to move out, you can ask for a lease-back clause from the buyer that permits you to remain in your home for a certain period of time for which you credit them at closing. There is almost always a solution that will permit the sale to occur, but turn to your attorney for guidance on what makes the most sense for you and what best protects your rights.

Online Closing Resources

An attorney is a valuable advisor in the home sale process, so check all your options before settling on one. These directories are great starting points for locating a lawyer in your area who specializes in real estate transactions:

- ◆ www.lawyers.com. Another online directory of national attorneys you can search. You'll want to follow up with your own research to determine their reputation and areas of expertise.

- ◆ www.martindale.com. This online directory from Martindale-Hubbell is a great resource for finding local attorneys to handle your closing (see the following figure).

- ◆ www.ForSaleByOwner.com/attorneys. You can find a directory of local real estate attorneys who frequently work with FSBO sellers here.

Search this national data-base by name, geographic location, or specialty to find potential real estate attorneys qualified to assist you.

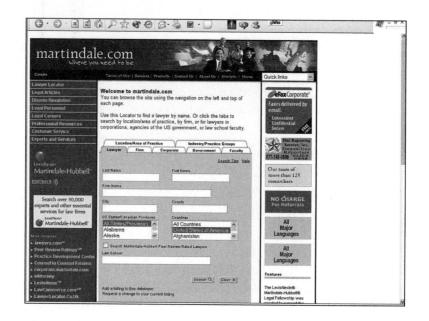

The Least You Need to Know

◆ After you and the buyer have signed a Purchase and Sale Agreement, the closing process begins and will take about 30 to 45 days to complete. The closing itself is usually a two-hour meeting in which your hand will cramp from the number of times you have to sign your name.

◆ To avoid problems with closing on time, stay in close contact with your attorney, who will be monitoring the situation closely.

◆ You and the buyer may sign the paperwork separately, or you may sign them in the presence of one another. The only real difference is that unless you sign them together, you generally won't walk out of the closing with a check for the sale proceeds in your hand.

◆ Immediately following the closing, all the signed documents are recorded at your local courthouse, and ownership of your home transfers to the buyer.

◆ If either you or the buyer decides part-way through the process to back out, you can halt the closing proceedings, but it will be expensive. The buyer will lose his deposit and maybe more, and you may open yourself up to a lawsuit.

Chapter

Now That You're Done— Tax Time!

In This Chapter

- ◆ Capital gains checklist
- ◆ IRS reporting do's and don'ts
- ◆ Tax deferral options
- ◆ Expert help when you need it

Taxes on profits from a home sale used to be a major concern for home-owners, with the IRS claiming a portion of any appreciation. Fortunately, Congress passed the Taxpayer Relief Act in 1997, which effectively allows tax-free capital gains of up to $500,000 per couple, or $250,000 for single homeowners, on the sale of a primary residence. That's good news for most homeowners because the average home price in the United States is only slightly above $250,000, at $264,540, according to the Federal Housing Finance Board, as of October 2004. This means you may be able to pocket most if not all of any gains on your home sale.

Of course, there are a bunch of conditions and caveats we'll run through in this chapter to make sure you qualify. And if the price of your home exceeds the $250,000/$500,000 limit, you may still be able to postpone paying taxes on any capital gains. The bottom line is that you may owe less than you expected.

The Tax Impact of a Home Sale

As of 1997, qualifying homeowners receive as much as $500,000 in tax-free capital gains, depending on their filing status. Single taxpayers or married couples filing separately are eligible to exclude up to $250,000 in capital gains from their incomes, while married couples filing jointly can exclude up to $500,000. Being able to earn up to $500,000 in income from the sale of your home, but not have to claim it as such on your tax return, is a nice chunk of change, tax-free.

Unfortunately, if you sold your home at a loss, you can't take a deduction for that loss.

To stay out of tax trouble, it's always a good idea to see what the IRS has to say about the sale of your home (see the following figure). IRS Publication 523 spells out everything you need to know about reporting the sale of your home and is available online at www.irs.gov/publications/p523/ar02.html.

The Internal Revenue Service (IRS) website is an excellent resource for up-to-date information on tax-related issues as well as downloadable publications and forms.

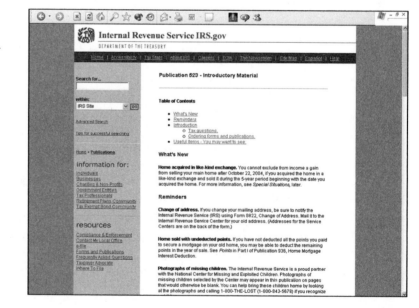

To qualify for this major tax relief, you need to meet three criteria, according to the IRS:

◆ Use. The property must have been your primary residence for at least two of the five years prior to the sale.

◆ Ownership. You must have owned the home at least two of the five years prior to the sale. However, those two years need not be consecutive—a total of at least 730 days or 24 months of ownership qualifies you.

◆ Timing. You must not have taken the same exclusion on a home sale within the last two years.

Each of these criterion are discussed in the sections that follow.

Use

Your main home or primary residence may be a house, or it could be a houseboat, mobile home, co-op, or condo, according to the IRS. In most cases, however, vacant land does not qualify because you likely resided (ate and slept) somewhere else. And if you own more than one home, you'll need to determine where you spend more of your time—that is typically your main home from the IRS's perspective.

But in addition to how much time you spend in a particular home, also consider the following when trying to sort out which place is your primary residence:

◆ Where you work and how far it is from each property

◆ Where your immediate family lives

◆ Which address you use for bills and correspondence

◆ Which address you use for official documents, such as tax returns, your driver's license, and car registration

◆ Where your primary banks are located

◆ Where religious organizations and private clubs you belong to are located

Choosing which home to designate as your main home is important because you can only exclude taxes on capital gains on the sale of your main home. So if you are fortunate enough to also own a beach home, a summer cottage, or deer camp, for example, you'll face paying taxes on any profit if they are not also your main home. But don't feel too bad—at least you have a beach home, summer cottage, or deer camp to enjoy!

After determining which property is your main home, you need to verify that you've spent at least two of the last five years living there. It doesn't have to be the last two, specifically, but 24 of the last 60 months need to have been there.

> ### FSBO Facts
>
> If you've sold a home you inherited, rather than purchased, the basis is generally the fair market value at the time the previous owner died. Appraisals are typically done as part of the probate process, to establish a price, and you should be able to refer back to that figure as a starting point. As with any property, if you live in it as your primary residence for at least two years, you can exclude either $250,000 or $500,000 of any gain on the sale, depending on your tax filing status.

Ownership

If you intend to try to take the $500,000 exclusion for married couples, you'll need to be sure that:

◆ You file a joint tax return the same year you take the exclusion—you can't file separately and qualify.

◆ One or both of you own the home.

◆ Both of you have lived in the home.

Only if you meet all three of these criteria can you take the $500,000 capital gains exclusion. However, you may still be able to take the $250,000 exclusion if you own the home as an individual and used it as your primary residence for at least the last two years.

Timing

With the housing boom of the 1990s and early 2000s, savvy home buyers in some markets have been able to sell a home for a tidy profit after owning it for only a couple years—sometimes even less.

Flipping homes, or buying and reselling them shortly thereafter, is perfectly legitimate, but you can't do it more frequently than every two years or you lose the exclusion privilege. You also must live in the home for two years or more in order to qualify.

Special Circumstances

Although the tax relief rules are fairly clear, there are some exceptions you'll want to read through if you didn't qualify based on the initial three tests. You may also qualify for the gain exclusion if:

◆ You and your spouse have divorced and one of you has transferred ownership of the home to the other; whoever is living in the home can count the days the other spouse lived in the home in addition to their own in order to meet the Ownership and Use criteria.

◆ You postponed paying taxes on the sale of a previous home when you bought your current home, you can count the days you lived in your previous home toward the Ownership and Use requirement for your current home.

◆ Your spouse died and you have not remarried before selling your home, you can count the days your spouse owned and lived in the home toward the Ownership and Use criteria.

And even if you didn't qualify for the full $250,000/$500,000 exclusion, if you sold your home for health, employment, or other unforeseen circumstances, such as if you lost your job or your financial situation changed significantly, you may still qualify for a partial exclusion.

Calculating Your Gain

Now that you know whether or not you qualify to take an exclusion, you're probably wondering how much it's worth to you. That is, what is the capital gain on the sale of your home?

To determine whether you have a gain or a loss on the sale of your home, you need to know two things: the cost of your home and the sale price. When you subtract the cost from the sale price, you get the gain or loss.

While the sale price is pretty simple—it's whatever the buyers agreed to pay you—the cost side of the equation can get a little tricky. That's because what you paid for your home is only one piece of the puzzle.

In addition to what you originally paid for your home, you'll need to add in the cost of improvements and subtract any credits to get your *adjusted basis*.

Tools of the Trade

Your **adjusted basis** is an accounting of costs you incurred versus monies or credits you received, which determines your capital gain or loss. To arrive at a figure, you must calculate the price you paid for your home plus the cost of any improvements you made, which increases your total cost and lowers any taxable capital gain. You then must subtract any tax credits you've received as well as other items that lowered your overall costs, therefore increasing any taxable capital gain.

The cost of improvements with a useful life of more than a year can be added to your original purchase price, as well as special assessments you paid for local improvements. You can also count money spent to make repairs to your home following major damage, such as the result of an earthquake or ice storm.

Increases to Your Basis

Your basis is the original cost of your home. Some examples of improvement costs that should be added to your basis include:

◆ Additions, such as a bedroom, bathroom, garage, porch, or deck

◆ Heating and air conditioning work, such as a new heating or air conditioning system, a new furnace or duct work, or a central humidifier or filtration system

◆ Plumbing work, including a new septic system, water heater, or filtration system

◆ Renovations, such as a new kitchen, new appliances, or new flooring

◆ Insulation in the attic, walls, or floors

◆ Upgrades or replacements, such as new storm windows or doors, a new roof, central vacuum system, internal wiring upgrades, or a security system

◆ Landscaping work, including new trees and shrubs, an irrigation system, a new driveway or walkway, a fence, or swimming pool

A big exception to the list of improvements is routine upkeep and repair of your home, such as the cost to paint rooms or fix broken window screens. Tackling these jobs doesn't add to the value of your home, they merely help maintain it.

Expenses incurred while selling your home also help to reduce your adjusted basis.

Sales Snafu _____

Be sure you don't double up on some of your credits for improvements. Let's say you've lived in your home for 10 years and, when you moved in, you paid $8,000 to replace all the carpeting. That $8,000 became part of your adjusted basis. But if you replaced the carpeting again, say, right before you sold your home, you can add the cost of the second round of carpet replacements, but you cannot claim the $8,000 you spent the first time. After you replaced the $8,000 carpeting, it is no longer part of your adjusted basis—only the newer carpeting is.

Decreases to Your Basis

After adding in the cost of improvements you've made to your home, you need to be sure you subtract from your basis any tax credits you've received through the years as well as other items that lowered your total costs. These may include:

- Any postponed gains from the sale of a home before May 7, 1997, the date on which the Taxpayer Relief Act was enacted

- Payments you've received for granting an easement or right-of-way

- *Casualty loss* tax deductions

- Insurance payments you have received or expect to receive for casualty losses

- Depreciation allowed if you used your home for business or rental purposes

Tools of the Trade _____

A **casualty loss** is damage that is done to your property due to a "sudden, unexpected, and unusual event," according to the IRS. This includes such disasters as a tornado, flood, hurricane, earthquake, fire, volcanic eruption, ice storm, or tsunami. As a result of such a loss,

- A residential energy credit claimed for the cost of energy improvements made (these were generally allowed between 1977 and 1987)

- An adoption credit you claimed for improvements made

- Nontaxable payments from your employer's adoption assistance program, which aids employees in the process of adopting a child, that you used to make improvements to your home, such as adding another bedroom or bath

- A first-time homebuyer credit given to residents of the District of Columbia

◆ An energy conservation subsidy, that you didn't report as taxable income, which you received from a public utility after 1992 to buy or install energy conservation measures

These items need to be subtracted from your home's cost (basis) because you've already received the benefit. Claiming them again is the equivalent of double-dipping.

FSBO Facts

A new IRS ruling in 2005 gave additional relief to the more than 2.5 million homeowners with home offices, as well as others who rent all or part of their homes. Revenue Procedure 2005-14 allows homeowners with a home office or rental space who sell their homes to defer all or part of the capital gain above the $250,000/$500,000 maximum by purchasing a property with at least as much commercial space within 180 days. Check with your accountant to see if this applies to you.

Doing the Math

Now that you have all the parts of the equation, you can calculate whether you have a gain or a loss on the sale of your home:

Start with the price you paid for your home $_____

Add (+):

◆ Cost of improvements

◆ Payments made for special tax assessments

◆ Cost of repairs made following a casualty loss   _____

Subtract (-):

◆ Depreciation for business use of your home

◆ Energy credits

◆ Payments for easements or rights-of-way

◆ Insurance payments for casualty losses

◆ Adoption credits

- ◆ First-time homebuyer credits
- ◆ Energy conservation subsidies   _____

Total (=):

- ◆ Your adjusted basis $_____

Should You Take the Exclusion?

In most cases, it makes perfect financial sense to claim the capital gains exclusion you're entitled to and pocket the cash you made from the sale. But there are a couple circumstances under which you may want to skip the exclusion.

1. If you expect to sell another, more expensive, home in the next two years and want to save the exclusion for that property.

2. If you and your spouse each own a home and want to sell both the same year. If one had higher capital gains than the other, you might want to take the $500,000 on one, assuming you are filing jointly, and not take the exclusion on the other.

Sales Snafu _____

Rather than take a chance that your tax return is incorrect, if you have a question, call the Taxpayer Advocate at the IRS at *877-777-4778* directly. It's better to clarify anything that you're unsure of now, than to be audited later and hit with penalties for an error.

If you take the exclusion and have no gains above the $250,000/$500,000 cap, you do not need to report the sale on your tax return. You only need to report the sale if your gains exceeded the maximum allowable OR if you didn't take the exclusion and need to report all of the gains.

Partial Exclusion

If you didn't pass all three tests—use, ownership, and timing—required for the maximum exclusion on capital gains, you may still qualify for a partial exclusion, which the IRS calls a "reduced maximum exclusion," if you passed one or two of the tests.

The IRS has a worksheet in Publication 523 to help you calculate how much of an exclusion you are entitled to. Check out part of it in the figure that follows.

IRS Publication 523 includes this helpful worksheet for determining how much of an exclusion you are entitled to.

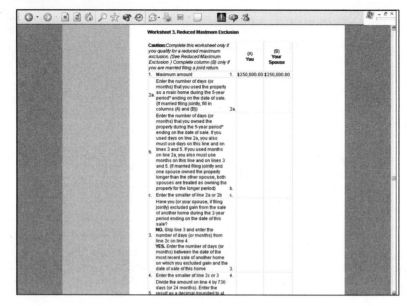

Postponed Gains

Prior to 1997, you had the option to postpone paying gains on the sale of a home. However, if you are now selling that home, you'll need to cough up the tax on those previous gains. Unfortunately, prior gains weren't grandfathered with the new 1997 laws, so you still owe for the previous sale.

Before 1997, you could postpone paying taxes on the sale of your home if you bought a new home within two years that cost at least as much as the adjusted price of the one you sold. But eventually, you'd need to pay the piper—in this case, the IRS.

Other Issues

Although you know you qualify for the exclusion, your attorney, title company, escrow agent, or whoever is completing the closing paperwork may not. To ensure you do not have to report the income, you need to tell the agent or attorney that they do not need to issue a Form 1099-S, Proceeds from Real Estate Transactions because:

- ◆ You owned and lived in your home for at least two of the past five years.

- ◆ You have not sold another property in which you took a gains exclusion during the previous two years.

◆ The home was not used in whole or in part for business or rental purposes. If it was, you'll need to pay taxes on any gain from the portion of the property used for business. So if 10 percent of the building was used as a home office, for instance, you'll have to pay taxes on any gain on the 10 percent.

◆ You are married filing jointly and the gains on the home are less than $500,000 OR you are single and the gains on the home are less than $250,000.

These days, it's rare for attorneys and accountants to issue a 1099-S for the sale of a personal residence. But if you do get one, just ignore it. If the IRS questions you about it later, you can explain that you didn't report the sale because you qualified for the exclusion and it was, therefore, not a taxable event.

FSBO Facts

Although it can be costly, you can also change your mind about taking the exclusion. You have three years from the date your tax return is due from the year of the sale to revoke the exclusion, or to accept it. That means, if you sell your home in 2006, you have three years from April 15, 2007, to accept or revoke the capital gains exclusion, which you'd do by amending your return.

Online Tax Resources

If anything is fuzzy about any taxes owed on the sale of your home, turn to these two websites to help sort them out:

◆ www.irs.gov. When in doubt about the specifics of your situation, it's always best to check with the source. The IRS website has just about everything you need to know about tax issues, including publications, news, FAQs, and forms. You can even get in touch with your local tax office if you don't find the answer you need online.

◆ www.turbotax.com/articles. TurboTax offers a great overview of the tax implications of selling your home in an easy-to-read article, if you want to read more.

The Least You Need to Know

◆ The IRS allows you to keep up to $500,000 in capital gains from the sale of your home tax free if you're married filing a joint tax return, and up to $250,000 if you're single. You do not have to report any of this tax-free income on your tax return.

◆ To qualify for the exclusion, you must meet the use, ownership, and timing tests to confirm you've owned and lived in the home long enough—a minimum of two years.

◆ To calculate your gain or loss on the sale of your home, you'll need to take the price you paid for the home, add the value of improvements you've made through the years, and subtract credits you've earned and taken to arrive at your adjusted basis.

◆ If you have a loss, you cannot deduct it. But if your gain exceeds the $250,000/ $500,000 exclusion, you must report it and pay taxes on it.

◆ You can choose not to take the exclusion, too, which is smart if you plan to sell another home in the next two years with a higher gain than your current one, or if you and your spouse are both selling homes and one has a higher gain where you could apply the $500,000 maximum.

Part 5

The Problem House: The Less Than Perfect Buyer and Other Final Details

Much of what we've covered so far has addressed items that are largely business as usual. As we all know, that's what happens until real life intervenes, so in this part, we talk about some problems that can occur and what you can do about them. We start with the home that, try as you might, just doesn't seem to sell. From there, the problem buyer who, for whatever reason, seems intent on making things as challenging as possible. Next we move on to a common challenge—the business of selling a home and buying another one at roughly the same time. Then we close out with a chapter that we fervently hope you never have to even lay eyes on—when to decide if you may benefit from a real estate agent and, if so, how to find one who's right for you.

Chapter 18

Don't Be Difficult—The House That Just Won't Sell

In This Chapter

◆ Possible reasons offers are scarce

◆ Strategies for drumming up interest

◆ Solutions for common turn-offs

◆ Your fall-back position

Despite your best efforts, it's still possible your home may not sell as quickly as you'd like. It happens. And if it happens to you, take comfort in the fact that you're not alone.

The challenge, of course, is diagnosing what's keeping offers at bay and then fixing them—pronto! And if that doesn't work, there may be some financial inducements you can offer to attract new buyers. Take heart, it's by no means a lost cause. This chapter gives you strategies to help you come up with solutions for selling your home.

What's the Problem?

If you've done everything we've suggested—decluttering, cleaning, rearranging, and brightening—and your home still has the "For Sale By Owner" sign on your lawn weeks after it first went up, it's time to take a long, hard look at what's going on. Is there something about the home that is frightening buyers away?

Interest rates have been low, the housing market has been hot, so unless your particular local real estate market is dead, there may be something buyers are noticing about your home that is turning them off. You haven't noticed it, of course, so it's always a good idea to bring in a friend or two, or some real estate agents, to get a fresh perspective.

Ask what they notice when they come in, what they see as the advantages and disadvantages your home has to offer, and what price they would expect your home to fetch. Then match that up to how you perceive your home. Are the two views in sync, or are your expectations unrealistic?

Things to Do When a House Won't Sell

Depending on what your friends, colleagues, and agents tell you, or what you've heard from buyers who've toured your home, you may be able to quickly identify a problem area, or two, or three. Some of the most common are odors, busy traffic, or a design defect, such as one bathroom in a four bedroom home. But there are others to watch for as well, most of which have at least partial remedies.

De-Clutter and De-Dirt

The most obvious turn-off for prospective buyers is a home that is dirty and cluttered. For one, it raises the question of how well you've maintained the home and whether they'll have problems because you've ignored basic upkeep. Some buyers don't want to take a chance that they'll have to do some big repairs after closing because it appears you're not on top of things. For another, it's hard to see past piles of paper, clothing, and junk to envision the home as anything but messy. And if buyers can't picture themselves living in your home, they'll move on to another one.

The solution, of course, is to further reduce the amount of extra papers, magazines, books, supplies, kitchen tools, toys, and furniture so the home looks bare. Less is more, as they say. If you can't store it somewhere, box it up and put it in storage.

If you're concerned about showing a home that looks nothing like how you live in it, don't be. When buyers are touring a home, they expect to see it at it's best, which may not necessarily be how you've lived in the space the past few years. So do what's necessary to show off your home's best features, even if it seems ridiculous to pack up half your closet of clothes or to remove most of your personal photos.

Get Rid of Odors

Although your countertops may be spotless and your closets super organized, if visitors get a whiff of a noxious odor, they'll be out the door before even getting beyond the front hallway. As someone who has been living in the home, breathing the air regularly, you probably can't detect pet odors, dirty baby diapers, or the smell of tobacco or cigarette smoke. But someone walking through the door for the first time will pick up the scent immediately. If you or someone in the home smokes, you need to try to remove the existing smell that has seeped into carpeting, walls, and furniture. There are a number of easy ways to do that, such as regularly vacuuming the carpeting, cleaning and painting the walls, spraying upholstered furniture with odor remover or freshener, opening all the windows just before a showing or open house, and regularly emptying ashtrays outside. Better yet, move any smoking outdoors, away from the home's living areas.

Long-term smoking indoors will be tough to eliminate, however. You may need to hire a professional smoke residue cleaning service, which can cost anywhere from $1,000 to more than $10,000, to try to rid the home of its smoky scent. But if no one is willing to consider buying your home as it is because of the smell, a few hundred dollars may be all that stands between you and a sale.

Sales Snafu _____

It's become quite common for home sellers to try to win over the noses of buyers by having potpourri simmering on the kitchen stove, warm cookies baking in the oven, or strong coffee percolating, but don't overdo it. A few candles, some flowers, and fresh Pine Sol in the toilet is one thing. Air freshener in every room, candles spread about, coffee brewing, and vinegar strategically placed may make buyers concerned that there's a serious odor problem you're trying to cover up. At the very least, you don't want your home to be so perfumed it turns off buyers.

Fortunately, the smell of dirty diapers is much easier to get rid of—simply dispose of diapers in outdoor garbage cans, rather than indoors, and open some windows to clear out the smell. If the scent lingers, you may need to steam clean the carpeting or do a wipe down of furniture with polish or cleanser to be rid of it.

Pet odors, on the other hand, are tougher. You can steam clean your carpeting to try to get rid of the smell of cat urine, for example, but sometimes it just won't come out. Try pet odor cleansers first, but realize you may be facing a losing battle. Depending on how offensive the odor is, it may be smarter just to pull the carpeting up and put down rugs.

Even if you manage to get the smell out, anyone who is allergic to pets will have a reaction after they walk in the door—smell or no smell. It's the dog and cat dander that causes noses to get stuffy and eyes to water, and besides cleaning religiously, there's not much more you can do. Having a professional carpet cleaning give the home a once-over will certainly help, but don't expect miracles. If you and your cat have lived in your home for the last 15 years, it'll be nearly impossible to erase all traces of your friend. Your best bet is to do a thorough cleaning and then make sure kitty isn't in the building during showings and open houses.

One quick fix is to move any litter boxes somewhere out of the main living area, such as to a garage, if possible. If you can't do that, at least change the litter or paper more frequently, such as daily.

In addition, you can try to mask trace odors with a few scented candles lighted around the home, air freshener sprayed into the air, and using scented cleaning products when you do last-minute cleaning in each room.

Eliminate Extra Noise

Another potential problem homes on busy roads face is noise. Loud street noise or air traffic can be distracting to buyers.

Unless you're prepared to relocate the building, there's little you can do about the noise besides blocking it or covering it up. Soundproofing measures, or adding another layer of drywall or insulation on walls facing the street, can help make the home's interior quieter. Replacing windows and frames can also significantly reduce noise—double-paned glass windows provide a 20 percent improvement over single pane glass, and new vinyl frames can reduce noise up to 50 percent.

In addition, playing soft music inside can also partially drown out the sounds of cars, buses, and overhead planes. Keep windows and doors closed, too, to help reduce outdoor noise.

Too Much Personality

Sometimes the problem with a home is simply decorating style. When the personality of its current owner is overwhelming, or very different from a buyer's, it can be difficult for the buyer to imagine the home as their own. For example, bold colors, lots of personal photos, or unusual artwork can be a buyer turnoff.

Yes, there is probably a buyer out there who would love your place just as it is, but unless you're willing to wait it out, hoping that such a buyer happens to be looking for a home in your neighborhood, you'd be smarter to make your place more neutral. Neutral appeals to a wider cross-section of buyers.

To neutralize your place, you'll want to consider painting your walls and trim a shade of white or off-white—don't go bright white though because it's jarring. Paint will make the biggest difference, and you may not need to do anything else.

However, if you have a lot of bright upholstery and fabrics, you can tone them down with slipcovers or solid color throws. Take down wall hangings and remove personal mementos. You're going for an almost sterile appearance. Let buyers envision their own belongings in the rooms, rather than being overwhelmed by yours.

Uninvited Guests

If your home happens to be inhabited by ghosts, or it has been stigmatized by a murder, suicide, or illness, you may find it will take longer to sell. Two business professors at Wright State University studied 100 such "psychologically impacted" homes and found they take about 50 percent longer to sell, for an average of 2.4 percent less than comparable homes in the area. The impact of an event is also greatly affected by how much media exposure it has received. A well-publicized murder, for instance, can reduce a home's

> **FSBO Facts**
>
> State rules regarding disclosure of ghosts, murders, suicides, natural deaths, or felonies varies widely. In some states you are required to alert potential buyers to such events while in other states there is no such requirement. Check first with your attorney to learn what your particular state demands you tell buyers about your home's past.

value by 15 to 35 percent, the professors report, for up to 5 to 7 years. After that, however, the stigma begins to subside.

Fortunately, not everyone is turned off by the prospect of living side-by-side with the supernatural—some might even be more attracted to such a home. You may want to try to get a sense of how a buyer feels about ghosts to know how to break the news.

Design Issues

Sometimes a home stays on the market because of a perceived design defect, such as a lone bathroom in a four-bedroom home, or the lack of an attached garage. There's little you can do to fix this, unless you want to hire a contractor and shell out thousands of dollars, but you may be able to highlight the possibilities as a way to help buyers see beyond the current situation.

One family we know that lives in a warm climate owned an older home without central air conditioning. Many homes in the area featured central air, so their lack of it stood out to buyers touring the home. But instead of forging ahead to have the A/C installed, which would have taken three weeks and $15,000, they gathered quotes from local contractors regarding what it would take to have the home converted. When visitors expressed interest in the home, the information about the option to install central air was presented. They showed buyers that although the home didn't currently have air conditioning, it could, and they priced it accordingly. The home sold.

The same approach could be used to help buyers see beyond a home's current layout. Collecting quotes from contractors or architects regarding adding a bathroom, adding a bedroom, expanding the kitchen, building over the garage, or finishing the basement, for instance, may help buyers see the home's potential.

Too Many Contingencies

It's very possible that there is nothing wrong with your home and that it is priced appropriately, but you have too many *contingencies* on the sale.

If buyers seem to like your home but don't end up making an offer, take a look at your list of contingencies to see if there's a way to remove, or at least limit, them. If you won't be able to move into your home for several months, for instance, and you want to continue to live in your existing home after closing, that may be a major deterrent to someone being relocated into your city—they may not be able to wait months for a home.

Tools of the Trade

A **contingency** is a condition placed on a sale. Common contingencies are a buyer's offer to purchase a home contingent on the sale of their existing home, or securing a mortgage. On the seller's side, a contingency could be when the home will be available for occupancy by the buyer or the buyer's assumption of all their closing costs.

Consider eliminating your contingencies as a way to interest buyers on a fast track to a purchase.

Not Affordable

A more common problem with homes on the market is an overly optimistic asking price. Especially in fast appreciating housing markets, some sellers price their home on the high side as a test. Unfortunately, after a home has been listed at a price that's well beyond its market value, it may take several price drops before it sells.

If you're committed to selling your home for a fair price, be extremely familiar with what comparable homes in your area have recently sold for—*recently* being the key word. What homes sold for a year or two ago is irrelevant today. Look at what homes have sold for in the last three months as a better guide. Be able to explain to buyers why you set the price at the level you did.

If you think you've priced it fairly and can't come down much in price without losing money, you have a couple of options—they won't get you money in the short-term, but may help prevent you from losing your shirt. One is offering the home as a lease with an option to buy and the other is renting it.

Leasing your home with an option to buy it after a specified period of time has a number of advantages. One is that you get a tenant who may have a greater interest in the upkeep of the home because he or she may end up buying it. Another is that you can charge an up front fee for the option, or add it into the monthly rent. Even if the renter later decides not to buy, you get to keep the extra cash you've collected.

FSBO Facts
Real estate prices nationwide rose an average of 11 percent in 2004, according to the Office of Federal Housing Enterprise Oversight, but then started to level off in 2005. Markets that have seen double-digit growth the last few years may start to see appreciation slow down considerably.

Turning your home into a rental can be tricky, depending on the neighborhood. If you're in an area with a lot of rentals already, it may be better to sell now at a small loss than to get stuck with a home that has a better chance of depreciating than appreciating in value. However, if you're in a decent area, you may be able to charge higher than average rents—enough to cover your mortgage—especially if you have new executives moving into the area in need of short-term housing.

Timing Is Everything

Although a home's price has the biggest impact on buyers, another big factor is when the home goes on the market. Putting your home up for sale when many folks are beginning to look will significantly improve the odds of it selling. It's a numbers game.

Pick your best season to sell, if you can. If you live in the northeast, early spring is when most buyers start looking, whereas late spring is the proper time to go house hunting in the Midwest. Late fall is when buyers are hot to purchase in Florida, before the snow flies, that is, just like in South Texas.

If you live in Vermont or Maine, putting your home on the market in January or February, when there are several inches of snow on the ground, may limit the number of potential buyers to bold folks who are relocating and simply have to find a home, no matter what the weather. Waiting until the snow melts will likely increase the number of people interested in seeing your place.

Likewise, it's tougher to sell homes in hotter climates during the scorching summer sun. Some people leave the area during that time and fewer people are looking to move in then. Wait until the area is hopping again, when it cools off, to put your home on the market, if you can.

The time of year you choose to make your home available for sale can affect the number of offers you receive and, therefore, how close they come to your asking price. If you've had difficulty selling your home, it may simply be that it's not the best season.

Drop the Price? How Much? How Often?

If your home is on the market beyond when you thought it would sell, don't panic. Being in a hurry to sell can only push you to accept a lower offer than you might otherwise, which may not be in your best interest.

Of course, if you've priced it reasonably to begin with, you're less likely to need to drop the price later. If you've priced it high in the hopes of landing an eager buyer, when you drop the price weeks later, buyers will assume it was overpriced to begin with. They'll assume that it still is. The situation becomes like a price war, where customers just sit back and wait for the price to bottom out. If you've dropped the price once, it may be hard not to do it again.

Instead of starting too high and having to reduce the price later, simply set the price in line with what other area homes have sold for to begin with and you'll sell much quicker—probably for more than if you listed it high and had to reduce it. You may even get into a bidding war with interested buyers that drives UP the price!

When you set your price, also determine your lowest acceptable selling price. The difference between your asking price and your minimum selling price will help you decide when to reduce the price and by how much.

In general, you'll want to have your home on the market for at least three to four weeks, depending on the activity in your local housing market, before you consider reducing your asking price. Of course, this is a guideline and will vary according to how desperate you are to sell and whether you're in a *buyer's* or *seller's market*.

The amount by which you drop the price really depends on how far away you are from asking prices of comparable homes in your area. If most homes are selling for between $250,000 and $280,000, for instance, and yours is currently listed at $320,000, you may want to drop it to under $300,000, such as $298,000, to bring it more in line with what's been selling.

Tools of the Trade

When a housing market is deemed a **seller's market,** there are more buyers than there are homes—finding a home available for sale is tougher. In a **buyer's market,** there are many homes on the market, some that have been there for months, and they are in a strong negotiating position—meaning they can often buy for less than the asking price.

In general, around five percent is considered a standard percentage by which to reduce the asking price.

On the other hand, if your home is priced at $255,000 in the same market, you'll want to drop it far less, such as to $249,000, unless you've identified a glaring problem with the home that would further reduce its value.

Of course, some homeowners elect not to drop the price—ever. Instead, they keep the house on the market for many weeks, hoping the right buyer will come along who is willing to pay their asking price. Some ultimately take the home off the market and decide to stay.

Others pull the home off the market temporarily, to try to get rid of its stale reputation, and then put it back on a few weeks later, when a whole new crop of buyers are looking. If you decide to go this route, seriously consider dropping the price when you try to sell it again. The combination of the home being a new listing again with a more reasonable price may be just what you need to snare a buyer.

Online Problem House Resources

For help in finding the tools or services you need to improve your home's attractiveness to buyers, visit these websites:

- ◆ www.extremesoundproofing.com. If you like do-it-yourself projects, you may want to take a look at the soundproofing products this company offers.
- ◆ www.servicemaster.com/library/tips/disaster/fireSmoke.dsp. Tips for reducing smoke residue in your home, as well as what not to do to make the situation worse.
- ◆ www.pureayre.com/pet-odors.htm. One do-it-yourself product for pet odor elimination is described here, but there are many on the market.
- ◆ www.airfiltrationsolutions.com. To help reduce airborne particles, such as smoke and other odors, you may want to investigate a residential filtration system, such as those featured at this website.

The Least You Need to Know

- ◆ If your home has been on the market far longer than other homes in your area, it's time to get an outsider's perspective on what's wrong. Ask friends, neighbors, and real estate agents over for a tour and get their honest opinion regarding what's holding buyer's back.
- ◆ Except for design challenges, such as a tiny kitchen, or paranormal residents, there are plenty of things you can do to address perceived negatives.
- ◆ Eliminating contingencies, such as the date of possession, for example, can help interest buyers who were scared away by the additional terms of sale.
- ◆ Price your home appropriately at the outset—within the range of prices received for comparable homes in your area—to avoid pricing yourself out of the market.
- ◆ Remember that it only takes one serious buyer to make a sale.

Chapter **19**

The Problem Buyer

In This Chapter

- ◆ Yes, maybe, I don't know—The uncommitted buyer
- ◆ The buyer who won't tell all
- ◆ Dealing with the buyer who wants it all
- ◆ When to say enough is enough

Selling your home means you're going to run into all sorts of people. Some will be so mellow you'll wonder if they're even awake, while others will display an intensity that could saw steel in half. Hopefully, when you hook up with a buyer willing to buy your home, you'll be lucky enough to land somewhere in the middle—someone who's intent and committed but reasonable enough to respect the needs of others and the overall importance of seeing the sale through to a successful conclusion.

Notice we used the word *lucky*, because sometimes things don't work out that way. You will likely discover that not every buyer is ideal in every way—often, to be frank, rather flawed and hard to deal with.

Our sympathies. If you're reading this chapter, it's likely you've just hooked up with the "problem buyer"—one who, for whatever reason, comes across as intent on making things as needlessly difficult and unpleasant as possible—regardless of whether they intend to or whether they're even aware of their behavior.

But we've got you covered. In this chapter, we discuss the various types of problem buyers, the ways they can wreak mischief on the sales process, and effective ways for you to cope with their behavior.

What Next? The Prospective Buyer Who Won't Commit

Next time you have to hang around a car dealership for a while—say, your car is in for repairs—pay attention to shoppers in the showroom or out on the lot. If you look long enough, you're likely to spot a buyer who just cannot seem to make up his mind. There are all sorts of classic signs—he may circle the car repeatedly like a bird unsure of where to land. Perhaps he'll kick the tires several times or peer under the hood in a vain attempt to suggest he has the slightest notion of what he's doing. Whatever you see, you'll notice that he's going to great pains not to talk to the salesperson or, even worse, make a decision at all.

Unfortunately, there are buyers like this in the world of home selling as well—those who seem interested but, for whatever reason, just can't seem to make the call on whether or not they really want to buy your home. Like the car shopper, they can display some classic signs—maybe they come back repeatedly to look at the house, or maybe they ask for the same details and information over and over.

To a certain degree, that's both natural and expected. After all, buying a home is a huge financial commitment, one that should never be entered into lightly. With that in mind, you should be prepared to accept and deal with a certain degree of hesitancy and, on occasion, downright fear.

Sales Snafu _____

One strategy to nudge a hesitant buyer toward a commitment is to ask what other type of information they may need to help them reach a decision. Sometimes, the information they need may be completely new, such as proximity to a particular shopping area or place of worship that hasn't been covered. On the other hand, you may find yourself repeating old news that you know the buyer knows as well. Go with the flow—sometimes, a buyer has to hear certain things more than once before it really sinks in.

Hesitancy is only a problem when it crosses a certain line—when, in effect, a buyer's hesitancy becomes an impediment to selling your home as efficiently as possible. Warnings signs can include:

♦ You're spending too much time with this one buyer to the detriment of time with others who may be much more willing to commit.

♦ The buyer asks you not to accept any offers until he makes up his mind. He may go so far as to offer a small deposit to "hold" the house for him.

♦ The buyer keeps insisting an offer is on its way—except nothing ever actually arrives.

Countless other examples exist, but you get the picture. Maybe the buyer can't make up his mind, or perhaps he's over-reaching—expressing unrealistic interest in homes he can't possibly afford.

Selling Smarts

Loan preapproval can be an invaluable tool in helping you determine just how serious a hesitant buyer really is. With preapproval, at least you know the buyer is financially positioned to afford your home. This tells you the cold feet are coming from somewhere else. Check out a sample pre-approval form at www.yourloanhelper.com.

The problem, too, is that a hesitant buyer today may be a committed buyer tomorrow. You certainly don't want to run the risk of somehow discouraging or alienating someone who may be a few moments away from deciding on an offer.

It's important you have an effective strategy for dealing with hesitant buyers so you don't run the risk of getting tied down by someone who, in reality, isn't likely to buy your home. Here are a few tips:

♦ Never accept any money to take the house off the market unless it's a bona fide offer.

♦ Be upfront with a buyer who seems unwilling to move toward a commitment and is becoming a pest. Provide the information they need, but make it clear you'll accept any other competitive offers that may come in. In other words, let her knowing the house may be gone by the time she's ready to act.

♦ If in doubt, find out whether a buyer has been preapproved for a loan sufficient to buy your house. If he hasn't been, that's a red flag telling you he may be unable to afford your house and your time may be better spent elsewhere.

◆ If you know a buyer is financially capable of buying your home, follow the suggestion we made earlier in the chapter. Try to help the buyer identify what is holding him back from a decision. Sometimes, a little more information or just some reassurance may be all he needs.

◆ Finally, never downplay the problem a hesitant buyer poses. They waste your valuable time, get your hopes up, and divert your physical and emotional energy. Be polite and helpful, but never lose sight of your own interests.

It can be exceedingly helpful to break down a buyer's objections into smaller, more manageable issues. As we suggested in Chapter 11, a buyer who feels your home is $10,000 more than he can afford—even though his loan approval says otherwise—may be swayed if he hears that $10,000 boils down to a mere $59 a month on a 30-year mortgage at 6 percent interest. That's not even a night out in most cities.

I'm Shy—The Buyer Who Won't Disclose

We've stressed throughout this book the importance of knowing whether, in fact, a buyer can afford to buy your home. All other things being equal, nothing is really more essential. And that means financial disclosure—either through loan preapproval or by thoroughly documenting their capacity to buy the property.

That naturally leads us to the next type of problem buyer—the buyer who is shy about disclosing necessary financial details.

The problem here is that, to a certain extent, it's a very understandable reaction. For one thing, many people are exceedingly private about their financial lives—particularly when it comes to a complete stranger, which you likely are. Maybe they're nervous they won't be financially positioned to buy your home, even though they may, in fact, be perfectly qualified. Perhaps they are worried some financial problem from the past will prove both embarrassing and destructive to their hope of buying your home.

Whatever the reason, you may hear any number of things other than the financial specifics you're going to need. Maybe they say everything is okay, don't worry. By the same token, they may tell you they're very much at the beginning of their house hunt and haven't reached the financial stage yet.

Should you take that as a warning sign? Maybe, maybe not. As we said, some people just aren't keen on being that forthcoming. But there is always the chance their finances are not up to par in some way or another. Or by the same token, they may be hoping to get them back in shape before the time comes to show a financial commitment.

First rule of thumb: Bear in mind that, sooner or later, the buyer is going to have to tell you about how he intends to buy your home, provided they're serious. No way around it.

With that in mind, it's a reasonable course not to pay too much attention to a buyer who doesn't want to pass along financial details right away. Put your energy into other prospective buyers who are more upfront. If you want, only deal seriously with buyers who are preapproved for a sufficient size loan. That way, you don't have to guess whether they have the necessary funds.

Selling Smarts _____

Think a buyer who says he's preapproved—even as he waves an official-looking letter around—is really preapproved? One source contacted for this book offers an adamant "no." She urges all FSBOs to double check the legitimacy of preapproval. Look up the lender in the phone book or online. Call them or visit a real live office to confirm whether your buyer is, in fact, preapproved.

Why all the suspicion? Our source tells us she has known of many instances where a buyer faked preapproval—even going so far as to draft phony letters or have a friend at the other end of the phone line pose as a loan officer. The reasons can vary. Some people may simply get a kick out of feeling like they pulled one over on someone else. Others—a bit more legitimate—may be hoping to pull their real finances together while posing like qualified buyers so you stay interested.

It may seem a bit overblown, but it certainly never hurts to double check whether your buyer has genuine financial documents—just to make certain you're not wasting your valuable time and energy.

But if a buyer seems genuinely interested, you can always try to help him overcome his reticence to share financials. Here are some ideas:

- Ask if he's working with a bank or other lending institution. Ask his permission to contact them for financial details. If he's interested in your home—and that interest is genuine—he shouldn't object.

- Ask if your lawyer can contact his attorney, if he has one. Sometimes, people are more comfortable sharing financial details if their lawyer is involved.

- Make a particular effort to point out the financial summary you've prepared about your home. An overview of cost, property taxes, and other details may offer a subtle hint that, sometime soon, the buyer is going to need to prove to you that he can handle those sorts of numbers.

♦ Don't give him free reign. Like the buyer who's unwilling or incapable of making up his mind, be polite and thorough in your dealing with him, but at some point, let him know things simply are not going to move any further until he can prove his financial standing.

The Nitpicky Buyer—What You Should and Should Not Have to Do

There are some buyers who seem as though they wouldn't be able to decide whether or not to get out of the way of a speeding truck. And as we've seen, there's another buyer—shy as a newborn when it comes to sharing details that are central to moving ahead and completing the sale.

Then there's a third type of buyer, one who is every bit as frustrating and hard to deal with—the nitpicky buyer. This is the buyer who wants everything, just the way he wants it, and he wants it yesterday—until tomorrow, of course, when he'll change his mind and demand something else.

Granted, this kind of behavior can show up to a greater or lesser degree depending on the buyer. And to a certain extent, it's to be expected. After all, we're talking about a transaction of significant financial impact. Every one of us, within reason, has the right to expect certain things from a deal of that magnitude.

The key phrase there is "within reason." This is a characteristic that's in short supply with the nitpicky buyer. They have no sense of compromise or give and take. They want the house on *their* terms and no one else's. They demand things happen at the precise moment they demand they happen. Moreover, because things rarely hit on all cylinders at once during each phase of the sales process, they complain every step of the way and point fingers at everyone but themselves.

The problems with the nitpicky buyer are varied but no less destructive. First of all, they're only concerned about themselves, not about getting the deal done in a fair and equitable manner. Moreover, they can be grossly unrealistic in their expectations—every minor problem or issue that needs to be addressed is blown out of proportion. Not only can that threaten the entire deal, if nothing else, it makes an already challenging process unnecessarily stressful.

One classic sign of a nitpicky or unreasonable buyer is a habit of asking to talk with you or see your home at odd hours—say, early in the morning or late at night. Of course, these requests are rarely accompanied by any sort of apology for putting you out.

On the surface, not getting involved with a buyer whose manner and expectations are unreasonable seems the most commonsense choice. The problem is, many such buyers are often the ones with the best financial muscle. If you think about it, it stands to reason—for instance, if a buyer has the cash to buy a home outright, he has the leverage to demand more than he would if his position weren't so strong.

Selling Smarts _____

Keep in mind the risks of bad faith bargaining when dealing with nitpicky buyers. We mentioned this in Chapter 11—negotiating without a genuine intention of closing the deal. If you turn down legitimate offers from someone just because you think they're too demanding, it could lead to charges of bad faith bargaining—that you never had any intention of selling your house. Check with your attorney to be safe.

The simple truth is that nitpicky buyers who seem to demand everything are a fact of life when trying to sell your home. Rather than avoiding them altogether—and possibly passing up an opportunity to sell your home for a price you want—it's more effective to know how to deal with them. Here are a few ideas that may help:

♦ When you start out on selling your home, be sure to set limitations on what you're willing to do and where you draw the line. That makes it easier to work with all types of buyers, nitpicky and otherwise.

♦ Don't be afraid to shove back a bit if needed. It's not always the case, but many nitpicky and unduly demanding buyers are trying to bully their way into what they think is a better deal. And, like all bullies, they tend to back down when someone stands up to them. It doesn't have to be any sort of dramatic scene—just tell them you're not willing to agree to something or you find some of their requests unreasonable. You may be pleasantly surprised how quickly they back off.

FSBO Facts
Remember our earlier anecdote about the buyer who got all bent out of shape when three coat hangers were left in the closet (pun intended)? She even had the audacity to ask one of the authors—the person selling the home—to come over and take them out of the closet! The answer: a very blunt "no." Amazingly, the topic of coat hangers was never raised again.

◆ If a buyer seems genuinely interested in your home but is being maddeningly nitpicky in the process, hand her off to your attorney. Not only are they trained to handle all sorts of people, but your attorney will be able to work with the buyer without any emotion.

◆ Give on some things, but have them agree to give in as well. Another strategy is to accommodate some of your buyer's more reasonable demands. In return, have them agree in writing that they're satisfied and no further demands will be made.

◆ As we mentioned earlier, haggling over what stays and what goes from a house can prove a veritable feeding frenzy for the nitpicky buyer. If you fear the stay/go debate may prove a bottomless pit, remember our earlier suggestion about scheduling a walkthrough specific to that topic. On top of that, pick your battles carefully. If you truly value something, keep it out of sight. If you don't mind giving something up, leave it out—it may prove sufficient bait and give you negotiating leverage in the long run.

Here's another tip for pushing a problem buyer toward items in your home that you don't care about giving up. During the initial showing or walkthrough, mention how those items are particularly dear to your heart. If a buyer has his heart set on grinding you out of all you're worth, he may well ask you to throw them into the deal. If not, you can offer them as a "gesture of good will." Either way, you come off as generous and, in the process, soothe a buyer who, without that bone, could prove even more troublesome.

Other Headaches, Courtesy of the Buyer

Think we're done with our rundown of problem buyers? Not by a long shot! Sit down, take a deep breath, and check out some other types you may come across (and some ideas on how to best handle them):

◆ Buyer incommunicado. Someone tours your home, says she loves it, makes an offer, you counter, and then you don't hear anything. Another variation: a buyer with whom you commit to an offer is slow in getting back to you with information on how elements of the sale are progressing (indeed, if they even bother to get back with you at all.) It's a classic case of the buyer who doesn't maintain an adequate flow of communication. Possible solutions: inform them in no uncertain terms that they need to keep in better touch to ensure all goes ahead as planned. If that doesn't fly, have your attorney contact them—hearing from a lawyer that there's a problem needing correction often carries more weight.

♦ **The hyper buyer.** A buyer makes an offer on your home and wants the deal done as quickly as possible—often in an unreasonable timeframe. This can work, but be careful about allotting yourself adequate time to do everything that needs to be addressed. Also, if you can, find out just why the buyer is in such a rush.

♦ **The house hunting divorcee to be.** This isn't a problem so much with the buyer himself as it is with the circumstances connected to the house purchase. A soon-to-be divorced person makes an offer on your home. The offer is a fair one—at least so far as the price goes. Trouble is, the funds for purchasing your home are coming from the divorce settlement. Not surprisingly, this sets up a host of problems. First and foremost, divorce settlements are notorious for taking their own sweet time to come together—on top of that, the terms and specifics of the settlement can change at any time. And while many divorces are little more than a happy parole, for others, they are wrenching. This may put you in a position where you're dealing with a buyer who may not be in the best shape, emotionally speaking.

Here, you have to judge things according to the specifics of the situation. Find out when the divorce is slated to be completed. In some cases, things will come together in plenty of time to complete your deal. Others that are more shaky and less predictable are probably well avoided. Checking on details such as preapproval can help address these issues, too.

Cut Bait! When to Terminate Relations with a Buyer

Ideally, most headaches that a problem buyer presents can be handled in some manner. Just be more patient, more thorough, or do something a bit better or differently to keep the deal moving forward.

Unfortunately, that isn't always the case. As we've just seen, there are as many foreseeable problems with buyers as there are buyers themselves, and even more unforeseeable ones. And, sad to say, not every problem has a solution.

That means the time may come that, no matter how promising the deal may have appeared at first, it becomes apparent it's time to sever relations with a buyer.

The preceding discussion should have given you examples of the types of behavior and instances that could warrant calling it quits with a buyer. Some others include:

♦ Failure to keep appointments. This can be as maddening an issue as any you'll encounter. Nothing like taking off valuable time to meet with the buyer, only to deal with a no-show.

♦ Failure to adhere to deadlines. Somewhat similar to appointments, but these can have clear legal ramifications as well. For instance, failure to obtain suitable financing within a specified timeframe is one common reason why a buyer is dropped from the picture. Failing to complete necessary paperwork is another common one.

Selling Smarts

As we've mentioned numerous times throughout this book, various steps in the sales process can carry certain legal obligations—including when and how you can call it quits with a particular buyer. Be on the safe side and always check with your attorney to make certain you're on safe legal ground to discontinue your relationship with a particular buyer.

♦ Intruding on your time. Of course, you should make yourself reasonably available to work with the buyer in any way possible. But some take advantage of that openness—they may call you repeatedly at all hours or, even worse, simply appear at your door with questions. Don't be nervous about setting parameters as to when you're open for business and when it's time off for other things.

♦ Having you do things they should be looking after themselves. It may seem strange, buy buyers have been known to ask the sellers to schedule a home inspection or see to some other detail that buyers almost always handle. Don't play nursemaid to any buyer.

♦ Believe it or not, some buyers ask the sellers to complete the necessary paperwork—such as disclosure statements—claiming they simply don't know how to do it or are unable to afford an attorney to do it for them. No further discussion needed here.

♦ A general inability to hold up their end. As a rule, look into dropping a buyer who consistently fails to do what they're called upon to do. If they're really committed and motivated to buy your home, they should certainly prove capable of seeing to whatever obligations the process involves. If, time and again, they don't, check with your attorney about cutting them loose as quickly as possible.

As is the case with most anything related to selling your home, never just tell a buyer that things have come to an end. Put it in writing. Don't forget to return whatever deposits or other funds the buyer may have put up in the process.

Online Problem Buyer Resources

Much of your success in dealing effectively with the problem buyer boils down to being assertive—not aggressive but standing up for yourself in a positive, productive fashion. Some websites that offer information on how to be assertive in any number of situations are found at:

- ◆ www.couns.uiuc.edu/Brochures/assertiv.htm
- ◆ http://mentalhelp.net/psyhelp/chap13/chap13e.htm
- ◆ www.albernstein.com/id21.htm

The Least You Need to Know

- ◆ Problem buyers are a part of selling your home. Prepare to deal with them.
- ◆ If a buyer just seems incapable of making up his mind, ask if there's any additional information you can provide that may help.
- ◆ Be careful with buyers who hold back on financial disclosure. That can hint at all sorts of significant problems.
- ◆ Dealing with a nitpicky or bullying buyer can be done several ways. Ask them to back off or hand them off to your attorney.
- ◆ You may want to terminate relations with a buyer for a number of reasons. But be careful and check with your attorney to make sure you're in a legal position to do so.

First Sell, Then Buy— Juggling the Two

In This Chapter

♦ Buying time

♦ Staying in place

♦ Multiple moves

♦ Financial incentives to make it work

In the best of all possible worlds, you find a home you love and you buy it. You move in. Then you put your current home on the market and it quickly sells. Such a scenario avoids all the hassles of trying to time closings and move-out dates, which can drive homeowners batty. But not everyone has the assets to afford two mortgages at once, which this situation requires. Most homeowners need to buy and sell simultaneously and sometimes find themselves squeezed between two homes.

Fortunately, this chapter covers the options that allow you to straddle your two homes without moving twice, which no one wants to do. From staying in your current home longer to negotiating pre-possession, most homeowners find a way to make it work without moving into temporary housing.

Setting the Timing—How to Juggle a Sale and Purchase Smoothly

To avoid moving out of your current home and putting everything into storage, try to schedule the closing for your purchase and sale on the same date—one after the other. Closing on the same day ensures you can move your belongings right into your new home, rather than storing them indefinitely. If that won't work, storing your stuff is one option, as is trying to get permission to stay in your old home until your new home is available.

A number of possible timing scenarios exist. These include:

◆ **Move in early.** If your new place will be available soon, you can start to cart belongings over there for storage before you have to close on your current home. You may be able to do a fair amount of moving yourself, because you have the extra time.

◆ **Move in and out the same day.** If you won't be able to get into your new place until the day you close on your existing home, you need to begin checking out who will be available to assist you. Believe me, you'll need help!

◆ **Move out after closing.** If you can't move to your new address until after you sell your current home, you'll want to try to negotiate with the buyers to give you some extra time to move out. There are several ways this arrangement can be structured.

Tools of the Trade

A **sale-leaseback** is an agreement in which the buyer of a home consents to allow the former owner to remain in the home for a specified period of time beyond the official closing date. In some cases, the buyer receives a payment, similar to a rental fee, and in others, such an arrangement is part of the sale negotiation.

Staying Put

If you know it will be several weeks, generally no more than 60 days, before you can move into your new home (and you want to avoid moving twice), you can try to negotiate with the buyer to get some additional time. For instance, if you're building a new home and its completion has been delayed, you may be able to lease or rent your home from the new owner after closing, called a sale-leaseback, or rent-back. In some cases, *sale-leasebacks* call for the seller to pay the buyer for the additional time in the house, while other deals are simply part of the purchase agreement.

Because of horror stories about sellers refusing to get out of the house after closing, some buyers may be reluctant to allow you to stay in the home after closing, fearful that you'll never leave or that they'll end up without a place to live. But it's worth asking if you know you'll need the extra time after closing.

Move in Early

Similarly, as the buyer of your new home, you should inquire about early possession. Just as sellers may be granted permission to stay in their residence after the official closing date, buyers may be granted permission to move in early. In one family's case, they received permission to move some of their belongings into their new home's garage the week before closing, which helped them get everything out of their old house on time.

Another way to close on your new home before moving out of the old one is to arrange *bridge*, or swing, financing, which would allow you to buy the new home before you've sold the old one, giving you a window of a few days or weeks to get settled.

Tools of the Trade _____

A **bridge loan** is a financing tool that bridges the gap between when you close on your old home and your new home. Many sellers need the funds from their home sale in order to close on the new home, but sometimes it's just not possible to schedule them simultaneously. By using your current home as collateral, you may be able to get a bridge loan to enable you to buy your new home, which you then pay off along with your old mortgage when your current home sells. Of course, the longer the loan, the higher the fees.

Because of the higher cost of bridge loans, you may want to check into less expensive, traditional financing options, such as a home equity loan, second mortgage, or cash-out refinance on your current home. The only downside is that having such debts on your credit record may make it more difficult to qualify for the mortgage on your new home.

Or if you have the finances to afford it, you can save the cost of the bridge loan by qualifying for a mortgage on your new place while you still own the old one. Holding two mortgages, even just for a week or two until the first home sells, will generally end up saving you money because bridge loans are made at higher interest rates.

Tools for Dealing with Timing Problems

If you discover you need extra time in your current home or want to try to move into your new home early, you may have difficulty convincing the buyer or seller to agree. However, there are a couple of legal documents that can help you in your quest.

Indemnification Agreement

If you find that staying in your home after the closing date would be advantageous, because you can't move into your new space yet, ask the buyer as soon as possible. No one likes to be surprised at the eleventh hour, so the earlier the subject is broached, the better. Generally, those unwilling to allow you to stay take that position because they have nowhere else to go or because they are nervous about damage occurring to their property after they've bought it.

To calm those fears, offer to sign an *indemnification agreement.* Such a document promises you will leave the residence in the same condition it was in before closing, when they did their final walkthrough, and if any damage does occur, you will have it repaired at your expense.

Be aware that this does create a risk for you, the seller. If that refrigerator you sold with the house suddenly dies, or starts leaking, the indemnification agreement requires you repair or replace it. Or if your toddler one night spills paint all over the off-white carpeting, you are now responsible for cleaning or replacing it. Any misstep can be costly, now that you're effectively renting your old home.

Tools of the Trade

An **indemnification agreement** is a legal document buyers and sellers sign in which the seller agrees to maintain the home in its current state, repairing or replacing anything that becomes damaged or broken during the time they possessed it.

Before you start worrying about sale-leasebacks and indemnification agreements, keep in mind that most buyers want to move into their new home as soon as possible, so this will likely not be an issue for you. For many buyers, any potential delay in a move-in date will discourage them from making an offer in the first place.

Keep in mind, you'll be in a much better negotiating position if a sale-leaseback isn't a requirement of the sale.

Offer to Pay for Temporary Housing

If you find the buyer would be willing to let you stay in your home if they didn't need a place to go, you may want to offer to pay for their temporary housing until your home is ready for move-in.

When you realize that you're going to need temporary housing, either in a hotel or furnished apartment, offering to pay for the buyer's expenses may earn you permission to stay where you are until you can get into your new place. It comes down to a question of who's going to the hotel, and if they've already moved out of their place, they may be more willing to wait it out in a hotel a couple of days, especially if you make it worth their while. Either way, you'll have to pay housing costs, but at least this way you don't have to move twice. That's certainly worth something!

The Path of Least Resistance—Options If You Don't Want to Buy Right Away

Of course, in some situations, it may be advantageous to sell your current home before you've even found a new one, such as if the housing market is booming and you want to cash out at the top.

In that case, you can consider moving in with friends or relatives, signing a month-to-month lease on another home, moving into your vacation home at the beach, if you have one, or simply putting your stuff into storage and traveling.

And when you're ready to buy a new place, you'll have the added advantage of not having to make an offer to purchase contingent on the sale of your home—it's already sold—which in some markets can make you a more attractive buyer. In some cases, contingencies can make or break an offer.

Getting Out of Dodge—Relocation Resources

As soon as you have a signed contract to buy or sell a home, whichever comes first, you'll want to start planning your move. Whether you're headed down the street or across the country, relocating your household takes time and effort.

Many websites are out there that can help you map out your moving timetable, calculate moving costs, create an action checklist, and gather important information about your new home base. Some you may find useful include:

♦ www.relocationessentials.com/home.htm—Whether you have a new job or are exploring the possibilities of a move, this site has everything from moving planners to community data to school recommendations and mortgage calculators (see the following figure).

Websites can give you a great head start on your moving plans and help get you organized well in advance of move-out day.

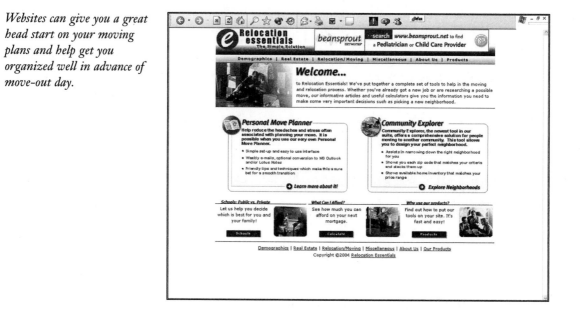

♦ www.monstermoving.monster.com. Plan your move, get quotes from local companies, and make use of their free address changer.

♦ www.homefair.com/homefair. Offers moving help, checklists, calculators, and community information.

♦ www.dod.mil/mapsite/relocate.html. Help for relocating military personnel.

Obtain as much information as you can when you compare price quotes, look into storage and moving, explore schools and neighborhoods, and get set for the exciting journey.

To Move or Be Moved?

Of course, after deciding to sell your home, one of the first decisions you have to make is whether to move yourself to your new place, or whether you should turn over the process to a professional moving company.

Even then there are different levels of involvement—from pack, load, unload, and unpack, to just load and unload. Generally, the amount of time, energy, and money you have will determine how much help you should get—the more time and energy you have, the less you may want to pay someone else for assistance.

Self-Service Move

The biggest advantage of handling a move yourself is the savings. Except for the cost of a truck or van to haul your belongings to your destination, which is optional if you already own or have access to a truck, you may have no other expenses.

However, to make your move smoother and less painful, you may want to consider:

- Asking friends and family to lend their brawn in getting large pieces of furniture on and off the truck.

- Buying boxes, or collecting them from area retailers for free, to pack up smaller household items.

- Arranging for a short-term storage facility to hold items you must get out of your place but which you're not sure will fit in your new home.

- Hiring professionals, at an hourly rate, to handle the heavy lifting.

- Turning over the heaviest, or most valuable items, to a professional mover to relocate for you.

Selling Smarts

Summer is the most expensive time to move because professional moving companies are busy. Waiting until after Labor Day can yield a savings of up to 30 percent. If you need to move during the summer, ask about mid-month or weekday rates, which are generally cheaper.

Although an investment in a professional mover may increase your expenses, your important possessions will also be insured against damage—something you give up when you ask your buddies to help you out. You also reduce your liability in case one of your helpers becomes injured while carrying your grandmother's antique bureau down several flights of stairs.

A compromise between moving yourself and a professional mover is a self-service move, where you are responsible for loading and unloading your possessions on the truck, but the mover handles transportation to your new home. If you have a lot of stuff to move, or are moving several hours away, this may be a better alternative than trying to handle the move yourself in several trips back and forth.

Full-Service Move

If you decide to explore having a professional moving company handle your move, here are some recommendations for finding a good one:

- ◆ Ask for recommendations from friends, family, neighbors, and local real estate agents, who have some influence if anything goes wrong.

- ◆ Get a list of certified movers who are members of the American Moving and Storage Association, which can be found at: www.moving.org (see the following figure). Click on the Mover Referral Service button.

Selecting a quality mover can make the difference between furniture and important possessions arriving in one piece or several. Choose your moving company carefully.

- ◆ Verify whether a business is reputable by calling your local Chamber of Commerce to ask about any complaints and by visiting the Better Business Bureau online at www.bbb.com to investigate each company's business practices (see the following figure).

Finding and hiring a reputable mover is half the battle, and you get what you pay for in many respects. Don't base your choice of a mover on cost alone—check out the Better Business Bureau's records first to learn how many former customers were happy with the company's service.

◆ Be wary of Internet databases listing movers—There is no way to distinguish a quality moving company from a fly-by-night crew.

◆ Ask movers to provide references, and take the time to call them!

After you've put together a list of possible movers, you'll want to:

◆ Call several—don't settle on the first one.

◆ Ask them to come to your home to give you a price quote based on the amount of furniture, boxes, and miscellaneous items to be moved.

◆ Ask if the quote is *binding*—that is, whether the final cost could be higher than what was quoted.

◆ Find out what each mover's formula is for calculating the price quote they've given you. Is it based on the number of pieces of furniture? Does it factor in the distance you're moving? Is it based on the estimated weight of your belongings? And what is the weight?

Sales Snafu

Costs-per-pound vary widely from mover-to-mover. For example, one mover in California quoted $.11 per pound for 8,000 or more pounds moved, or $.14 per pound for 1,000 to 2,000 pounds. A mover in New York, however, quoted $.30 per pound. There is frequently a premium for stairs climbed as well.

Knowing how each mover came up with your quote will make it easier to compare several movers.

♦ Learn whether the mover offers "full value protection" or "full replacement value." If so, the mover will be responsible for compensating you based on the cost to replace anything damaged in transit, rather than the current market value of the item, which is frequently far less than what you paid to buy it.

♦ Ask for and complete a "High Declaration Value" form to itemize priceless or precious belongings prior to the move. This brings attention to your high value items and establishes their value up front in case anything gets damaged in transit.

The most expensive type of move includes packing up your home in boxes, loading it on the moving truck, driving it to your new place, unloading the boxes and furniture, and unpacking it for you. Clearly, this involves the least amount of effort on your part, which is the way some families choose to go.

 Tools of the Trade _____

A **binding** quote is a price the moving company agrees to charge for your move; that price cannot change unless the terms of the move change, such as the addition of several more pieces of furniture. A non-binding quote is more of an estimate, which can go higher or lower come moving day. Some movers use not-to-exceed quotes, which guarantee the final cost of your move will be either the original quote or less—but it won't be more. If you have the option, this is the type of quote you want to see.

However, you can also choose to take care of the packing and unpacking yourself, thereby reducing your moving bill while still preserving your body from unnecessary punishment. Whether your company is pitching in to pay for a relocation may also factor into whether or not you spring for the packing service.

Moving is time-consuming, hard work, not to mention stressful. But everyone gets through it, and you will too.

Online Relocation Resources

For more information about topics covered in this chapter, check out the following websites:

◆ www.irs.gov. Check out IRS Publication 521 "Moving Expenses" to learn whether your move is totally or partially tax deductible.

◆ www.moving.org/before/handbook.pdf. The website for the American Moving and Storage Association offers a free consumer moving guide. Download it here.

◆ www.usps.com. Complete change of address forms are available online. Fill these out so your mail is forwarded to your new residence (see the figure that follows).

Make sure your mail is forwarded to your new address by completing the online mail forwarding forms here.

◆ www.moving.org. Get a list of certified movers who are members of the American Moving and Storage Association by clicking on the Mover Referral Service button.

The Least You Need to Know

◆ If you can afford to hold two mortgages simultaneously, so you can buy a new place before selling your current home, you'll find the whole issue of moving and relocating your possessions to be much simpler.

◆ If you can't afford two mortgages, you can still explore a bridge loan, which allows you to close on your new home before you sell the current one.

◆ If you can't move into your new home until after you have to be out of your old one, ask the buyers for a sale-leaseback, which means you rent your old home until your new one is available.

◆ Don't wait until after you've moved into your new place to decide what to keep and what to throw away—you'll waste time, energy, and money packing items you may end up tossing later.

◆ Although relying on a rented truck and friends to help you move may be cheaper, you take a risk with valuables, which aren't covered by insurance, and with your back, which may not be up to hauling huge furniture to and from the moving van.

Chapter 21

Bailing Out–Opting for an Agent

In This Chapter

- ◆ Signs you may benefit from an agent
- ◆ I just need a little help
- ◆ Know your agreement options
- ◆ Be sure to share all you've learned

Hopefully, this is the only chapter in this book you will never, ever have to put to use. But in the interest of being thorough …

Like most everything else in life, selling your home on your own is by no means a sure thing. Granted, in this book we've tried to give you every possible tool to ensure your success. But for one reason or another, not every home is built to sell quickly or at the best possible price—FSBO or otherwise.

By the same token, you may immerse yourself in the process to a certain degree, only to discover it simply isn't your cup of tea. Or that you don't have the time. Or that you're tired of dealing one-on-one with buyers who would make saints grit their teeth.

Whatever the reason, you're giving some thought to using a real estate agent to help sell your home, at least in some capacity. Although we sincerely hope the following information proves unnecessary to you—however enlightening—here are some strategies to bear in mind when you suspect the sale of your home would benefit from the presence and skill of a professional agent.

> **Selling Smarts** _____
>
> Before we get into the meat of the issue, giving some thought to bringing an agent on board shouldn't be equated with failure. As you've no doubt learned, selling your home successfully hinges on a number of factors—some under your control, many that are not. There are simply too many factors in the mix to warrant any sort of guilt trip. Remember: the goal is to *sell* your house.

When to Bail—Signs That It Won't Go

The idea can occur to you at almost any point in the process of selling your home. Maybe you've only been at it for a little while, perhaps you've been working hard for quite some time. Regardless of when it happens, a slightly unnerving thought hits you: This just doesn't seem to be working out. My house just doesn't seem to be selling.

Obviously, the notion that you may do well to opt for Plan B is a highly subjective one. What one homeowner would consider maddeningly frustrating another would only see as mildly inconvenient if, indeed, nothing more than a challenge.

> **Selling Smarts** _____
>
> A refresher: one of the first questions a buyer will ask is how long a home has been on the market. The longer the time-frame, the greater a buyer's suspicions about why it hasn't sold—and why they may not be interested as well. Moreover, it only gets worse the longer the home stays on the market.

Still, there are some rather universal signs that suggest the sale of your home isn't necessarily bound for utter success, and you may want to consider your options. Here are a few to consider:

- **Time on the market.** This is very subjective sign, indeed, one that will vary according to the dynamics of the local marketplace. But as a general rule of thumb, if your home has been for sale for more than a few months, it would be wise to rethink what you've been doing. For many, six months without a sale is a sure sign that what you've been trying so far isn't working.

◆ Time with little or no buyer traffic. Maybe you started out with a steady stream of prospective buyers, but now a buyer calling for a look is fast becoming the exception rather than the rule.

◆ No one seems to be qualified. A variant on the prior problem. You're seemingly getting enough interested parties, but they all inevitably turn out to be incapable of buying your home. (This can be a sign of a poor marketing strategy—attracting the wrong types of buyers—or a home that is simply priced out of its league.)

◆ You sense that some buyers are antsy without an agent in the picture. We warned you about this earlier and, although attitudes are changing, there are still some buyers who are apprehensive about dealing directly with an owner.

◆ You've had a couple of deals fall through. Here, you accepted offers, only to have the sale fall apart for any number of reasons—perhaps something was uncovered during the home inspection, or some other point of follow up negotiation nixed the sale. In any case, you've experienced the frustration of coming close without closing.

◆ You've made some paperwork mistakes. Hopefully, the guidance offered in this book makes this a distant possibility but, if it does occur, this is a good argument in favor of having someone else help you with the necessary documentation.

◆ You have to move more quickly than you originally expected. Not so much a problem as a change in circumstances. In this case, a new job or some other obligation in another location requires your presence sooner than you anticipated, making it necessary to sell your home faster than you planned.

◆ You've found a new home you simply can't live without. Ditto the dynamics of the prior scenario. You've got to sell your current home in the fastest way possible or you'll lose out on your dream home.

Any number of other possibilities exist, but the bottom line is a common one—selling your home simply has not gone the way you expected and hoped it would. And it seems to you that working with a real estate agent in some capacity might be your best option.

We covered the various advantages and drawbacks of working with a real estate agent back in Chapter 1. The advantages include contacts, experience with real estate in your area, and marketing savvy, among others.

Selling Smarts

If you're considering working with an agent in some way, it can be helpful to think back and try to identify just what didn't measure up with your FSBO. Was it the price, marketing, advertising, negotiation, or some other problem? Pinpointing what you think went awry can help you identify the sort of agent you want to work with as well as how you think you may be able to work with him most effectively.

How to Find the Right Agent

Even if you're merely considering the possibility of working with an agent, it's important to know how to partner with one who will serve your needs.

The first issue is where to start. One reliable way is to ask for referrals from friends, relatives, and colleagues. The reasoning here is that they have worked with an agent in the past with whom they've been happy and feel confident in recommending.

One possible pitfall in obtaining referrals is that others' homes may be substantially different from yours. For instance, your friend's house may be quite a bit more expensive than yours or vice versa—or it may be set in the country while yours is in a subdivision. So it's a good idea to try to pick the brain of someone whose home is, at the very least, somewhat similar to yours.

Another resource is a variety of regional and national associations dealing with real estate agents, for example, www.realestateagent.com (see the following figure). We provide additional websites at the conclusion of this chapter that offer search engines to pair you up with an agent who works in your area.

Another way to get a lead on solid agents in your area is to drive around and look for listing signs on front lawns. If you see a name over and over, that means that particular agent is, if nothing else, busy. While this doesn't necessarily indicate the agent who's best for you, it's at least a reasonable indicator warranting further investigation.

After you have a lead on several candidates, it's essential to meet with them to get to know their approach and credentials. That means a face-to-face meeting with each—loaded with some pointed questions that should give you a good idea about who will work and who won't.

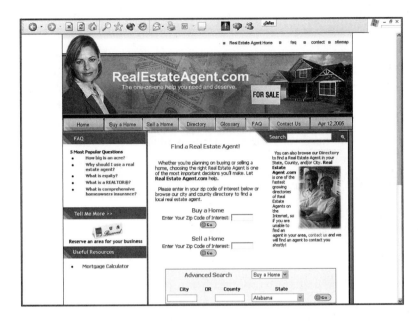

Search engines, such as this one at Realestateagent.com, let you find agents working in your area.

Here's a lineup of suggested questions that can prove helpful in getting not just a good agent, but the right one for you—one who may be willing to take a former FSBO into consideration:

♦ Have them outline their experience, particularly local. How long have they worked in the area where your home is located?

♦ Have them review any special designations or training they may have received. Also professional memberships and associations.

♦ How many deals have they actually closed—not working on, but done and finished—during the past two months or so?

Selling Smarts _____

The list of questions here are anything but run of the mill, stereotypical, tell-me-about-your-self questions. They're carefully worded to lead you to your next step—considering what type of arrangement you can work out with a real estate agent.

♦ Have they always worked as a real estate agent? If not, then what other experience might they have? (This is an excellent way to uncover skills and other traits that may prove helpful.)

♦ What is their ratio of buyers represented to sellers represented? (Some agents are particularly good or more comfortable with one or the other.)

♦ How do you cancel whatever relationship you may have with the agent if you're not satisfied?

♦ Have them offer their opinion of people who try to sell their homes without an agent. This can be very telling. Many real estate agents are very understanding that people want to save money any way they can. Others, on the other hand, may resent anyone's perceived intrusion on their livelihood. If you get that feeling with an agent, it may be hard to work with him—particularly if you try to work out an alternative arrangement.

♦ What is their standard fee or commission?

♦ Has the agent ever agreed to some sort of alternative agreement with a seller? If so, what were the details of that?

Like any sort of interview process, it's always important to obtain and check into a few references. In your case, try to find a client who initially attempted to sell his home by himself, then opted for the agent. Find out how the experience went and if he would do the same thing again.

Asking for Help, Not a Listing

The preceding list of questions has two primary objectives. The first is to find an agent who's qualified, experienced in selling homes such as yours, and sufficiently aggressive to offer a good chance of success.

The second point is determining whether an agent is agreeable to arrangements that fall outside the conventional, full-fee listing. Know upfront when you approach a real estate agent that—regardless of whether you're a FSBO or otherwise—he's going to want to sign your house on for a full listing.

That's understandable. Real estate agents, like everyone else, are trying to earn a good living in a very competitive environment. Never fault them for wanting a deal that offers the best paycheck they can reasonably get.

The downside for you, of course, is the 6 to 7 percent commission that attaches itself to conventional listing services. As we've reviewed before, that can prove a tidy sum—and, the more expensive the home, the greater the commission cut.

> **Sales Snafu** _____
>
> When considering a full-service agent, bear in mind the problem of a sudden jump in the asking price of your home. That's not because the house has suddenly soared in value—rather, you may choose to try upping the price to offset the expense of the sales commission. That can raise eyebrows from buyers who may remember a lower FSBO price. In the end, with a full-service agent, you may have to settle for pocketing less than you originally hoped for.

If the cost of a sales commission seems a reasonable price to pay, go for it. After all, that only becomes an issue if your house is sold—and that's the whole point of putting your home on the market in the first place.

But you may wish to pursue other options. Start by asking for an agent's help, not necessarily a listing, at least at first. If you have a friend or relative who's an agent—or, by chance, you found a sympathetic agent through your course of interviews—ask them to critique what you've done so far. That may offer additional insight into how your FSBO may have misfired and, in turn, how an agent may be able to best assist you from here on.

Things being what they are, don't expect a friendly agent to necessarily tell you everything you need to know to revive your FSBO. One contact for this book reports that many agents are rather prudent in what information they're willing to share with any prospective client, let alone a FSBO. An agent may give you just enough information to whet your appetite and underscore her credentials, but not so much that you can necessarily proceed on your own. Understandably, they'd prefer the listing.

It never hurts to inquire about financial arrangements other than the going sales commission cut. Look back at some of the issues relating to agents in Chapter 1—it's possible an agent has, on occasion, trimmed his fee to get an appealing home. Many agents are open to cutting their commission up to 1 percent or so. Not exactly a windfall, but every little bit makes a difference.

Few, if any, solid agents will be willing to consider a flat fee in lieu of a percentage-based sales commission. Understandably, there's simply insufficient financial incentive to warrant their time and energy. As we mentioned in Chapter 1, there are so-called "discount" brokers who operate fee-based services. But their services can be notoriously uneven.

One of the pluses you bring to the challenge of working out some sort of alternative arrangement with an agent is your experience in attempting to sell your home on your own. For one thing, you likely know more about your home than many other homeowners (see the following section on helping your agent.) On top of that, you may have research, information, or available materials so she doesn't have to compile them from square one.

These and other advantages may make you a particularly attractive client for many agents—and, in turn, make them more amenable to trimming down their conventional commission. So in chatting with agents, play up all that you, as an experienced FSBO, may be able to bring to the relationship. It may make the agent's job a good deal less challenging and a better fit to a lower commission.

Selling Smarts _____

Once more, keep local conditions in mind when pursuing alternative commission arrangements. A hot market where homes are selling quickly may prompt agents to discount their commission. A lesser paycheck but, hopefully, for less effort. On the other hand, a slow market where agents are struggling to move houses may mandate full commissions. The reasoning would be that a tough market requires a greater amount of time and effort.

One way to leverage all that you may already have in place is to offer a relatively modest cut to any broker who brings you a buyer—a finder's fee of sorts ranging from 2 to 4 percent. Position this approach by pointing out what steps you have taken to date—including advertisements, listings, marketing, and other efforts—and that you'd be happy to compensate any agent who provides you with a qualified buyer.

Another way to entice agents toward a lower commission is the prospect of work beyond just selling your home. If you know of other homeowners who may be on the lookout for an agent, mention that you'd be happy to pass his name along. Moreover, don't forget yourself. If you're buying a new home after selling this one, you'll need a good agent to help see that through, right?

One final possibility breaks the commission structure down according to the price of your home. Some agents may be willing to charge a certain commission rate for, say, the first $100,000 or $150,000 of the price and then a discounted rate for any amount beyond that. The obvious drawback is that this arrangement is only workable with more expensive homes.

Business As Usual? Agent Agreement Options

Another part of the relationship between seller and an agent is the formal agreement that outlines their relationship. This is known as the *listing agreement*.

There are basically two types of listing agreements—an exclusive agreement and an open listing. An exclusive agreement breaks down into two subcategories—the exclusive right to sell and an exclusive agency. The exclusive right to sell is by far the most advantageous to the real estate agent and agency. This guarantees that your agent is going to get his commission no matter how the property is actually sold. In return, the exclusive right to sell requires the agency to actively promote the sale of your home.

Tools of the Trade

A listing agreement defines various aspects of a real estate agent's work with a seller. Details include commission rates, how long the listing will remain in place, who gets paid under various circumstances, and other information. Once signed, this is a binding contract.

If you break down the exclusive right to sell a bit, it's easy to see why this is the agent's arrangement of choice. Say you sign the agreement with the agent. The next day, a buyer who looked at your home back when you were trying to sell it on your own appears and offers the full purchase price. Your agent—who may have done little more than hand you the pen to sign the listing agreement—gets his commission. Nice work if you can get it.

The exclusive agency arrangement narrows this somewhat, but not by much. Here, the only time the agent doesn't get paid is if you find the buyer yourself. Under any other circumstances, the full commission is paid.

The second option is known as the open listing. Here, the dynamics are in your favor. Under this contract, the only time your agent earns her full commission is if she, herself, finds the buyer. Anything else—nada.

It's no great revelation that real estate agents avoid an open listing at every foreseeable turn. Not only does it offer the least chance of actually earning a commission, it also lets you list your home with other real estate agencies at the same time—and, for that matter, to continue to try to sell your home on your own.

That said, an open listing is one you should pursue when working out your listing agreement with your agent. It combines the best of both worlds—the resources of a professional agent along with the continued possibility that you may sell your home without the agent and save the commission in the long run.

Selling Smarts

Try to gauge how your agent will react to working under an open listing. Some may take it as added incentive to work particularly hard to earn their commission. Others may not go too far out of their way to sell your home, reasoning that the odds are stacked against them. In that case, you may end up saddling yourself with an agent who, in the end, may do little to help move your house.

Other elements of the listing arrangement warrant your attention. These include:

- Length of the agreement. Many agencies will push for terms as long as six months, reasoning that the law of averages will produce a buyer within half a year. Unfortunately, that can limit how aggressive they may be in trying to sell your home. Look for shorter terms, such as 60 or 90 days.

- When the commission must be paid. Make sure your listing stipulates that any commissions will be paid when the sale is completed and you have the money in hand. Some arrangements set payment at the time an offer to purchase is signed.

- Who's responsible for advertising and marketing expenses. This should be your agent's responsibility, not yours.

Have your attorney review any listing agreement before you sign it. For one thing, she'll be aware of local legal limitations or customs that may impact the agreement. Also, she should make sure the contract contains clear provisions that allow you to terminate the arrangement. For instance, many contracts really don't mention any specific responsibilities that an agent must perform, such as hosting open houses, advertising the home in the local paper, and other duties. These should be spelled out. If unfulfilled, they should also be mentioned as a justifiable cause to cancel the listing.

Helping Your Agent with What You Know

As we've mentioned, you're going to be unlike most sellers an agent works with. Because you've put the time and effort into attempting to sell your home on your own, chances are good you'll know more about your home than other buyers—and, in the process, prove a valuable resource for your real estate agent.

If you followed our suggested agent interview questions listed earlier in this chapter, chances are also very good that you've paired with an agent who has a certain degree of respect for the experience and insight you've acquired. Ultimately, that should lead to a working relationship that's more of a partnership instead of your agent telling you what to do at every single turn.

So, don't be the least bit shy about sharing any knowledge or experience you may have picked up along the way that you think may be of use to your agent. Notice that open houses got a better turnout on a Sunday instead of a Saturday? Mention that. Did you find that buyers seemed particularly drawn to the features of your kitchen and less so to the family room? Suggest that tours with prospective buyers play that up as well.

The point here is that you can bring more to the table than many other owners—information and perspective that your agent can use to his decided advantage. Moreover, don't limit it to your personal experience. If you have any materials—sales flyers, research, and other items—that you thought were helpful, be sure to pass those along as well.

 Sales Snafu

It's helpful to be as involved in the sale of your home as possible. But don't go overboard to the point of monitoring your agent's every single move. Even the most open agent will begin to resent a seller who can't seem to tell the difference between involved and intrusive. And any bad feelings between you and your agent will only hinder the sale of your home.

Not only can your experience as a FSBO prove helpful to your agent, it also makes you a more informed consumer. Because you have a particular appreciation for what goes into the successful sale of a home, you also are aware of what you can reasonably expect a competent agent to do on your behalf. And, in the end, that can only contribute to your ultimate goal—the sale of your home with a fair profit in your pocket.

Online Resources for Choosing an Agent

Here are a few websites that can prove helpful in selecting and working with a real estate agent:

◆ Realestateagent.com (www.realestateagent.com) lets you search for local real estate agents using your zip code. It's also a useful source for other real estate-related information.

- Another excellent source for finding an agent is at: www.realestate.com. It also serves as a handy starting point for information about refinancing and other financial details.

- Another excellent starting point for identifying and finding a solid agent is located at: www.ewoss.com/search.aspx?k=real+estate+agents&s=5.

The Least You Need to Know

- Get to know certain warning signs that suggest your efforts to sell your home may benefit from an agent. Some of the more obvious ones are a long time on the market without a sale or dwindling buyer traffic.

- Interview agents aggressively. In particular, find out how they feel about sellers who first tried to sell their homes themselves.

- Try to negotiate commission structures. See if they'd be open to less expensive finder's fee or other options that are less pricey than conventional commissions.

- Check your listing contract carefully. Avoid exclusive right to sell arrangements if at all possible. Also, check how long the contract will be in effect and what the agent is legally obligated to do on your behalf.

- Serve as a resource for your agent. Share what you've learned about your home so he ultimately can do a better job of selling it.

Appendix A

Glossary

adjusted basis   This is the price you paid for your home plus any additions. This boosts the total cost and also lowers taxable gain on the property.

amortization   The breakdown of a debt into specific, scheduled payments, including principal and interest.

appraiser   A professional trained to estimate what your home is worth. An appraiser goes through your home in some detail, noting various features and the condition of the home, then compares your property with others with similar features.

bad faith bargaining   This refers to someone involved in a sale who is not bargaining seriously; put another way, they don't have any real intention of completing the transaction. Bad faith bargaining can lead to legal action if someone feels they were intentionally misled.

benefit   This term refers to what an owner enjoys as a result of a home's features, such as a good school system or room to add on to a home.

binding quote   A binding quote is a price the moving company agrees to charge for your move; that price cannot change unless the terms of the move change, such as the addition of several more pieces of furniture.

bridge loan   A short-term loan that lets a homeseller buy a new home before receiving the proceeds from the sale of the current home.

broom clean   This term means a rather thorough house cleaning—countertops washed, bathrooms cleaned, and all garbage and remnants removed and hauled away. Usually applies to the condition of a home prior to the final walkthrough.

buyer's broker   An agent hired by a buyer to help them find a home. Without such an agreement, agents are bound to represent the seller first and foremost. With a buyer's broker, the buyer pays half the commission in exchange for the knowledge that the agent is working on their behalf, not the seller's.

buyer's market   A market that's generally favorable to those shopping for a home. For instance, a large number of attractive, competitive homes can work in a buyer's favor.

casualty loss   Damage resulting from a sudden, unexpected, or unusual event, including tornados, floods, hurricanes, and ice storms.

closing   The point at which real estate formally changes ownership. A variety of documents are signed by the seller and buyer. Various related charges and fees are also settled.

closing costs   Various costs, fees, and other expenses connected to the final closing on a property.

comparables   Short for comparable properties. Also known as "comps." These are homes that have recently been sold and are very much like yours in terms of size, location, and features. In effect, they set the pricing parameters for your home by having preceded you in the marketplace.

competitive market analysis   This study compares your home with other similar, recently sold homes to establish a target price range. The formula takes in the size of the home, location, number of bedrooms, and other amenities.

contingency   A condition placed on the sale of a home.

co-op   When you agree to co-op an agent, you are agreeing to give them their "cut" or their half of the commission, if they end up selling your home.

deed   The legal document that conveys title to a property.

down payment   A one-time payment the buyer makes toward the purchase of your house. It reduces the amount the buyer needs to finance with a mortgage.

duty to disclose   This refers to material facts about your home or the neighborhood, which would not be evident to the buyer, that you are required to share. As the seller, it is your duty to make sure the buyer is aware of this information.

earnest money   Money that accompanies the presentation of an offer. By including a check with an offer, a buyer is indicating she is in earnest in her desire to buy your home.

equity   This refers to the difference between the market value of your home and the claims that exist against it, such as the outstanding amount of a mortgage, a home equity loan or line of credit, and other charges.

escrow   A third party involved in a real estate transaction who holds funds and documents for delivery after specific conditions have been met.

escrow closing   A closing where the buyer and seller do not sign at the same time. The buyer frequently does not collect proceeds from the sale on the same day.

fair market value   The price a buyer will agree to pay for your home.

feature   A facet of a home, such as a pool, hot tub, or even the amount of space a home contains.

FSBO   For Sale By Owner.

indemnification agreement   A legal document buyers and sellers sign if the seller is going to stay in the home after the closing date. In this agreement, the seller agrees to maintain the home in its current state and repair or replace anything that becomes damaged or broken during the time they possessed it.

lien   This refers to any sort of legal claim that must be paid off when the property is sold. A lien can take in everything from an existing mortgage to a legal judgment against the property owner which has yet to be paid off.

listing agreement   This defines various aspects of a real estate agent's work with a seller. Details include commission rates, how long the listing will remain in place, who gets paid under various circumstances, and other information. Once signed, this is a binding contract.

mortgage banking institution   A banking institution lends its own money, although it can also sell the loan later.

mortgage lender   This is more of a go-between. He or she shops for loan providers and pairs them with the buyer.

mortgage payoff   The amount owed on a mortgage as of the closing date.

nonbinding quote   Unlike a binding quote, here a moving company provides more of an estimate. The actual charge can go higher or lower when the move actually takes place.

not-to-exceed quote   A mover guarantees that the final moving cost will not exceed a certain quote and, in fact, may be lower than the quote.

prequalifying   This involves various financial calculations to determine whether a particular buyer is in a financial position to afford a home. As the term suggests, it happens relatively early in the sales process rather than later. However, it doesn't guarantee a loan—other factors such as employment and credit history figure into whether a lender will actually approve a loan.

private mortgage insurance (PMI)   A form of insurance a buyer has to obtain if he cannot manage at least a 20 percent down payment. Usually tacked on to a monthly mortgage payment, the going average is between $50 to $100 a month for a median priced home.

prorated amount   An amount that is adjusted according to the amount of time you actually own a home. For instance, property tax bills, utility expenses, and other costs may be prorated at closing to adjust for the time of year.

purchase and sale agreement   A Purchase and Sale Agreement is drawn up to cover every single term and condition that applies to the sale of a home. Depending on where you live, the document may go by a slightly different name.

purchase money mortgage   This means the owner is offering financing of some sort to the buyer.

radon   A radioactive gas that has been found in homes throughout the country. Naturally produced through the breakdown of uranium in the soil, it can seep into homes through cracks in the foundation and other areas. Breathing radon in sufficient quantity has been connected with lung cancer and other illnesses.

Realtor®   Although both real estate agents and Realtors are trained and have to be licensed, a Realtor has taken certain training courses and shown expertise in a particular area of real estate. All Realtors are members of the National Association of Realtors and subscribe to that group's code of ethics. Among other issues, the code pledges loyalty to clients, fiduciary honesty, and cooperation with competitors.

relos   Buyers who are moving to a new city for work are called relocations, or "relos" (pronounced ree-lows) for short.

round table closing   The buyer and seller sign at the same time. The seller receives sales proceeds when everything is completed.

sale-leaseback   An agreement in which the buyer of a home consents to allow the former owner to remain in the home for a specified period of time beyond the official closing date. In some cases, the buyer receives a payment, similar to a rental fee, and in others, such an arrangement is part of the sale negotiation.

seller's market   These are market conditions that work in favor of those trying to sell a home.

settlement statement   Also known as a HUD-1 statement, the settlement statement itemizes all funds that are payable at closing. The totals identify what you, as the seller, will receive as well as what the buyer has to pay at the closing.

special power of attorney   This document transfers authority to sign at a closing when one of the parties is not available to sign. Out of town buyers often use special power of attorney.

Staging®   A registered trademark of StagedHomes.com, this describes the process of preparing a home for sale, making it as appealing as possible by cleaning, rearranging, and decorating it for maximum impact.

title   This refers to the legal ownership of a piece of property.

title policy   A legal guarantee of the buyer's ownership of the property. It's essential in case someone in the future files a legal challenge to the ownership of the property.

title report   The title report identifies any liens, encumbrances, judgments, or other issues that may impact your legal capacity to transfer ownership of a piece of property.

traffic   Websites count the number of people who visit their site and report it as traffic. On a home selling website, this would be the number of potential buyers who stopped by to take a look.

virtual tour   An Internet-based system through which buyers visually tour a home by clicking on individual photos of a house. The virtual tour can lead a buyer through an entire house.

walkthrough   The buyer and the seller walk through the home and surrounding property in as complete a fashion as possible prior to the closing. The idea is to make certain everything is the same as what was agreed to.

warranty   A home warranty is a service contract purchased to protect the seller from a major household expense while the home is listed for sale and up to a year after closing. Generally, major systems like heating and air conditioning units, plumbing, and electrical, as well as appliances, are covered against breakdown.

Appendix B

Resources

When it comes to the challenge and opportunity afforded by selling your home yourself, you can never have too much solid information. Here are a few additional resources that can further your knowledge of, and ultimate success in, the FSBO world.

Books

American Bar Association, *The American Bar Association Family Legal Guide*. Random House Reference, 2004.

By no means a substitute for face-to-face legal advice, but nonetheless a user-friendly insight into the legal issues that impact the sale of your home. Also a helpful reference source for a host of other legal issues.

Fisher, Roger, and William Ury, *Getting to Yes: Negotiating Agreement Without Giving in*. Penguin, 1991.

As we discuss in Chapter 11, negotiating is an essential element of selling your home efficiently and for the best possible price. Unfortunately, it's a skill that many lack. This benchmark book on the topic can prove exceedingly helpful in honing your negotiating skills to their sharpest edge possible.

O'Hara, Shelley, and Nancy D. Lewis, *The Complete Idiot's Guide to Buying and Selling a Home*. Alpha Books, Fourth Edition, 2003.

While not focused exclusively on the FSBO market, this sister book offers a comprehensive look into the dynamics of buying and selling a home. It does touch on many issues of particular interest to homesellers, including the importance of prequalification, closing cost breakdowns, and other essentials.

Glink, Ilyce R., *100 Questions Every Home Seller Should Ask*. Three Rivers Press, 1995.

This book raises some provocative issues about selling your home that may eventually have far reaching consequences, such as seller greed, disclosure, and other issues. Glink brings them to your attention and provides answers offered by professional real estate brokers.

Miller, Peter V., *The Common Sense Mortgage*. McGraw-Hill, 1999.

After you've sold your home, chances are rather high you're going to need to buy another home. This excellent book goes into great detail about various strategies and techniques to help you obtain the best mortgage possible.

Ward, Schar, *Coming Clean: Dirty Little Secrets from a Professional Housecleaner*. Book Peddlers, 2002.

One of the least appealing aspects of selling a home—no matter how you choose to do it—is giving your home a thorough cleaning. This book from a cleaning professional is highly recommended for organizational and cleaning tips to take some of the sting out of the chore.

Websites

Homestore.com (www.homestore.com) offers a nice, central location for a number of information sources and services, including relocation search engines, mortgage calculators, and other handy tools.

Homebuying.about has a handy page that summarizes many of the steps we address in exhaustive detail. You can find a quick, easy to follow overview at http://homebuying.about.com/cs/sellerarticles/a/home_selling.htm.

Another handy, if general, real estate website is Yahoo! Real Estate (http://realestate.yahoo.com). Classified ads, mortgage and loan resources links, homeowner's insurance, and other resources are all available. If you feel like looking for a bargain, there's even a search engine for foreclosures.

Still another comprehensive real estate destination on the Internet is the Real Estate Library (www.relibrary.com). The site provides a variety of tools of interest to both buyers and sellers as well as a downright exhaustive array of links to a number of other real estate-related websites.

The federal government offers a good amount of information and further resources for homesellers on the Internet. One place worth a look is "Life Advice About Selling A Home," located at www.pueblo.gsa.gov/cic_text/housing/sellhome/sellhome.htm. There, you'll find basic information, free pamphlets, and other advice.

As we mention in Chapter 12, solid credit—reflected in a solid credit report—is an essential element in home buying. The three credit reporting agencies are Experian, Equifax, and TransUnion. All three have helpful and informative websites. They're located at www.experian.com, www.equifax.com, and www.transunion.com.

Not every home seller knows exactly where they want to go after the closing is complete. Want to find your dream town? CNN and Money have a useful Best Places to Live website at www.money.cnn.com/best/bplive. You can search according to housing costs, weather, and other issues that can impact your relocation decision. For that matter, the main CNN and Money homepage (www.money.cnn.com) has a section specific to real estate that addresses buying and selling, home improvement, and other topics. Also a nice resource for real estate-related articles.

Newsletters and Publications

www.fsbobasics.com offers a free monthly newsletter addressing real estate trends, interest rates, and other issues of interest to home sellers and buyers. Sign up at www.fsbobasics.com/new.html.

Likewise, www.homesaletips.com offers a free newsletter that touches on advertising strategies, negotiations, and similar topics for FSBOs. It's available at www.homesaletips.com/newsletter.html.

Mentioned in the website section, Homebuying.about has a free newsletter covering home buying and selling. Go to their URL, which was previously listed, and look for the link to newsletter sign up. Even better, you can also sign up for newsletters covering a variety of other topics.

The Internal Revenue Service has a wide variety of home selling-related information on the web, including Publication 523, which addresses the possible tax implications of selling your home. It's available at www.irs.gov/pub/irs-pdf/p523.pdf.

Sample Home Inspection Report

This sample of a home inspection report details what repairs need to be addressed and their costs. This gives you a reasonable idea of just how thorough and detailed an inspection report can be—and, as a result, what you as the seller may need to do in order to satisfy the report's guidelines and move forward with the sale of your home.

ENGINEERING, P.C.

2171 JERICHO TURNPIKE, SUITE 230, COMMACK, NY 11725
PHONE: 631-858-5500 • FAX: 631-858-5599

WEB: www.heimer.com • **EMAIL:** pe@heimer.com

ENGINEERS • CONSULTANTS • BUILDING INSPECTORS
LICENSED BY NEW YORK, NEW JERSEY, AND CONNECTICUT
2171 JERICHO TURNPIKE, COMMACK, NY 11725 • 631-858-5500
620 MIDDLE NECK ROAD, GREAT NECK, NY 11023 • 516-487-2100
370 SEVENTH AVENUE, NEW YORK, NY 10001 • 212-563-4777
16 COURT STREET, BROOKLYN, NY 11241 • 718-237-7777
2810 OLENVILLE AVENUE, BRONX, NY 10467 • 718-547-2000
71-34 AUSTIN STREET, FOREST HILLS, NY 11375 • 718-544-3000
901 HUGUENOT AVENUE, STATEN ISLAND, NY 10312 • 718-227-5000
48E MAIN STREET, WESTHAMPTON BEACH, NY 11978 • 631-288-3900
459 MAIN STREET, NEW ROCHELLE, NY 10801 • 914-576-6100

Our File Number: 218052
Date of Report: 1/24/2005

LICENSED PROFESSIONAL ENGINEER'S CERTIFIED REPORT

for

ADAM NONAMEE

ABSTRACT: The house at 11 Main Street, Anytown, New York, was inspected by the firm of Heimer Engineering, P.C., on January 22, 2005. The estimated repair expenses are as follows:

	Amount
NECESSARY EXPENSES	$11,670
UPCOMING EXPENSES	$17,640
POTENTIAL EXPENSES	$32,000
OTHER EXPENSES	$5,070
TOTAL EXPENSES	$69,180

THE HEIMER RATING™

7.8

ON THE HEIMER SCALE
OF ENGINEERING ATTRIBUTES

> *This annotated virtual sample report was abstracted from a full 86-page report. Some parts of the original report have been omitted, reduced in scope, or revised for clarity.*

This report is certified under the principal Professional Engineer's seal. The certification is found on page 80.

NONAMEE
1/24/2005
218052

This virtual sample report was abstracted from a full 86-page inspection report performed by <u>Heimer Engineering, P.C.</u> The names, dates, and locations have been changed.

This virtual sample report contains only significant highlights taken from the full inspection report. It is about 30 percent of the size of the inspection report upon which this virtual sample report is based. Many of the technical details, as well as all identifying information, have been omitted.

In creating this virtual sample report, page numbers and item numbers have been changed, so there may be some conflicting numbering. This conflicting numbering is <u>not</u> present in the full report.

The Summary of Costs is based upon the actual summary of costs in the full report. Due to the changes made in this virtual sample report, numbering conflicts may also be present.

This report is subject to the Terms of Use available at http://www.heimer.com/legal.

V I R T U A L   S A M P L E   R E P O R T

Licensed Professional Engineers – Heimer Engineering, P.C.
Call 1-800-640-8090 for more information or to set up an appointment.

Virtual Sample Report

NONAMEE
1/24/2005
218052

VIRTUAL SAMPLE REPORT

This is the actual TABLE OF CONTENTS from the original report. The original report upon which this sample was based is 86 pages in length.

TABLE OF CONTENTS

Licensed Professional Engineers – Heimer Engineering, P.C.
Call 1-800-640-8090 for more information or to set up an appointment.

Virtual Sample Report

NONAMEE
1/24/2005
218052

V
I
R
T
U
A
L

S
A
M
P
L
E

R
E
P
O
R
T

> *The INTRODUCTION AND DESCRIPTION gives you a description of the house and tells you where various utilities are located. The description helps in understanding which rooms are being referenced when they are mentioned in the report.*

INTRODUCTION AND DESCRIPTION

On Thursday, January 24, 2005, the home at 11 Main Street, Anytown, New York, was inspected on behalf of Adam Nonamee of Hometown, New York.

This 1950's vintage, two story, two-unit home is located on the westerly side of a pleasant residential street. It is on property reported to be 80 front feet by 100 feet deep.

The exterior accessories and the improvements to the site (besides the house) include, but are not limited to, the blacktop driveway, the concrete sidewalk, the concrete street curb, the detached two-car garage, the concrete driveway apron, the belgian block driveway curb, the brick and concrete front stoop, the concrete path thereto, the chain link, stockade, split rail and wood fencing, the blacktop path to the back, the bluestone, brick, and concrete back stoop, the concrete block and wood retaining walls, and general landscaping.

The house itself has four principal levels. These are as follows:

1. The basement, which is partitioned into north and south basement areas. On this level are located two furnaces, two oil tanks, the gas main, the gas meters, the water main, two circuit breaker panels, the main drain lines, the hot water heaters, the clothes washer, the clothes dryer, and a slop sink. (The water meter and two electric meters are located outside the house.)

2. The first floor, which is divided into a north and south side. The north side contains a kitchen, a dining room, a living room with heat thermostat, a shared entry foyer, a rear half-bathroom, and a rear connecting hallway. The south side contains a kitchen, a dining room, a living room with heat thermostat, a rear half-bathroom, and a rear connecting hallway.

3. The second floor, which is divided into a north and south side. The north side contains a master bedroom, two other bedrooms, a connecting hallway, and a hall bathroom. The south

Licensed Professional Engineers – Heimer Engineering, P.C.
Call 1-800-640-8090 for more information or to set up an appointment.

Virtual Sample Report

NONAMEE
1/24/2005
218052

side contains a master bedroom, one other bedroom, a connecting hallway, and a hall bathroom.

4. The crawl attic, which is accessible via a hatch located in the ceiling of the front bedroom closet of the north-side apartment.

> *The INITIAL RECOMMENDATIONS AND OBSERVATIONS contain recommendations involving observations that are not related to specific defects.*

INITIAL RECOMMENDATIONS AND OBSERVATIONS

Before we begin the section of this report wherein costs of repairs are estimated, we should like to recommend that you:

> *The recommendation below regards the existence of a Certificate of Occupancy, which helps assure you that the building complies with all applicable building codes and municipal regulations. The inspection report tells you specifically what to check in the Certificate of Occupancy (in this case, that the house is a legal two-family house).*

a) Make sure a current up-to-date Certificate of Occupancy exists for the entire house as it is presently constituted, including the use of the home as a two-family house. This should be on file with the local Building Department. The Certificate of Occupancy should confirm that the building and any alterations were constructed in accordance with the building code and zoning resolutions in force at the time of the construction…

**Licensed Professional Engineers – Heimer Engineering, P.C.
Call 1-800-640-8090 for more information or to set up an appointment.**

Virtual Sample Report

NONAMEE
1/24/2005
218052

V
I
R
T
U
A
L

Just as with the Certificate of Occupancy, evidence of an electrical inspection helps assure you that the home or building was wired safely. Again, our reports tell you what to look for in the electrical inspection certificate.

b) Make sure that a New York Board of Fire Underwriters Certificates exist for the 100 amp services, the electrical sub-panel hookups, the newer wiring, the basement wiring, the garage wiring, the outdoor wiring, the room air-conditioner hookups, the outdoor lighting, the electric hot water heater hookups, the electric dryer hookup, the washer hookup, the and all the wiring throughout the house…

In addition to the essential technical information reported in a engineering report, the reports include additional helpful information.

S
A
M
P
L
E

c) Realize that some of the electrical outlets throughout the house do not have a U-ground…

d) …smoke detectors (and other fire protection equipment) that should be in this building…

e) Realize that there is only one-zone heating. For this reason, the second floor will usually be warmer than the first…

f) Obtain the past oil bills…

R
E
P
O
R
T

Licensed Professional Engineers – Heimer Engineering, P.C.
Call 1-800-640-8090 for more information or to set up an appointment.

Virtual Sample Report

NONAMEE
1/24/2005
218052

V I R T U A L   S A M P L E   R E P O R T

> *Our reports warn you of potential environmentally related health issues such as those from Radon, Lead Paint, and Asbestos, if they are relevant problems in your new home or building.*

g) …radon gas is likely to be a problem in this area. Radon is a naturally occurring gas that cannot be seen or smelled. Radon's radioactive decay products are inhaled…

h) …***Protect Your Family From Lead in Your Home***. As of December 1996, Federal law requires the seller to disclose known information on lead-based paint hazards…

i) …materials that have been identified by the EPA as containing asbestos…

> *There is always some information that you need to obtain from the seller before you purchase the home.*

j) Ask the owner for an explanation of what all the individual light switches control…

> *Obtaining warranties for comparatively new items will protect you against future problems and expenses.*

k) Obtain the bills of sale and warranty for the roof, the latest windows, the new wood retaining wall…

**Licensed Professional Engineers – Heimer Engineering, P.C.
Call 1-800-640-8090 for more information or to set up an appointment.**

Virtual Sample Report

NONAMEE
1/24/2005
218052

V
I
R
T
U
A
L

S
A
M
P
L
E

R
E
P
O
R
T

> *Our reports advise you of things that need to be done before you purchase the home or building.*

l) Request that all of the personal property, debris, furniture, and stored material in the north-side basement, closets, garage, under the steps, storage rooms, cabinets under the sink, on the floors, blocking the basement and garage walls, …

m) Establish who owns the fence located on the borders of the property…

n) Establish who owns the retaining wall…

o) Obtain an inventory of all the screens stored in the basement and have instructions provided…

p) Realize that there are some tall trees close to this building. Make sure that your insurance policy…

q) Realize that this house utilizes double glazed windows. These windows serve as their own storm windows…

r) Return to the house, if possible, during a heavy rain…

s) Return to the house, if possible, during a hot, humid day…

t) Contact the building department and find out if there are any outstanding permits, permit applications…

u) Require that you be allowed a pre-Closing inspection…

**Licensed Professional Engineers – Heimer Engineering, P.C.
Call 1-800-640-8090 for more information or to set up an appointment.**

Virtual Sample Report

NONAMEE
1/24/2005
218052

> *The SPECIFIC FINDINGS section details the defects that the Licensed Professional Engineer observed.*

SPECIFIC FINDINGS

The inspection was conducted in all directly accessible and observable areas. In general, the house was found to be in reasonably clean, relatively well-maintained, fundamentally sound condition. Some significant problems were detected, as well as some moderate and minor problems. Our specific findings were as follows:

> *Our Licensed Professional Engineers look for evidence of termite activity. We also check for structural damage caused by termites. Only Licensed Professional Engineers can state if the structural damage renders the building structurally unsound.*

1. Evidence of termite infestation and/or activity was detected on the garage wall sheathing in the form of mud tube scars and in the northwest basement corner in the form of mud tube scars on the sill plate. Fortunately, no structurally significant damage was noted…

Licensed Professional Engineers – Heimer Engineering, P.C. Call 1-800-640-8090 for more information or to set up an appointment.

Virtual Sample Report

NONAMEE
1/24/2005
218052

Cost estimates are provided for repairs. The actual numbers have been omitted from this virtual sample report. The inspection report that is sent to you includes written dollar cost estimates.

Termite-proofing the entire house is recommended at an estimated cost of at least…

A termite form is provided to you at no additional cost. The termite form is usually required when applying for a mortgage.

The termite form we prepare is provided at no additional cost to you…

Safety recommendations are also included.

2. The duplex electric outlets located in the kitchens, the garage, the slop sink, and at the exterior are not fitted with Ground Fault Circuit Interrupters (GFCIs). By today's standards, outlets so located are safer with GFCIs…

Our reports inform you of older items, so that you can prepare for upcoming expenses.

3. The furnaces are beyond their rated life expectancy. Strictly based on their age, we recommend budgeting at least…

**Licensed Professional Engineers – Heimer Engineering, P.C.
Call 1-800-640-8090 for more information or to set up an appointment.**

Virtual Sample Report

VIRTUAL SAMPLE REPORT

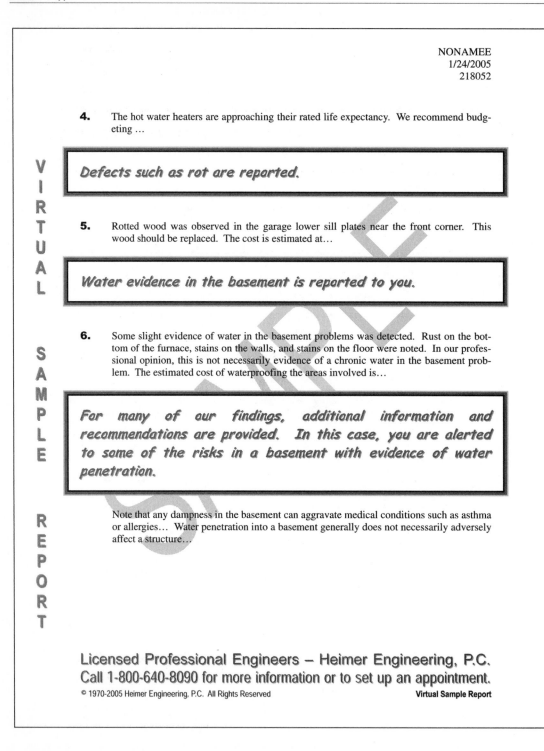

NONAMEE
1/24/2005
218052

4. The hot water heaters are approaching their rated life expectancy. We recommend budgeting …

> *Defects such as rot are reported.*

5. Rotted wood was observed in the garage lower sill plates near the front corner. This wood should be replaced. The cost is estimated at…

> *Water evidence in the basement is reported to you.*

6. Some slight evidence of water in the basement problems was detected. Rust on the bottom of the furnace, stains on the walls, and stains on the floor were noted. In our professional opinion, this is not necessarily evidence of a chronic water in the basement problem. The estimated cost of waterproofing the areas involved is…

> *For many of our findings, additional information and recommendations are provided. In this case, you are alerted to some of the risks in a basement with evidence of water penetration.*

Note that any dampness in the basement can aggravate medical conditions such as asthma or allergies… Water penetration into a basement generally does not necessarily adversely affect a structure…

Licensed Professional Engineers – Heimer Engineering, P.C.
Call 1-800-640-8090 for more information or to set up an appointment.

Virtual Sample Report

NONAMEE
1/24/2005
218052

**V
I
R
T
U
A
L

S
A
M
P
L
E

R
E
P
O
R
T**

In addition to the major defects, our reports also point out smaller, annoying, but still vital, defects.

7. We noted the following plumbing problems:

   a) The drain stoppers in the tubs are not functional.

   b) The south half-bathroom sink stopper needs adjustment.

We estimate the cost of repair at…

8. We observed the following electrical problems:

   a) The rear exterior outlet box is loose.

   b) The south-side apartment rear bedroom wall outlet is loose.

We estimate the cost of correcting these problems at…

9. The bluestone on the back stoop was observed to be loose and damaged. We estimate the cost of repair to be…

10. We noted the following minor problems:

   a) The north-side basement door sticks.

   b) The south master bedroom door sticks.

These can be repaired at an estimated…

11. The above-ground oil storage tanks are approaching their rated life expectancy…

**Licensed Professional Engineers – Heimer Engineering, P.C.
Call 1-800-640-8090 for more information or to set up an appointment.**

Virtual Sample Report

NONAMEE
1/24/2005
218052

Because of the narrative nature of our reports, information is included that does not fit in a obsolete checklist format.

V
I
R
T
U
A
L

S
A
M
P
L
E

R
E
P
O
R
T

12. There are two tall trees very close to the house. One is near the electric meters and the other is near the northwest corner. These trees should be removed to prevent damage at an estimated cost...

13. The kitchen ceilings are damaged below the hall bathrooms. Repair of the pipe leaks in the ceilings above is estimated at...

14. The three-wire overhead service hookup is too close to the south side window and the wiring at the masthead connection is loose. The hookup appears temporary. Proper installation of the overhead service per electric code is estimated at...

15. The retaining walls along the south side of the property are worn and have shifted. When retaining walls are in this condition, they are subject to localized failures at any time. The estimated cost of rebuilding these retaining walls is...

16. The south-side doorbell does not work properly. The repair cost is estimated at...

17. Part of the driveway is extremely worn and deteriorated. We estimate...

18. There are no rain caps or pest screens on the chimneys. Rain caps and pest screens should be installed to prevent rain and animals from entering the chimneys...

19. Safety wires should be installed in the garage door springs. Should a garage door spring break, it could injure the person operating the door. Deaths have been caused by breaking garage door springs. The estimated cost of installing safety wires is...

Licensed Professional Engineers – Heimer Engineering, P.C.
Call 1-800-640-8090 for more information or to set up an appointment.

Virtual Sample Report

NONAMEE
1/24/2005
218052

V
I
R
T
U
A
L

S
A
M
P
L
E

R
E
P
O
R
T

27.   Point of Information: Old gas lines sometimes develop leaks at the gas service entrance to the building…

28.   The north-side kitchen sink spray device was not operating properly. Repair is estimated...

29.   The porcelain on the south-side kitchen sink is chipped…

30.   Point of Information: The handrails on the steps to the basement are <u>not</u> child safe. We recommend that you carefully watch any children playing in these areas…

31.   Point of Information: Some of the floors in the building were uneven. It is our professional opinion that the unevenness is within normal limits for a building of this size, age, and construction type. Thus, the uneven floors do not, by themselves, render the building as being unsound…

32.   The cutoff and emergency valves for the fixtures and plumbing lines are old. If the valves are ever needed, they may be difficult or impossible to operate…

33.   Some of the cover plates for the electrical outlets were missing. Without cover plates, these areas represent a safety hazard…

> *Recommendations for pre-Closing checks are also included.*

34.   If you choose <u>not</u> to have the house rechecked by us (or another qualified Licensed Professional Engineer) prior to Closing, you should be aware that many areas are subject to developing problems…

  ✓ All feed and drainpipes should be rechecked for new leaks…

  ✓ All electric lights, fixtures, and switches should be rechecked. Check…

  ✓ The roof, the flashing, and roof sheathing should be rechecked for new leaks…

**Licensed Professional Engineers – Heimer Engineering, P.C.
Call 1-800-640-8090 for more information or to set up an appointment.**

Virtual Sample Report

NONAMEE
1/24/2005
218052

✓ All appliances should be …

✓ Windows and doors should be rechecked to see if the…

✓ Heating equipment should be rechecked…

✓ Hot water equipment should…

✓ Currently inaccessible areas should be…

✓ The basement should be rechecked for…

✓ All areas now blocked by personal property, debris,…

✓ The air conditioning should…

The above areas are all subject to developing problems and/or may have problems that cannot be fully checked until Closing…

In addition to reporting about specific problems and defects, you are provided with a description of the technical systems in the house or building.

UTILITIES AND STRUCTURE

A.   **FURNACE, HOT WATER, AND HEATING:**   These two one-zone, oil fired, Weil McLain systems each have a rating of 100,500 BTUs per hour. This is sufficient for the production of heat and domestic hot water, in conjunction with hot water boosters, considering rough estimates of the size of the premises, insulation present, window heat loss, and other heat losses…

No visual problems were detected in any radiators in this house. In order to maintain peak operation, radiators should be thoroughly vacuumed at least every other year. Odor or uneven heating in a house is often the…

Puffbacks are a potential problem in this furnace. A puffback is a small, slow explosion of oil in the furnace combustion chamber. Puffbacks are caused by improper furnace

**Licensed Professional Engineers – Heimer Engineering, P.C.
Call 1-800-640-8090 for more information or to set up an appointment.**

Virtual Sample Report

NONAMEE
1/24/2005
218052

maintenance, inadequate air supply or furnace draft, or contaminated fuel. To help prevent puffbacks…

OIL TANK: The condition of the two 275 gallon oil tanks was…

B. **HOT WATER BOOSTER:** These 40 gallon capacity, Bradford and Ford Products hot water boosters are used in conjunction with the furnace and will not be sufficient for use alone. The booster tank, along with the furnace, should produce sufficient hot water for normal needs considering the number of hot water outlets available. The hot water heaters were operating during the inspection and were producing, in conjunction with the furnace, 119 degree hot water…

C. **ELECTRIC SERVICE AND MAIN PANELS:** These two three-wire, 220 volt, 100 amp, overhead services are sufficient for the existing electrical requirements of this house. The condition of the accessible areas of the main circuit breaker panels and the accessible wiring was satisfactory from an electrical standpoint…

D. **PLUMBING AND GAS:** Mostly copper water lines, mostly cast iron and galvanized drain lines, and the mostly black iron main gas lines were observed to be in acceptable condition. Main drain drainage tests indicated satisfactory performance during the inspection. The water pressure was sufficient. The operation of the four toilets, seven sinks, and two tubs was normal except as noted…

There were no active gas leaks detected in the house. **If you ever smell gas,** *or even think you may smell gas,* **contact the gas company** immediately. Do not hesitate…

E. **STRUCTURE:** The accessible walls were plumb and the accessible floors were level within normal tolerances for a building of this size, age, and construction type. The condition of the accessible concrete and concrete block foundation walls, the accessible wood sill plates, the accessible floor joists was satisfactory. Indirect examination…

**Licensed Professional Engineers – Heimer Engineering, P.C.
Call 1-800-640-8090 for more information or to set up an appointment.**

Virtual Sample Report

V I R T U A L   S A M P L E   R E P O R T

NONAMEE
1/24/2005
218052

APPURTENANCES AND MISCELLANEOUS

F.   **FLOORING:** Functional…

G.   **WALLS AND CEILINGS:** Functional…

H.   **BLACKTOP DRIVEWAY:** Minor cracks…

I.   **CONCRETE SIDEWALK PAVEMENT:** Acceptable…

J.   **STREET CURBING:** Normal…

K.   **DETACHED TWO-CAR GARAGE STRUCTURE:** Acceptable…

L.   **CONCRETE GARAGE FLOOR:** Minor cracks…

M.   **GARAGE FLOOR PITCH:** Acceptable…

N.   **CONCRETE DRIVEWAY APRON:** Satisfactory…

O.   **BELGIAN BLOCK DRIVEWAY CURBING:** Satisfactory…

P.   **BRICK AND CONCRETE FRONT STOOP:** Minor cracks…

Q.   **CONCRETE PATH TO THE FRONT STOOP:** Acceptable…

R.   **CHAIN LINK, STOCKADE, SPLIT RAIL AND WOOD FENCING:** Sturdy…

S.   **BLACKTOP PATH TO THE BACK:** Satisfactory…

Licensed Professional Engineers – Heimer Engineering, P.C.
Call 1-800-640-8090 for more information or to set up an appointment.

NONAMEE
1/24/2005
218052

T. **BLUESTONE, BRICK AND CONCRETE BACK STOOPS:** Cracked…

U. **LANDSCAPING:** Blends with other landscaping…

Some people have misconceptions about how serious a problem may be. In addition to reporting problems, we explain, where appropriate, why some problems are only minor.

V. **FOUNDATION CRACKS:** Some detected in accessible areas of the foundation, none professionally judged to be structurally significant.

In fact, one could say that there are many more non-structural foundation cracks. A typical foundation is very strong under the forces of compression, but is much weaker against tension forces. Therefore, tiny cracks (many visually imperceptible) develop any place that there are slight differences in loading and support. Cracks typically develop…

W. **SCREENS:** Functional. Note that a small amount of air leakage…

X. **FLASHING:** No active leakage…

Y. **OUTDOOR ELECTRICAL OUTLETS:** One…

Z. **HOSE BIBB:** One observed. Make sure that the hose bibb is…

AA. **WROUGHT IRON EXTERIOR RAILINGS:** Sturdy…

BB. **PAINTED CEDAR SIDING:** Satisfactory…

CC. **GRADING:** Acceptable except…

Licensed Professional Engineers – Heimer Engineering, P.C.
Call 1-800-640-8090 for more information or to set up an appointment.

Virtual Sample Report

V
I
R
T
U
A
L

S
A
M
P
L
E

R
E
P
O
R
T

NONAMEE
1/24/2005
218052

V
I
R
T
U
A
L

S
A
M
P
L
E

R
E
P
O
R
T

DD. **LEADERS AND GUTTERS:** No holes…

EE. **ROOF:** There was no evidence indicating that the roof has present active leakage…

FF. **BRICK CHIMNEY:** Structurally sound…

GG. **BASEMENT WINDOW WELLS:** Normal…

HH. **UNUSUAL ODORS:** Normal odors detected. All houses have some odors, and…

II. **ORNAMENTAL WOOD SHUTTERS:** Normal…

JJ. **WOOD TRIM:** No need for immediate painting…

Warnings are provided about relevant potential hazards.

KK. **TWO OVERHEAD GARAGE DOORS:** Operable.

WARNING: Improper operation of garage doors can be hazardous, so you (and other users) should exercise caution when the garage door is in motion. Keep hands clear of the gaps between the garage door panels and any other moving parts…

Appliances and other interior items are also checked.

LL. The following items were checked and found to be in working order:

a) Ceiling fan

b) Westinghouse vented electric dryer

**Licensed Professional Engineers – Heimer Engineering, P.C.
Call 1-800-640-8090 for more information or to set up an appointment.**

Virtual Sample Report

NONAMEE
1/24/2005
218052

**V
I
R
T
U
A
L**

**S
A
M
P
L
E**

**R
E
P
O
R
T**

c) Kitchen exhaust fan

d) Magic Chef gas range

e) Broan range hood fan

f) General Electric refrigerator

MM. **WOOD INTERIOR BANISTERS:** Sturdy…

NN. **SAMPLED WINDOW OPERATION:** Satisfactory…

OO. **SAMPLED DOOR OPERATION:** Satisfactory considering…

PP. **CONDITION OF WINDOWS:** Acceptable…

QQ. **CONDITION OF DOORS:** Acceptable considering…

RR. **ELECTRICAL GROUND CONNECTION TO THE MAIN WATER PIPE:** …

SS. **SAMPLED ELECTRIC OUTLETS AND LIGHTS:** Operated…

TT. **MAIN STEPS:** Level within normal limits for this type construction…

UU. **EVIDENCE OF RODENTS:** None detected in accessible and observable areas.

Because rodent droppings can promote the spread of diseases,…

**Licensed Professional Engineers – Heimer Engineering, P.C.
Call 1-800-640-8090 for more information or to set up an appointment.**

Virtual Sample Report

NONAMEE
1/24/2005
218052

A SUMMARY OF EXPENSES is provided. This SUMMARY OF EXPENSES is based upon the SUMMARY OF EXPENSES in the actual report. Due to the changes made for clarity in this virtual sample report, numbering conflicts may be found.

SUMMARY OF EXPENSES

Many Real Estate Brokers have developed a large network of contacts over the years. Your Real Estate Broker may know contractors in the neighborhood who are willing to perform this work at a lower cost.

The total estimated expenses are $69,180. The breakdown of the expenses is as follows:

A. NECESSARY EXPENSES

These $5,670 in high priority expenses are necessary to either repair conditions which are hazardous to the structure, hazardous to people, or may cause harm or damage to the structure, people, property…

	COST	ITEM
Electrician	$ 5120	2, 9, 15, 28, 40
Garage Door Contractor	$ 150	22
General Contractor	$ 2380	6, 7
Mason	$ 1800	10, 21
Pest Control Specialist	$ 1750	1
Plumber	$ 470	8, 39
TOTAL	$ 11670	

Licensed Professional Engineers – Heimer Engineering, P.C.
Call 1-800-640-8090 for more information or to set up an appointment.

Virtual Sample Report

V I R T U A L   S A M P L E   R E P O R T

NONAMEE
1/24/2005
218052

B. UPCOMING EXPENSES

The new owner will probably encounter these expenses within the next several years because of the age of the equipment or other reasons. Hopefully, these $14,440 in expenses will be in the future…

	COST	ITEM
General Contractor...$	6800	17
Heating Contractor...$	2800	3, 24
Plumber...$	4100	5
Tree Service ....$	2200	12
TOTAL...$	17640	

C. POTENTIAL EXPENSES

These are expenses for which a limited inspection, such as this one, does <u>not</u> provide sufficient information to allow the Licensed Professional Engineer to formulate a proper evaluation. Note that when more information is obtained…

	COST	ITEM
General Contractor...$	24000	19
Heating Contractor...$	800	14
Plumber...$	1200	13
Waterproofing Contractor ....$	6000	7
TOTAL...$	32000	

D. OTHER SIGNIFICANT EXPENSES

These $5,070 in expenses are related to repairs which are of desirable nature but which are <u>not</u> imperative in an engineering sense. However…

	COST	ITEM
Driveway Contractor...$	2200	20
Electrician ....$	880	18, 25, 27
Handyman..$	1400	26
Plumber...$	590	25, 33, 34
TOTAL...$	5070	

Licensed Professional Engineers – Heimer Engineering, P.C.
Call 1-800-640-8090 for more information or to set up an appointment.

Virtual Sample Report

VIRTUAL SAMPLE REPORT

NONAMEE
1/24/2005
218052

The ANALYSIS AND CONCLUSIONS summarizes the findings of the Licensed Professional Engineer.

VIRTUAL SAMPLE REPORT

ANALYSIS AND CONCLUSIONS

The total expenses are $69,180. There are $11,670 in **NECESSARY EXPENSES** itemized on page 53 and $17,640 in **UPCOMING EXPENSES** itemized on page 53. Hopefully, the **UPCOMING EXPENSES** will not be required for several years. One way to prepare for these costs would be to establish a three-year sinking fund with monthly deposits of at least $500. That way when the costs in the **UPCOMING EXPENSES** category are required, hopefully you will be ready. As far as the $32,000 in **POTENTIAL EXPENSES** itemized on page 54 are concerned…

You should also review the **OTHER SIGNIFICANT EXPENSES** of $5,070 itemized on page 54, determine which are important to you *personally*, and budget accordingly. In addition, you should budget for any maintenance, redecoration, refurbishment, upgrading, modernizing, remodeling, reconditioning, exterior landscaping, new appliances…

THE HEIMER RATING™

The sum of the above **NECESSARY EXPENSES** and **UPCOMING EXPENSES** is in the less than normal category for a house of this size, age, and construction type. Because of this, because of the fact that the house is in a relatively clean and reasonably maintained state, and for other more subjective reasons, we give this house a Heimer Rating™ of:

7.8

ON THE HEIMER SCALE*

all things considered (and assuming, for the moment, that the **POTENTIAL EXPENSES** will not be necessary, that our **INITIAL RECOMMENDATIONS** (beginning on page 5) are satisfied, and…

The Heimer Rating™ scale is as follows:

```
9.5  —  10.0  —  OUTSTANDING
9.0  —   9.4  —  EXCELLENT
8.0  —   8.9  —  GOOD
```

**Licensed Professional Engineers – Heimer Engineering, P.C.
Call 1-800-640-8090 for more information or to set up an appointment.**

Virtual Sample Report

NONAMEE
1/24/2005
218052

V
I
R
T
U
A
L

7.0	—	7.9	— FAIR TO GOOD
6.0	—	6.9	— FAIR
5.0	—	5.9	— POOR TO FAIR
4.0	—	4.9	— POOR
3.0	—	3.9	— VERY POOR TO POOR
2.0	—	2.9	— VERY POOR
1.0	—	1.9	— EXTREMELY POOR TO VERY POOR
0.1	—	1.0	— EXTREMELY POOR
0.0			— UNACCEPTABLE

A glossary of terms is provided.

S
A
M
P
L
E

GLOSSARY AND ADDITIONAL INFORMATION

The following glossary is included to help you understand terms that may be used in the report…

It is important that you understand that we disclose important limitations in pre-purchase home and building inspections. The ADDITIONAL RECOMMENDATIONS AND DISCLOSURE OF LIMITATIONS includes this disclosure. Some inspection companies choose to leave out these limitations, even though they exist in all inspections. We state the limitations clearly for your protection.

R
E
P
O
R
T

ADDITIONAL RECOMMENDATIONS AND DISCLOSURE OF LIMITATIONS

This report represents the professional opinion of the Licensed Professional Engineer at the time of the inspection and the reviewing Licensed Professional Engineer following the inspection, and is furnished as an aid in determining the physical condition of the inspected premises and reported aspects thereof…

Licensed Professional Engineers – Heimer Engineering, P.C. Call 1-800-640-8090 for more information or to set up an appointment.

Virtual Sample Report

NONAMEE
1/24/2005
218052

All of our reports are certified by a Licensed Professional Engineer. An ENGINEER'S CERTIFICATION is also provided. This is rarely done by our competition.

ENGINEER'S CERTIFICATION

We certify as follows:

We have read this entire report, investigated the facts set forth in the report and the facts underlying the report, and conducted the visual inspection referred to above with due diligence in order to form a basis for this certification.

We certify that this report which is prepared by us discloses all the material facts which were discernible from a one-engineer, limited time, limited observation, walk-through visual inspection of those accessible and observable areas of the building that were inspected. This certification is made for the benefit of the buyer. We certify that this report, which is based on our visual inspection:

(i)   sets forth in narrative form the physical condition of the accessible and observable areas of the building and is current and accurate as of the date of inspection;

(ii)   affords, in our professional opinion, potential purchasers an adequate basis upon which to base their judgment concerning the reported aspects of the physical condition of the building provided that the purchaser reads this report, follows our recommendations, and calls our offices with any questions that might result from that reading;

(iii)   does not omit any material fact;

(iv)   does not contain any untrue statement of a material fact;

(v)   does not contain any fraud, deception, concealment, or suppression;

(vi)   does not contain any promise or representation as to the future which is beyond reasonable expectation or unwarranted by existing circumstances;

(vii)   does not contain any representation or statement which is false, where we:

(a) knew the truth;

(b) with reasonable effort could have known the truth;

(c) made no reasonable effort to ascertain the truth, or

Licensed Professional Engineers – Heimer Engineering, P.C.
Call 1-800-640-8090 for more information or to set up an appointment.

Virtual Sample Report

NONAMEE
1/24/2005
218052

(d) did not have knowledge concerning the representations or statement made.

It is to be understood that all aspects of the physical condition of the building cannot be determined by a one-engineer, limited time, limited observation walk-through visual inspection of accessible and observable areas, and that all statements contained in this certification are premised on and limited to such visual inspection.

We further certify that to our knowledge, we are not owned or controlled by and have no beneficial interest in the building owner.

HEIMER ENGINEERING, P.C.

Dated:

**Licensed Professional Engineers – Heimer Engineering, P.C.
Call 1-800-640-8090 for more information or to set up an appointment.**

Virtual Sample Report

(margin text, top to bottom) V I R T U A L   S A M P L E   R E P O R T

NONAMEE
1/24/2005
218052

V
I
R
T
U
A
L

S
A
M
P
L
E

R
E
P
O
R
T

> *Our reports include a SELLER'S CERTIFICATION. This is a list of questions that you should ask the Seller in order to obtain additional information on the house or building. Depending upon the type of inspection, this certification can have up to 60 specific questions.*

SELLER'S CERTIFICATION AND HEI-LITE™ QUESTIONS

SELLER: The inspection is limited to areas that are accessible and observable at the time of the inspection…

Licensed Professional Engineers – Heimer Engineering, P.C.
Call 1-800-640-8090 for more information or to set up an appointment.

Virtual Sample Report

Index